"Treat yourself to this movi
of the cutting-edge, healing
ing Angel Workshops™ an
novel captures the heart an
thriving."

—Kathryn Tull, M.A., LMFT, Author, *The Next Bold Step*

"The life of an abused woman can be seen from many different perspectives. Susan presents a captivating story that leaves you begging to discover what happens next as a variety of events and characters come together creating a sense of home, togetherness and possibility."

—Dorothy A. Martin-Neville, PhD, Author, *Dreams Are Only the Beginning* and *Your Soul Sings – Your Body Dances*

"What a journey the characters in Awaken *are on! We get to experience what they think and feel as we see the world around them through their eyes. This is a world where, yes, tragedy, grief, and pain can strike, but the characters also reach for positive, hopeful thoughts as they seek answers and forgiveness. I am excited to read the next book!"*

—Milena Erwin, MBA, CGBP, Women's Business Center

"Susan's book is a great teaching tool that shows women the importance of having self-respect and finding their true worth. The story illustrates the many types of abuse a woman can experience and its long-term impact on their lives. The book also gives hope and encouragement to victims that they can heal and not only survive, but thrive after abuse! I will be using this story to motivate the women I work with to reach new heights and free themselves from their past."

—Michele Hunt, domestic violence advocate counselor

"This book captured and held my attention to the end. I couldn't wait to find out what happened next. It is a powerful story that clearly illustrated the signs of abuse in a relationship without listing them like in a domestic violence pamphlet. The character development was awesome. I feel like I know everyone in the story and shared all their adventures. I can't wait to find out what's to come in the next books of the series."

—Teri Coughlin, *My Avenging Angel Workshops™* participant

"Awaken *is a page-turner of a book that should be shared with anyone who could be a victim. It is a fascinating window into the mind of all parties involved in an abusive relationship. The book is a must-read for anyone who works with victims as it provides an important, rare insight into the impact of violence and abuse on every character – their trauma, grief, courage and hope."*

— **Virginia A. Del Monaco, M.A. Program Manager for Domestic and Family Violence Curriculum**

"I loved Susan's book. I couldn't put it down. It is beautifully written — a very satisfying read. The characters are well-defined, and it is fun to watch them grow and change. This book should be a movie. I'm so glad I read it."

—**Elinor Welson, LCSW, MSW, retired social worker**

Awaken

The Awakening of the Human Spirit on a Healing Journey

Inspired by a True Event

by Susan M. Omilian JD

Butterfly Bliss Productions LLC
West Hartford, CT

Barbara!

You are awakening to the healing journey

5/4/2020

Butterfly Bliss Productions LLC
P.O. Box 330482, West Hartford, CT 06133
ButterflyBlissProductions.com
ThriverZone.com
SusanOmilian.com

This is a work of fiction. Names, characters, places, and incidents are the products of the author's imagination or are used fictitiously. Any resemblance to actual events, locales, or persons, living or dead, is entirely coincidental.

ISBN # 978-0-9985746-0-8 print book
ISBN # 978-0-9985746-1-5 e-book

Author photo by Cynthia Lang Photography
Cover and interior design by Anita Jones, Another Jones Graphics I AnotherJones.com

This book is available at quantity discounts for bulk purchase. Contact the publisher.

A portion of the proceeds of this book will be donated to services for women and children who have experienced abuse and violence.

Publisher's Cataloging-In-Publication Data
(Prepared by The Donohue Group, Inc.)

Names: Omilian, Susan M.
Title: Awaken : the awakening of the human spirit on a healing journey / by Susan
    M. Omilian JD.
Description: West Hartford, CT : Butterfly Bliss Productions LLC, [2017] I Series: The
    best revenge series ; [1] I "Inspired by a true event." I Includes bibliographical
    references.
Identifiers: ISBN 978-0-9985746-0-8 (print) I ISBN 978-0-9985746-1-5 (ebook)
Subjects: LCSH: Abused women--Psychology--Fiction. I Stripteasers--Fiction. I
    Spirits--Fiction. I Self-realization in women--Fiction. I Revenge--Fiction. I
    LCGFT: Domestic fiction. I Psychological fiction.
Classification: LCC PS3615.M55 A93 2017 (print) I LCC PS3615.M55 (ebook) I
    DDC 813/.6--dc23

Printed in the United States of America

For

Maggie

1980–1999

This is not your story.
But I hope this is the way you
would want this story told.

ACKNOWLEDGMENTS

Thanks to all those who have helped me tell this story and put it on the page so it can be of benefit to others. Thank you to Faye Schrater for her assistance with shamanic ritual scenes, Claudia Volkman for editing, and Anita Jones of Another Jones Graphics for the book covers and interior design.

Special thanks to Sharon Castlen of Integrated Book Marketing for getting what I do and helping me get it out into the world.

Note from the Author

In writing this novel, I employed one of the best tools that a fiction writer has — the "what if" method of finding the story. My thought process began with a true event: the murder of my nineteen-year-old niece Maggie in 1999 by her ex-boyfriend.

From that I imagined and constructed a story by asking myself questions. What if I put my fictional characters in a similar situation? What would they do? What would happen to them? How would they feel? Then what next, next, and next?

So "inspired by a true event" is the best way I can describe how I got the idea for this novel. But the characters and their back stories are all from my imagination. I have spun a story that starts with a horrific act of murder, then chronicles its traumatizing impact on those left behind. Ultimately, though, this is a story about taking the journey beyond abuse to grow, change, and heal in the aftermath of a tragedy.

Sadly, as in real life, not everyone in the novel will pursue a healing journey. But I like to think of this novel as a fictional dramatization of the journey many of us will take after a traumatic event from victim to survivor to "thriver." Since my niece's death and in her honor, I have worked with hundreds of women who have been impacted by domestic violence, sexual assault, and child abuse and helped them find a path forward in their lives. They have a longing for something else good and positive to happen to them, but they need someone to show them how to reclaim their lives after abuse. I have been inspired by their courage and strength to take the critical next step forward and amazed by the sheer magnitude of what they have accomplished.

In connecting with a part of themselves untouched by all that has happened, they have awakened to the positive thriver energy inside them. They have created new, exciting futures for themselves and their children by getting new or better jobs, going back to school, singing or painting again, and finding new, wonderful places to live. They also have healthy relationships that have filled their lives with love, peace, and joy.

In this novel and in the upcoming books in *The Best Revenge Series*™, I have invited my fictional characters, Lacey and Lisette, to awaken to this journey of thriving. Living well is indeed the best revenge! As a writer, it has been a joy for me to help them find their inner thriver energy, even if it is just in my imagination.

I invite you too, my readers, to take the journey to your own happy place inside and live out your dreams. That's what thriving is all about!

Susan M. Omilian

"My mission in life is not merely to survive, but to thrive; and to do so with some passion, some compassion, some humor, and some style."
"Surviving is important. Thriving is elegant."

— Maya Angelou

CONTENTS

Living well is the best revenge.

— George Herbert

What we have once enjoyed we can never lose.
All that we love deeply becomes a part of us.

— Helen Keller

Your vision will become clear when you look into your heart . . .
Who looks outside, dreams.
Who looks inside, awakens.

— Carl Jung

April 5, 1996

The Escape

She saw the flashing lights of the police car in the rearview mirror of her father's pickup truck when she was about half an hour out of town. She had gone to the pay phone down the street from the bar, where she called in a report of the fire without giving her name. Her plan was to drive the truck as far as she could on the tank of gas she had filled it with earlier that day and then just leave it where it stopped.

She had been crying ever since she had left her father's bar. There, less than an hour ago, she had been so calm and cool as she lit the match and watched the place go up in flames. Now she could feel the panic setting in. What had she done? Did she really think she'd get away with it? What was going to happen to her? There was no going back now. The cops would pull her over, and soon she would be under arrest for killing Ralph. He deserved it, she thought. He was a mean, miserable son of a bitch, and no father to her. She had killed him, and she didn't even feel sorry. In fact, she was glad, even relieved, that he was out of her life forever. She hated him that much.

Then she thought of her mother. How could her mother have ever loved a man like him? How could she have left her with him? Her mother never spoke much about Ralph when she was alive, and certainly not when she was dying of the cancer that slowly ate away her body. She must have thought that when she died Ralph would change – that he would love and take care of their daughter. But didn't she know that he always was and always would be a liar and a bastard? He lied about everything, and he didn't care who he hurt – not even her, his own daughter.

It was all Ralph's fault that she was stuck in this nightmare. If only he had been the kind of father who had cared and watched out for her, this wouldn't be happening to her now. If only. If only. If only.

"Step out of the truck, young lady," the tall police officer said as he came up to the driver's side and flashed a light in her eyes. "You're not going anywhere tonight."

She didn't recognize this cop as anyone who had ever come into Ralph's bar, and she was so exhausted she decided not to argue with him. Instead she dragged her weary body out of the truck and stood on the side of the road. A second cop, younger than the first and with short-cropped blonde hair, searched the truck from the passenger side.

The other officer spoke to her again. "You don't have a license, do you?"

"I've got a learner's permit. It's in my purse." She leaned against the truck and closed her eyes.

"Bob, can you get the purse?" He signaled with the light to his partner. Then he turned back to her. "Do you have any other identification?"

"Just my library card. But it's expired."

He asked gruffly, "Are you Lisa Rozniak?"

She stared at him blankly, but then remembered that he wouldn't have any way of knowing about the transformation she was planning. After tonight she would use another name instead of Lisa, a dorky name she always hated. She wanted a name that was more – what? Grown-up and sexy-sounding, not like a little kid.

Before she could respond, the cop added impatiently, "Is your father Ralph Rozniak?"

"Yes," she said in almost a whisper.

"Is that an affirmative to both of my questions?"

She looked puzzled, like she didn't understand what he was asking her.

"Look," he said slowly and loudly as if she was hard of hearing. "You're Lisa and your father's Ralph, right?"

"Yeah, right."

"How old are you, and what are you doing out here all by yourself?"

"I just turned sixteen today, and I'm –" She paused for a moment. "I'm going to my aunt's house. She lives over in Clark's Bay."

"Does she know that you're driving in the middle of the night without a driver's license?" He sneered at her. "I bet she doesn't. I bet you don't even have an aunt in Clark's Bay."

He didn't wait for a response. He looked up at his young partner standing next to him, who spoke for the first time.

"Not much in the truck, Pete. And only a little cash in her purse."

The older officer looked back at her. "You're going have to come with me in the squad car, young lady. Officer Martin here will drive your truck back."

"Am I under arrest?"

"Arrest? For what?" he asked quickly. "Is there something I should arrest you for?"

When she didn't reply, he grabbed her elbow and led her to the car. She eyed him as he opened the rear car door and she slid into the back. Her hands touched the cool leather of the seat and she looked down at her sneakers, scuffed and soiled. When she looked up through the wire mesh that separated her from the officer in the front seat, she saw him pull the radio handset off its perch on the dashboard.

"This is Unit Eight. Come in, over."

When a voice over the radio squawked back at him, he talked as he started the car's engine. "We've found the truck and the girl. She came quietly. We're bringing the truck in too. No sign of anything suspicious."

He snickered. "Unless you count an expired library card."

CHAPTER ONE

October 17, 1999

Caught Off Guard

The words and music from the Donna Summer's "Bad Girls" disco tune blared out from the speakers on the stage as all hell broke loose at the Bare Bottom Dance Club.

Lisette stood there, in her furry white bikini top and G-string, watching a wall of drunken, angry men, yelling and screaming, storm the stage and head straight for her.

This isn't supposed to happen, she thought in the split second she had to think. Then she screamed, a shrill, panic-stricken cry that instantly was drowned out by the loud music going on and on.

She loved to play the music loud when she danced, the louder the better. She liked to hear and feel the beat all around her. When it shook the stage under her feet and sent shock waves out into the audience, she was ready to dance. And she loved the song that was currently playing. She had added it to her act out in Los Angeles and the crowd there had gotten into it, singing along with all the whistles, beep-beeps, and toot-toots. But now the music was part of the deafening roar all around her – the sound of a sea of drunken men in heat, stampeding onto the stage, beating up on each other, and yelling in sharp, hoarse voices for her. Like a tidal wave, this roar was about to engulf her. Luckily, Erick, one of the club's bouncers, who had hands the size of Texas, was at her side, pulling one guy after another off her. But as quickly as he did, someone else came at her, trying to grab her, touch her, grope her.

"Get away from me, you little pervert," she screeched at one particularly nasty drunk who lunged at her from behind, yelling, "I love you, I love you!"

She turned around and elbowed him in the face. That sent him reeling backward, and he fell to the stage with a splat. In that moment, Lisette saw her chance to escape. But just as she turned to run off the stage, the guy she had decked reached up from the floor and grabbed her leg.

"Marry me, marry me," he slobbered, attaching himself to her ankle and pawing his way up her leg.

God, she hated her job on nights like this! Why had it been her dumb luck to open at the Bare Bottom Dance Club late on a Sunday night when the college students with fake IDs got two watered-down drinks for the price of one if they showed their school card? By the time she had gotten onstage as the headline stripper, the audience was pretty tanked up. Of course, she was used to having men go nuts over her long blonde hair, big breasts, and the kinky getup she wore. But tonight, as she was taking off her costume for the crowd, the audience was pushing and shoving each other down in front until one guy took a swing at another and a brawl broke out. Everyone leaped onto the stage, and now this idiot wouldn't let go of her leg.

She tried to pry his fingers off her almost-numb flesh, but he hung on to her with a grip like a steel trap. Desperate now, she yelled for Erick. "Get this asshole off me!"

On stage, she was always in charge, but this was way out of control!

When Lacey pushed open the door of Ari's college dorm room on Sunday night before midnight, Ari was slumped down in front of his computer. The door wasn't locked, and she hadn't knocked. She just barged in. She didn't care – she was that pissed at him.

The moment he saw her standing in the doorway, he bolted upright in his chair and his face lit up. He looked startled to see her, as though he had been expecting her but somehow now that she was there, he was surprised.

She stood there, backlit by the light in the hall, glaring down at him. He stared back, his eyes aglow like she was still the brightest spot in his life. But how could he think that? she wondered. They hadn't seen each other in about a week and as far as she was concerned, there was no magic left between them.

"I'm here like you asked," she said, "but I can't stay long. I told Sophie I'd be back in our room in ten minutes. I mean it, Ari. Ten minutes."

"In ten minutes, my angel," he said with a lilt in his voice that surprised her, "we can do a lot." He reached out to touch her, but she pulled her arm away and pushed herself back against the open door.

"Don't give me that 'angel' shit," she said. "How many times do I have to tell you? It's over between us!"

"You'll always be my angel. You can't change that."

"No, you're the one who can't change. When are you going to grow up?"

"I am all grown up." He grabbed his crotch and lowered his voice seductively. "Straight and tall, just for you. Can't you tell?"

She rolled her eyes. "Is that all you ever think of? Getting some girl into bed?"

"No, I think of you all the time. I can't get a damn thing done around here."

She leaned her head back against the door. "Jesus, Ari, it's not my fault!"

"Oh, no? If you hadn't been sucking face with that bastard at The Keg, none of this would have happened."

"I wasn't kissing Jack! I was dancing with him. You're the one who's a bastard."

"I'm the bastard because I get upset when I see the girl I love with another guy?"

"You don't love me, and you can't tell me what I can or can't do anymore." The agitation in Lacey's voice showed as the night at The Keg came rushing back to her now. Her body shook with rage. "If I want to dance with ten guys, you can't stop me. Jesus, Ari! Why do we keep going over this same old stuff? What do you want from me?"

"I don't want anything from you," he snapped and sank back down in his chair, his arms folded tightly across his chest.

God! How he infuriated her. Now he was going to sulk and show her how angry he was at her, but she was sick of his games. It was time for this to end. She had no future with Ari, and she'd never give in to what he wanted. It was over. She had to make him understand that. That's why she agreed to come here tonight. Why was he being so impossible?

"Look," she began, shoring up her voice so it sounded strong and firm. "If you think you can talk me into getting back together with you, forget it." She grabbed the doorknob and made a move back into the hall. "I'm out of here."

"No! No!" He leaped from his chair and jammed the palm of his hand against the door. "Please, don't go. Please," he begged. "Come and sit down over there." He motioned across the room to his roommate's bed. "And I'll sit here," he added, walking back to his desk chair, his eyes still glued on her. "I won't touch you, I promise."

Lacey stood in the doorway, her arms wrapped around her and her foot tapping the floor. She curled her lip and weighed her next move.

"I don't want to fight with you," he continued. "I just want you to read something for me like you used to. Remember? That's why I asked you to come here tonight."

She looked at him, then at his roommate's bed, and then back out into the hall. She wanted to storm out of there, but she knew that wouldn't solve anything. Suddenly she felt sorry for him. After all, she was the one who had dumped him. She wanted to let him down easy, but he was making it so hard. So she had to stay, play along with him for a while until she could say what she had come to say and then leave. Maybe that was the only way to settle this thing with him once and for all.

"I'm sorry I upset you," he went on. His voice was softer, and suddenly he sounded more like the Ari she knew. That made her feel a pang in her heart for him, like she had felt the day she first met him when he was so charming, so open, so much fun to be with. Maybe if she just tried harder now to let him know how sorry she was that he was taking this so hard.

She relented just a bit and said softly, "I'm not upset." Then she sighed and added, "All right. What do you want me to read?"

"I have to print it out. It will only take a minute."

She looked at him, this time with a little more kindness in her eyes.

"Okay," she said as she slowly moved away from the door and let it close behind her. "But then I have to get back. I still have homework."

"I never thought you studied so much," Ari said with a smile. "You're so smart. I'm the one who's stupid."

"You're not stupid," she said, crossing the room and settling down uneasily on the edge of the bed next to the door that led to the bathroom and Ari's suitemates' room. "You need to apply yourself more, that's all."

"No, compared to you, I'm an idiot. You're a wonderful writer, and I can't even keep my English words straight. That's why I need your help. I've got to get my grades up or my dad won't pay my tuition. You know what a bastard he is. He couldn't care less if I'm happy or well-educated. He's sure I'll end up an old wino, lying drunk in the gutter with nothing to show for my life. God! How he loves screwing with my head!"

"Look," Lacey hedged, trying not to get caught up in all his problems. "I said I'd help you. So can we just get on with this, please?"

"Sure, sure," he said breezily as he reached over to the keyboard of his computer and pushed a few buttons. Soon the printer started up, and he went on. "I appreciate you coming over. This damn paper is due tomorrow and I haven't been able to focus on it. I couldn't sleep a wink last night. I kept thinking about the Homecoming Dance last fall. Do you remember it?" He shut his eyes for a moment and spoke as if he was talking about a dream. "It was the first time I saw you. You were a freshman, and I asked you to dance. You said yes. I couldn't believe it. You were wearing that green velvet dress with your hair all piled up on top of your head. God, you looked beautiful, so beautiful."

His voice trailed off, but a few seconds later the bitterness he must have felt towards her since she broke up with him came spewing up like bile in his throat. His eyes popped open and his face went dark as he ripped into her. "How could things get so bad in just one year? You went from being the most loving, caring person in the whole world to such a cruel, heartless bitch. Did you ever really love me? Or do you just enjoy making me feel like a worthless piece of shit?"

She sat there stunned. What was he – crazy? He was twisting everything around, trying to make it all her fault. Did he really hate her that much and believe all those terrible things about her?

Suddenly she felt scared. For the first time since she walked into the room, she wondered how this was all going to end. She thought she'd tell him to leave her alone one more time and then leave. But maybe that was not what he was thinking. What was he thinking? Was he capable of doing something to hurt her? He had never hit her or anything like that. That wasn't Ari. But he had been pressuring her, pushing their relationship too far, too fast, and he got so jealous if she even talked to another guy. She just wanted it to stop. Why couldn't she make him stop? What was wrong with him? Maybe she should have listened to what Sophie had said to her about him after the episode at The Keg.

"This guy is creepy. He's trouble, big trouble!"

But how much trouble? Lacey's mind raced now. She knew that he was immature, but how far would he go with this rage he had against her? What was he capable of? His voice, loud and demanding, took her out of her thoughts.

"There's something I want to show you," he said, standing up and taking the few steps over to his bed.

She stood up too and, almost without thinking, launched into what she had come prepared to say because now she was shaking inside and wanted to leave. "I'm sorry that things have changed between us, Ari, but they have. You have to stop tormenting yourself about this and move on. You have to believe that someday you'll meet someone else and—"

"I don't want anyone else," his voice, flat and oddly detached, broke in. "I want you."

She hesitated, gauging his mood, but his eyes looked haunted and she felt a cold, scary distance between them.

"But you can't have me," she went on, her voice rising. "You have this idea that if you keep bugging me, I'll give in. But I won't. It's no use." Then her voice was loud and shrill. "You can't go on like this. It's not good!"

Suddenly she stopped and the room was silent except for the printer.

"I've got to go," Lacey said in a rush of words, her heart pumping and her stomach hurting. "This is getting way too crazy for me."

"But you have to see this first."

"I don't have time to read your paper tonight."

"Not my paper," he said with a twisted smile. "A surprise just for you."

He faced his bed and reached underneath it for something. He kept it close to his body as he raised it up to his waist. She strained to see what it was. At first, all she could tell was that it was long and shiny. By the time she realized it was a gun, a rifle, he had it pointed at his head.

"Oh my God!" she screamed and fell back. "Ari, what are you doing? Where did you get that?"

She took a step toward him, but then stopped when she saw his finger on the trigger. "Ari, don't! Don't!"

But he didn't stop. He closed his eyes, and suddenly she knew what was going to happen next. She lunged toward the bathroom door. She could get out that way. This bastard wasn't going to kill himself in front of her. She wasn't going to watch it. No way! This wasn't going to happen to her. But before she could reach the door, she heard a loud popping sound and felt a sharp pain in her back. Her legs went out from under her, and suddenly she was on the floor on her back, twisted around, looking up at him.

"If I can't have you," he said with no emotion at all in his voice, "no one can."

"Please, Ari!" she screamed, her heart pounding hard and her voice filled with terror. She had never had a gun pointed at her before. "I'm sorry. I'm so sorry."

She closed her eyes, thinking she'd feel something more but she didn't. This time, the sound was like fireworks going off, and it shattered the night as the screen before her eyes went red – blood red. Then, amazingly, her whole life flashed before her, from the time she was a little girl to only a few moments ago when she walked into Ari's room. It was like a movie, but it was going very, very fast. Almost too fast, but then it was her life, so she knew what was going on.

As she felt herself sinking deeper and deeper into this cinematic whirl, the story shifted and other people, people she didn't know or even recognize, filled the screen. She watched with fascination as another drama unfolded. This one felt so familiar, as though it had happened to her already but she couldn't remember how it ended. All the things she had been doing the last few days and much, much more were mixed up in what she was seeing, but what was she seeing? Was it a dream? Was Ari in this dream? Or was he someplace else? Did she hear another shot, or was it that blasted music that was pounding in her head now? God, it was loud. And there were people yelling on a stage somewhere. She felt danger there, like someone was trying to hurt her or someone else.

Where was she? Who were these people? What was happening to her? She tried to figure it out, but the music grew so loud that she couldn't hear herself think. If someone could just turn the damn music down! What was wrong with these people anyway?

What the *hell* was going on?

With the disco music still blasting up on the stage, Lisette looked down into the face of the man who had her leg in his grip. He wasn't letting go of her no matter what she did to shake him off and she was afraid. With the hungry look she saw in his eyes, maybe he wasn't going to let go until he got what he wanted from her. But what was that? Just when she feeling hopeless, suddenly Erick spun around and grabbed the guy off the floor, squeezing him around the chest so hard with his huge hands that it knocked the air out of him and he finally let go of her leg.

Then Erick yelled, "Get out of here, Lisette! Go to your dressing room and lock the door."

She didn't argue. She ran for the back curtain, scurried backstage, and raced down the hall. She told herself that when she got to her dressing room, she'd call Mo. She didn't care how late it was. Her agent was going to hear about this. This shouldn't be happening to her. She was a dancer, an artist. Her mother had taken her to too many dance classes when she was a kid to have her career end up like this.

She turned off the long main hallway that led from the stage to a shorter one that dead-ended at her dressing room door. She could feel herself relax a little, knowing she was almost there, almost safe. But when she got to the door and grabbed the knob, it wouldn't open.

"Damn it!" she screamed and kicked at the door. Who the hell locked this? she fumed. She didn't have a key. She stood back and jammed her shoulder against the door, hoping it was just stuck, but it wouldn't open. Then the music from the stage suddenly quieted down and she heard a noise coming from out in the hallway where she had just been. She stopped to listen for a moment. Was someone coming? Maybe it was Erick to see if she was okay. Then she definitely heard footsteps coming toward her down the long hallway.

"Who's there?" she called out, her voice shaking. "Is someone there?"

A man stepped out from around the corner and she gasped. It was the lunatic that had her leg in a death grip on the stage. How did he get back here? Where were the bouncers? Oh God! She shuddered; the guy had that same hungry, haunted look on his face as before. Had he come to get what he wanted from her now?

What could she do? She was trapped alone in this tiny hallway, with nowhere to run or hide. Should she scream? Would anyone hear her?

She held his gaze, trying to stare him down, but he didn't flinch; he didn't move.

"What do you want?" she finally said, hoping that the rage in her voice might scare him off. But he didn't reply, only moved closer to her, his dark, clouded eyes locked on hers. She watched his face as he looked down, and his hand came up from behind his back. That's when she saw the knife.

"Oh, God!" she screamed, falling back against the door and grabbing at the knob. She frantically wiggled it up and down, back and forth, desperately trying to get it open. But it wouldn't budge. The only way out was past the man with the knife.

She stood her ground, although her legs were shaking and her stomach was churning.

"What do you want?" she repeated, but she got no reply. She wanted to beg, "Don't hurt me. Please don't hurt me!" but suddenly a bright light blocked her view of him. In the first flash of the light, she saw a girl with long blonde hair, standing with her arms folded across her chest. Then she vanished and a voice came into her head.

Don't beg. Begging won't help. Stay calm. Never let a man trap you in a place where you can't get out. Think, girl, think. Whatever you do, don't make a sudden move. That could set him off. Back away from the door slowly, very slowly. That's it. Try to catch him off guard. You can do it.

Terrified, Lisette listened to the voice, trusting it as if her mother was talking to her. She backed off, but she could feel the man coming closer and her legs went limp. Was this the end? Was this how she was going to die? What should she do? Should she stop listening to the voice?

Suddenly, the sound of sirens outside jolted her and an idea came to her.

"Police!" she yelled into the light. "They're coming for you. Run now, run!"

She must have confused him, making him think the police were after him because he gasped and grunted, and then she heard his footsteps going down the hall to the back door of the club. When she looked again, the light was gone and so was he. Instead, Erick rushed toward her.

"Are you okay?" he asked. "I came as soon as I could."

"There was a man with a knife," she said, her breath coming in short gulps. "The sirens scared him away. He ran out the back door. The police will catch him."

She fell against Erick. Her whole body shook as he put his arms around her, and she stood there in his embrace, trying to take in what had just happened to her.

"It's okay," Erick whispered into her ear. "I'm here. You're safe now."

She let herself stand there for a while, and then she slowly pulled away from him.

"The police will get him, right?" she said. "He could hurt someone."

Erick shook his head. "The police aren't here," he said. "We didn't call them. Those sirens are going down to the campus." Lisette knew he was talking about the college that was only a few blocks from the club.

"Someone just came into the bar and said a girl was shot and killed there," Erick added. "The whole place emptied out real quick."

"Oh my God!" she gasped, and her thoughts went to a dark and scary place. She could have been murdered tonight too. If it weren't for the voice and that light, she'd be dead.

"Are you all right?" Erick asked her again. He turned toward her dressing room. "Why didn't you go inside like I told you to?"

She looked at him, barely understanding his words, and then muttered, "I tried. The door was locked. I couldn't get in."

He gave her a look and reached for the door handle. He jiggled it a bit, lifted it up a notch, and the door pushed open.

"It gets stuck sometimes," he said, his voice heavy and thick. "Someone should have told you. I'm sorry!"

"It doesn't matter now," she said, too exhausted to be mad and too relieved to do anything but stumble into her dressing room.

"Why don't you put some clothes on and I'll walk you back to your hotel?" Erick offered. "The night air will calm you down and you'll get a good night's sleep." She nodded and sighed. Then he gave her a smile and added, "You'll be okay now."

He closed the door behind him, and she sank into the chair in front of her dressing table. She looked at her face in the mirror and saw what a mess it was. Her eyes were red and bloodshot, her skin pale. Her hair was all over the place. But that didn't matter. She was alive! But if that voice hadn't come to her, the man with the crazed look in his eyes might have killed her for sure.

If whoever killed that girl tonight at the college was anything like him, Lisette had some idea of what she must have gone through.

What a horrible way to die! And there was no one there to save her.

Why was she the only one tonight lucky enough to be alive?

Lisette woke up the next morning in her hotel room with something ringing in her ear. It took her a moment to figure out it was the phone. As she reached to grab it on the nightstand by her bed, she saw on the clock radio dial that it was only eight o'clock. Who the hell was calling her at this hour of the morning?

She was tired. She had been too afraid to close her eyes last night, scared that she'd see the face of the man with the knife or dream about the girl who had been killed at the college. Without much sleep, she could feel a migraine headache coming on and she wished the damn phone would stop ringing!

She grabbed it, and said groggily, "Hello?"

"Lisette?" a familiar voice on the other end said. "Are you all right?"

It was Mo, her agent, and he sounded frantic. "I got your message this morning," he went on. "What the hell happened last night?"

She had called him from her dressing room as Erick waited outside to take her back to her hotel. She had forgotten about leaving him a message until now, but she knew that she had sounded pretty frantic last night.

"I almost got trampled onstage," she began, her head pounding. "Then there was this guy with a knife who cornered me by my dressing room, and if I hadn't seen this light and heard a voice, I would have… I wouldn't be…" Her voice dropped off as the emotions she had felt last night – shock, fear, and relief – flooded back and overwhelmed her. Then her mind shifted and she went on, "When I heard the sirens, I said the first thing that popped into my head and – "

"Wait a minute!" Mo broke in. "Slow down! You're not making any sense."

"Of course I'm not!" she snapped, sitting up in bed with a jolt. She moaned as the sudden movement brought a sharp pain to the front of her head, and she fell back on the pillow. "That's why I want out," she went on. "Do you hear me? I'm not going back to that club. A girl got killed near there last night. I'm scared, Mo. I'm really scared."

"But I can't tell Wiley you're quitting just because some guys rushed the stage. You know that can happen anywhere. And I heard about the girl. You know it's not Wiley's fault some girl was killed nearby. And why should you care? You didn't even know her."

"I do care. I'm serious. I'm not going back there. Period."

"Look," Mo said, his voice getting testy. "You're upset. Take some time, calm down, and call me back later. We'll talk."

"But you don't understand." Lisette's voice cracked. "I feel so… so…"

"So, so what?" His voice slowed down, as if he was trying to understand.

"I don't know. I feel like… like…" She paused, trying to find the right word, and then went on, "I feel bad, I guess. I feel bad about the girl who got killed."

"I know the story is all over the TV news today, but that's no reason for you to quit your job. What's that girl to you?"

"It's on the news?" Lisette asked eagerly. "What are they saying? What happened?"

"Only that her boyfriend shot her and then killed himself."

So the little coward did do it! I'm glad he's dead.

"So the little coward did do it!" Lisette blurted out, but the words felt like they had come from somewhere else.

"Yes, they said it was a lover's quarrel," Mo added.

A lover's quarrel? You've got to be kidding. The little bastard didn't love me. He trapped me in his room and then pulled a gun.

"It wasn't a lover's quarrel," Lisette insisted, but then she wondered how she could know that. What did she know about this girl? Suddenly, she had to know everything.

"Look, I've got to go," she told Mo, as she eyed the TV remote control on her nightstand. "You're right. I'm upset. I'll call you later."

"But wait! Don't hang up on me. What is going on?"

"Here's what's going on," she bristled. "I want out. I don't want to talk about it. I want you to fix it. Okay? Bye."

She slammed the phone down, reached for the remote, and switched on the set. She flipped through channels until she found a news program and the picture of the girl on the screen. Lisette couldn't believe it. She had long blonde hair and a face that she recognized instantly.

Oh my God, it's me. They're talking about me like I'm dead. Am I? Am I really?

It was the girl who had flashed before her eyes in the hallway last night. She was standing in the same way, with her arms folded across her chest.

That's my high school graduation picture. The photographer made me pose like that. I look like I'm in charge of the world, don't I? Hey, I like that!

This girl was wearing a heart-shaped locket around her neck, something Lisette had seen last night but didn't remember until now.

That's my mom's locket. I always wear it.

Lisette's mind raced. How could she have seen someone who was lying dead someplace else? Was that possible?

"Jesus!" she said aloud. "This is weird, too weird!"

Weird? Here's something weird. Our names both start with "L." What's with that?

The announcer said the girl's name was Lacey Lockhart and that she was only nineteen years old. Same age as me, Lisette thought. Same long blonde hair. Same everything I saw last night. But this Lacey was dead. How could I have seen her?

I get it now. I'm dreaming. I didn't go to Ari's room last night. I'm asleep in my dorm room, and soon the alarm clock will ring and Sophie will have to pull me out of bed because I'm always late. She'll tease me about how I'll be late for my own funeral, and I'll tell her I dreamed I was a stripper and danced for men who lusted after my body and fought over me until they got so crazy they attacked me up onstage. Sophie will tease me and say, "Yeah, sure! In your wildest dreams, Lacey! Sure!"

Then another picture flashed on the screen. "This is Ari," the announcer said, "the man who killed Lacey." Lisette gasped. He had dark hair and a scowl on his face. How could a girl like Lacey be with someone like him? Someone who could kill her?

Dead? I'm not dead. But seeing pictures of Ari and me on TV is strange.

The announcer added that the couple had broken up recently, and that there had been no prior reports of violence between them.

He's right. Ari never touched me. If he had, I would've beaten the snot out of him. Somehow he got a gun. I didn't see it there in his hand until the very end. The little bastard got me into his room and tried to kill himself! But I wouldn't watch it, no way!

So he was her ex-boyfriend. That made sense. Lacey had dumped the creep, and he wanted her back. But if he couldn't have her, no one could.

Ari's famous last words! How did you know that?

When she said no, he killed her. It was that simple.

Oh, my God, now I get it. He shot me! First in the back and then I fell down. He pointed the gun. I don't remember, but I felt the pain.

Suddenly, Lisette felt a sharp, terrible pain in her own back, so intense that tears came to her eyes. What was happening? Where did this pain come from? It hurt so much.

I remember feeling the pain and then floating off somewhere. Feeling like I was neither here nor there, like I was lost with no place to go.

Lisette couldn't stand the pain. She doubled over and gasped for breath. She gulped for air but the pain only got worse.

So I am dead. Ari killed me, and then he killed himself. This isn't a dream. I won't be waking up and telling Sophie anything. I'm not coming back. I'm never coming back. Oh, God! When will this pain end? Please, God, let it end.

Then a heave came up from Lisette's stomach. She was going to throw up. The pain was so unbearable.

But if I'm dead, then where am I? Am I in Lisette's body? How does this work? I can hear what she's saying, but can she hear me? She did last night, but now she's acting like she doesn't. Oh, God! Oh, God! What is happening to me?

"Oh, God! Oh, God!" Lisette cried, as she ran into the bathroom and got down on her knees in front of the toilet. "What is happening to me?" She felt her stomach churn and her chest get tighter and tighter. The pain in her back was so intense that she could hardly breathe.

She hears what I'm saying, and she feels my pain. If I get excited, her stomach gets upset. That's a start. We can do this. Ari is gone. I'm safe here with Lisette. I'm okay. I'm fine for now. It's okay, Lisette. We're fine.

Lisette didn't throw up. Instead, she sat down on the bathroom floor and held her head in her hands. Slowly, the jitters in her stomach and the pain in her back eased. She took a deep breath. Maybe this was from the migraine she felt coming on when she woke up. Maybe she needed to get something to eat. She could get dressed and go get some breakfast. It wasn't even nine o'clock in the morning, and she wasn't usually up so early when she worked the night before. But this morning was different. She needed to take some time, have a cup of coffee, try to relax. Then she'd call Mo, tell him she was better, and they'd talk about a new club date for her. Soon she'd be back at work, and what happened to her and this Lacey Lockhart would be forgotten. A prayer her mother had taught her when she was a kid came into her head.

"May the souls of the faithful departed, through the mercy of God, rest in peace, Amen." Yes, dear God! Lisette thought. Let Lacey rest in peace. There was nothing more to do for her.

But there is something you can do. Get me out of here! I'm in this crazy limbo place. Dead, but still here in the body of a stripper, for God's sake!

"Rest in peace, Lacey," Lisette whispered fervently. "It's over!"

But it's not over. I want out. Somebody help me! Please help me!

"Give it a rest, Lacey! Give it a rest."

CHAPTER TWO

A Lucky Day

When Ambrose walked into the Pussycat's Meow that Wednesday night, he remembered what he liked about the noisy, smelly club.

It was cheap. With no cover charge to see the dancers, he could buy a drink and nurse it slowly at a back table and watch the girls perform. Or he could sit in the bar and watch television. But tonight he had come for one reason – to check out an act, a very special act he thought.

When he had first seen the publicity poster for this act hanging in the front window of the club a few days ago, his jaw had dropped and eyes popped wide open. He read the top line, "Straight from Appearances in Los Angeles!" and then took in the photograph of the dancer below.

She was young, maybe nineteen or twenty, and had a sultry look on her face. Her wide, sensuous lips were set in a perpetual pout, and her long blonde hair hung down from a helmet-like hat on her head in tangled strands that he thought needed combing. Her breasts were large, probably surgically implanted, he noted, and her derriere was more than ample. She stood in profile, her chest and ass thrust out in opposite directions, with a scant, bikini-like outfit barely covering those areas of bountiful endowment. Fuzzy white fur framed those parts of the costume that touched the most intimate parts of her body.

Below the photo were the words: "Coming Soon – Attila the Hunny!"

At the sight of her stage name, he smirked. What was this Attila the Hunny shit? There's no "hunny" in Attila the Hun! What was this girl thinking? In the fourth century, the Huns would've raped any woman especially one who looked like her.

Tonight he bought a bottle of beer at the bar, walked to a table near the front by the stage, and took a seat. He'd have to wait a while for the real show to begin. First, Wiley, the club's owner, would bring out the dancers who were not as talented, experienced, or sexy as the headline stripper, and they'd entertain the crowd until the drinks flowed. Then, when there was little chance that watching the show might interfere with the sale of booze, Wiley would bring on the prize package. Although Ambrose knew this drill by heart, tonight every minute felt like an hour for him and every irritation was agony.

Like the fact that it was only mid-October, yet the club's heating system was already blasting out hot air as if it was the middle of winter. He had been inside for only a few minutes and already his tall, husky body was overheated. Sweat covered his brow and beads of perspiration ran down his face, falling into his bloodshot eyes and glistening on his large nose. Sweat also settled in the kinky gray strands of his beard that were almost as long as the matted, stringy brown hair hanging from his receding hairline to the middle of his back. But Ambrose didn't seem to care how the sweat mixed with the dirt and dust on his clothing and made his whole body reek. He leaned back in his chair, stretched out his six-foot frame, and folded his arms over the protruding belly barely covered by a faded Grateful Dead T-shirt and the black leather vest that he wore over it.

"Jesus, can't you clean yourself up?" a voice said from behind him.

Ambrose turned to see Wiley, the club's owner, cruising the larger-than-usual Wednesday night crowd with Webster, his bouncer, a routine Ambrose knew well. They'd harass a few guys so the rest wouldn't try any funny business, but no one would get thrown out. It was a delicate game that Wiley played well, but then, so did Ambrose.

"Like it's your business how I look," Ambrose shot back, pushing himself forward in his chair and taking a gulp of his beer. "I'm not here for a job interview."

"But you could go back to work," Wiley replied with a modicum of civility in his voice. Then he added with a snarl, "And not be such a drain on society."

Ambrose gave him a look. "You got a problem? I paid for the beer. When's the show going to start, anyway? I hope the new headliner is better than those two up there." Ambrose pointed to the girls lethargically dancing on the stage. "Even I can keep better time to the music than they can."

"This isn't the Arthur Murray Dance Studio. I don't hear you complain when they take it all off. That's what stripping is about. Tits and ass, not those stupid pirouettes."

"Stripping is about you getting rich off us poor folks," Ambrose said. Then he sighed, feigning disgust. "Jesus, I don't know why I come in here anymore."

"You come in here so you can go back to the gutter and whack off."

"At least I can get it up," Ambrose shot back, taking a gulp of his beer.

Wiley's eyes flared up, and Webster made a sudden move for Ambrose.

"Let me take him out of here, boss. He's a moocher. I caught him the last few days outside the club drooling all over the head-liner's picture."

"No, leave him be," Wiley said, waving Webster off. He lit into Ambrose. "Pay for more than one beer tonight, would you? Or Webster will kick you out of here."

"Yeah, yeah," Ambrose growled as the men walked away from him. Go bother some other poor slob, he fumed to himself, while he drank his overpriced beer. Ambrose's eyes returned to the stage as the so-called dancers were scurrying off to modest applause. He felt his heart thump as the stage announcer gave the cue.

"Ladies and gentlemen, the Pussycat's Meow is proud to pres-ent the most ferocious, the most fantastic, the most awesome dancer of them all, Attila the Hunny!"

Several loud booms came from the stage, causing Ambrose to jump in his seat. Puffs of smoke rolled up from the back and moved along the runway until they enveloped the round plat-form with a ceiling-to-floor brass pole set in the middle. Through the haze he could see nothing, but he heard the bold opening chords of the loud, crashing rock song "We Are the Champions" that proclaimed what Attila and his Huns would be when they conquered the world.

Slowly a figure emerged through the smoke, a girl dressed in a furry, white jacket that went down as far as the top of her hips. Recognizing her and all that fur from the poster as the headliner, Ambrose watched her walk with her arms up over her head and a dozen streamers of long white, gauze-like material blowing back from her shoulders. Two wind machines below her blew the streamers up and away from her body so that they looked like wings attached to her.

My God! Ambrose thought, with that and the wispy pillows of smoke floating around her, she looks like an angel perched up on heavenly clouds. Suddenly he felt a shiver go through him. Few people in this crummy strip joint would appreciate the true message of her act, but he got it. She moved something inside him that he had thought was long dead. It was as if the energy and boldness of Attila the Hun that he experienced as a kid playing soldiers in his backyard was coming back to him, and Attila the Hunny was showing him the way out of his misery.

Thank God! he sighed. She had come to rescue him.

She had come at last.

As the last chorus of the rock song thundered out into the audience and the smoke lingered on the stage, it was Lisette's cue to walk up to the brass pole, lean back against it, and look graceful and magnificent.

But the smoke wasn't clearing, probably because the explosions were too big, and the damn streamers on her arms were flying all over the place because the wind machines below her were blowing too hard in the wrong direction. This was a disaster, and it was all Jerry's fault. He was an idiot. She had warned him this morning about all this when she met him, the stupid stage manager of the strip joint that Mo had booked her into after the Bare Bottom Dance Club. But he didn't get it. Tonight the explosions were off, and the wind machines weren't set up right. Worst of all, right now Jerry was nowhere in sight, the little twit. She gritted her teeth, felt her way to the pole as the smoke cleared and tried to get the streamers under control. But suddenly the wind machine on her left picked up on one of them, causing it to fly up behind her, waving wildly. Trying to continue with her act, she took the Attila helmet off her head, but when she did, the wind blew her long hair right into her eyes. Now she couldn't see a damn thing.

What a complete disaster! This place was worse than the Bare Bottom. It smelled like dead socks in her dressing room, and everyone was so incompetent. Why had Mo sent her here? Didn't he know how much she needed her act to be perfect? It meant something to her, no matter where she danced or for whom. She wasn't stupid. She knew why the goons in the audience came to see her, but was it so unreasonable for her to want to do something artistic before she took her clothes off? It was that part of the show that got her through the rest. But tonight, there was no hope for anything coming off right. The runaway streamer was whipping around behind her so wildly that she decided to let all the streamers go and have the wind blow them to the back of the stage, out of her way. That's what happened, except one of them caught the wind and went flying into the audience. A man down in front stood up and grabbed it as it flew by. Then, like an idiot, he flapped it up and down on his arm.

"Look, I'm the flying stripper," he yelled, slurring his words, obviously drunk. Once he did, several other men joined in heckling her.

"Hey, baby!" one shouted. "When are you gonna take it off?"

Another chimed in. "Show us your tits!" Then they all thrust dollar bills at her and taunted her to come get them.

"Hey, Hunny!" the first man said, flipping the streamer. "You blow me away!"

"Christ," she moaned, as the music of her opening song faded and the driving beat of the next song came on. She hated it when some joker in the crowd upstaged her. Once a heckler got started, he'd never stop until somebody shut him up, and it never worked for her to try to do that from up on the stage. So she went on, dancing across the stage, acting like nothing was wrong. When she spun herself around the brass pole and a whoop came up from the audience, that made her feel good until the heckler put the streamer over his face and screeched at her. "Hey! Attila the Hunny! Yoo-hoo! Peek-a-boo! I see you!"

As he pulled it away from his face, she glared at him. How was she going to shut this asshole up? Suddenly, a man – a big, tall guy with long hair and a beard – came out of nowhere and went up to this guy's table. He wasn't a bouncer, because they only approached customers when they touched a girl or got up onstage. No, this long-haired guy didn't care about that. He was there to help her and so he grabbed the heckler, pulled him down off the chair, and sat on him. Lisette couldn't believe it. The guy shut up, and Lisette was able to go on with her act, pouting and strutting around the stage, bending over and taunting the audience through her legs. As she did, she danced over to the big guy who had just helped her out. She opened her furry white jacket and flashed him a preview of coming attractions. She could tell he loved it. His eyes bugged out and his mouth gaped open at the sight of her body gyrating just for him. He must not be getting any these days, she laughed to herself. Then he surprised her. He got a silly little grin on his face, put his hand up and gave her a little wave – like she was his new best friend, or like he'd follow her anywhere and do anything for her. Who was he kidding? she smirked. That wasn't going to happen. Sure, you helped me out, but dream on, sucker, she thought, as she danced away across the stage.

This is striptease, buddy.

Nothing more.

Ambrose stared up in amazement at this incredible young woman dancing right in front of him.

This Attila the Hunny had breasts to die for and an ass that she wiggled like she was giving every guy in the place a piece of it. It was clear to him that she was paying attention to him for taking care of that heckler business, but he was sure it was more than that. They were connecting, and he felt useful for the first time in a long time. Then the drunk he was sitting on got feisty again and pounded on his leg.

"Get off me!" he snarled. "This is *my* seat."

Ambrose let up a little, and the man scrambled out from under him.

"She ain't Attila," the man blurted out, butting his short, fat body right up against Ambrose's. "He'd never wave any damn silly white curtains around." Then the man grabbed at the tangle of white material from around him and threw it in a wad on the floor behind him.

"Sit down and shut up!" Ambrose snapped. "You don't know shit about Attila."

"I know he killed a lot of people, and they called him the Sponge of God."

"*Scourge* of God, you asshole. Shut up or get out – I'm watching the show."

"No, I'm going to take a piss," the man announced, his eyes rolling back into his head.

"Good. You go wee-wee and come back when you're not being such a jerk," Ambrose said to the guy as he disappeared in the crowd. Ambrose settled into his front-row seat as the show continued.

Now Attila the Hunny had taken her furry white jacket off her shoulders, down her arms, and was tossing it from one hand to the other until she flung it out into the audience. A cheer went up from the crowd as it sailed up and then down into a group of men who scrambled for it as if it were a home-run ball hit into the upper deck of left field. Then she pranced away, showing off her large, full breasts, pink and pushed up against the white fur of her skimpy bikini top, and began tugging at the fuzzy G-string that caressed her flat stomach. She turned around so that everyone could see the thong that barely covered the crack of her ass and shook her buns, tight, round, and glistening with sweat. It was as if she wanted them to see the sweat pouring off her body and notice how the lust, like heat, was rising up in that room. Then, with a flash of lights and a puff of smoke, she pushed away and the music changed. "War, What Is It Good For?" – a tune that Ambrose recognized as Sixties anti-war song popularized by Edwin Starr– came through the speakers.

At each proclamation of "WAR" in the chorus of the song, she stood with an Attila-like sword and held it high over her head. Her hips wiggled their way down to the floor as the chorus continued until the next drum beat gave her another *"WAR!"* and she was up again, standing strong and defiant. It was Attila's war cry, and all the ferociousness that Attila felt as he plundered the Roman Empire was right there on her face. Then her pout turned even fiercer, as she crossed the stage, jabbing and poking the sword at the audience. This only provoked them more, and now everyone was standing, stomping, and clapping to the insistent beat. At the chorus, they all shouted out loud again, "WAR!"

This sultry bitch had the place so riled up that Ambrose wasn't sure they could take anymore. But then the music switched again, and a song with a slower beat came on. She was bringing it down just in time as Wilson Pickett began crooning "In the Midnight Hour."

The slow, grinding beat of the music and the words sung with a suggestiveness matched perfectly the wavy, rhythmic movements of her pelvis and hips. As she worked her body up and down the brass pole, she moved with such fluidity that Ambrose longed to touch and caress her. Her every action caused a reaction in his body, and when he saw how the muscles of her slender torso and flat pelvis rippled to the beat of the music, he knew that he and every other guy in the place wanted to be standing right now somewhere between her and that damn pole.

But Ambrose also got the significance of the song's lyrics about the midnight hour. Attila died on his wedding night, sometime after midnight, and Ambrose had to smile. Choosing this song told him that this girl knew something about Attila. But suddenly Ambrose didn't care what she knew. Screw history! He wanted to see her take it all off. After all, she had been playing with him all night, coming back time and again to catch his eye and send a special little bump and grind his way. Now she was in front of him, holding his eyes as she reached back to unfasten her top, bending forward and releasing her full, ripe breasts. Her boobs jumped forward, catching gravity, and settled down in all their majesty. Ambrose stared in disbelief at the most amazing breasts he had ever seen – white alabaster skin ringed with large pink nipples and a firm red tip. They weren't surgically enhanced, he could tell that now, and they didn't sag or droop. They were all natural and perfectly shaped. He struggled to hold himself back from wanting to reach out and touch their soft, warm plumpness. As if she read his thoughts, she winked at him and slowly shook her head, as if to say, "No, no! Look, but don't touch!" As she moved around the stage, thrusting her breasts out on every uptake of the song's driving beat, the crowd went crazy, rushing toward the stage and throwing bills of all denominations at her.

God, she was incredible, Ambrose thought. Beautiful, talented, sexy, and artistic. She could work an audience while still being true to the real Attila the Hun. He wondered if there was some way to harness her energy and take advantage of her amazing ability to capture Attila's spirit with every move of her body. Then it came to him with such clarity – an idea so brilliant that he wondered why he hadn't thought of it before. It was perfect. Attila the Hun would be proud of him. Did he dare go see her after the show and tell her? Or would she just blow him off as another guy who admired the way she danced, trying to get it on with her? He had to try. A chance like this only came once in a lifetime. In his head, he rehearsed the words he'd use to explain his idea to her. Then he imagined what she'd say and thought of a response to all of it. He was deep in this imaginary conversation with her when he felt a hand clamp onto his shoulder. Ambrose turned, barely able to tear his eyes off the stage, and saw Wiley eyeing him.

Can't you see I'm busy? Ambrose wanted to yell at him. I'm planning the rest of my life here.

"Have you been bothering this customer?" Wiley screamed over the roar of the crowd. Ambrose looked over to see the guy who had gone to take a piss cowering between Wiley and Webster. Was this little twerp going to make him miss the end of the show? No way, he fumed as he lunged at the guy. Ambrose had his hands around his neck before Webster could stop him. The bouncer's hand was on Ambrose's arm squeezing it so hard in a vice grip that Ambrose had to let go of the guy's neck.

"Get out of here," Webster snarled.

"Her act's almost over," Ambrose whined. "When she's finished, I'll go!"

"No! Go now," Webster said, flashing his teeth and squeezing his arm again.

"All right!" Ambrose said, annoyed. "I've seen what I came for."

"Then see that you don't come back," Wiley added as Ambrose brushed by him.

As he turned to walk away, Ambrose could hear John Denver's "Annie's Song," coming from the stage. One particular line got to him. It was the one about dying in someone's arms. Oh, God, if I could work with this girl, he thought, I wouldn't care whose arms I died in. He wanted to stay and see the rest of her act. He wanted to go back to her dressing room and talk with her. But with Webster's eyes on him, Ambrose had no choice but to lumber out of the front door of the club and take off into the night. He stood there on the sidewalk for a moment, staring at the picture of Attila the Hunny on the publicity poster in the window, and he felt a rush go through his body. He recognized that it was a life force, something that he thought had died in him so long ago.

"Oh man," he groaned, "she is the only way to get my life back."

He had to find a way to talk to her tonight. She liked him; he had helped her. She wouldn't forget. Attila the Hun would never turn down a friend – she wouldn't either. She'd listen to his idea.

Ambrose thought there might be a basement window at the back of the building that Wiley hadn't boarded up. He was pretty sure he could ease his way through it and get back inside the club tonight.

Suddenly, a loud commotion started up inside the club, and Ambrose smiled to himself. Good! he thought. Wiley and Webster would be too busy dealing with whatever was going on to hear him jam his foot through the window and climb down into the basement. From there, he'd find his way to the back of the club and her dressing room. So sure of his plan, he hummed a few notes from the last song of her act as he headed down the alley to the back of the club. He felt lighthearted and confident.

Why not? he thought.

It was his lucky day, after all.

CHAPTER THREE

Barely a Proposal

Somewhere in the middle of the last song of her act as the lilting music wafted over the rickety stage of the Pussycat's Meow, Lisette felt trouble brewing.

For the second time in a week, something twisted in the pit of her stomach as she looked out at the audience of drunken, horny men eyeing her with tortured looks on their faces as she danced bare-breasted, and this time, she took it as a sign. Maybe it wasn't a fluke that she got mobbed last Sunday. Maybe it could happen again tonight.

But there wasn't much she could do about it. Jerry still wasn't around, and Webster had left his place on the side of the stage a while ago. Not even Wiley, the owner whom she had met briefly that afternoon, was there. She could have hurried off the stage now, but she was no quitter. With only her G-string to take off, she was waiting for the audience to calm down with her last slow song, the one her mother loved, "Annie's Song." Then she'd grab the dollar bills stuffed in the elastic band of her G-string with one hand and give the string a quick tug in front with the other. She'd twirl it up and over her head, and then around on her finger while the audience cheered and applauded. Then it was one more tour around the stage to pick up the rest of her tips and head to her dressing room. She had learned years ago not to show off too much of a good thing. How else could she tease these jerks into coming back for more the next night and next night after that?

With a whiff of trouble in the air, she eyed the group of businessmen in expensive suits down in front who had been rowdy and as goofy as those college kids at the Bare Bottom the other night. But these guys had money, so she thumbed her G-string at them, like she wouldn't do anything more until they cooled down and gave her a tip. She hoped they'd get the message, but the guys took her gesture as a dare and instead jumped up onstage, heading straight for her. They grabbed at her, falling over each other and yanking at the elastic band of her G-string until she couldn't take it anymore. Seeing her Attila sword on the floor behind her, she lunged down to get it and came up fighting.

"Get away, you assholes! Or I'll chop your balls off."

A whoop came up from the bunch of them, as if they were making fun of her or taunting her, so she swung at them again. This time they took her more seriously as she forced them into a tight half-circle in front of her.

"Who's going to be first? Come on. Show me what you've got."

She poked at their crotches and laughed as they scrambled off the stage. They were afraid of a girl with a toy sword. What a joke! She was relieved until she looked up and felt something happening in the room around her. It was as though no one had ever seen anything like it before, because the whole club, even the guys who had been watching TV in the sports bar, came running to see her. They pressed up against the stage and shouted at her. Fear gripped her as the jeers from the audience got louder, and her heart pounded. Alone on the stage with her boobs hanging out, she felt as trapped as she was when the guy with the knife cornered her in the hallway the other night. What had the voice told her to do then?

Don't make any sudden moves. Back away slowly. Catch them off guard.

So slowly, she picked up the sword again and held it out in front of her as she edged herself to the back of the stage, ready to make her escape. But then another idea came to her. She was sick and tired of what she had put up with in this job and she wanted to get some revenge. She wanted these assholes tonight to feel as scared of her as she might be of them. She thought for a moment. How would Attila the Hun show how mad he was? Wouldn't he give out a yell, a howl so loud that everyone there would feel his power? She could do that. Not scream like a girl or yell like boys on a playground. No, she'd have to roar from deep down inside and let everyone know that she was pissed.

She ran to the front of the stage, threw her head back, and let out a cry that Attila would have been proud of. It was long and shrill and made the top of her head ring. When she was done, everyone and everything in the place was silent. The music had stopped, the crowd had quit yelling, and all eyes were upon her as she waved the sword over her head.

"All right," she commanded. "Everyone back away or I'll…"

Before she could go on, Webster rushed onto the stage out of nowhere.

"What the hell are you doing?" He grabbed her arm. "I could hear you outside!"

"What? You were out there for a smoke?" she snapped.

"You're nothing but a troublemaker, do you know that?"

"And you're an asshole!"

Suddenly Wiley's voice broke in from behind her. "That's enough! Take your stuff and go to your dressing room." He added gruffly, "I'll get back to you later."

"You'll get back to me?" she exploded. "I'll get back to you when I'm ready to dance again in your lousy club."

"You are threatening my customers!"

"Your customers are worth shit. You know what? I quit!" Lisette turned and walked away. She was livid. But as she did, one of the customers down in front of the stage chanted, "Hun-ny! Hun-ny!" and soon others joined in, punching their fists into the air like they were cheering for the star quarterback at a football game. Did they really love her that much? Excited, she stepped toward the men but Wiley grabbed her wrist and pulled her back.

"You're done for the night. You're not going anywhere."

"But they want me," she protested. "They're calling for me."

"I don't care if they adore you! This is my club. Customers come to see the striptease, not some crazy lady letting loose with all her anger against men. If they wanted that, they'd stay home with their wives."

"Fine," Lisette huffed, and then dug her fingernails into his hand around her wrist.

"Ow!" he yelped. He let go of her as he cursed, "You bitch!"

She ran off the stage and back to her dressing room, her head pounding like it had that night at the Bare Bottom. What was going on? Why was this happening to her? She didn't deserve it. Even if she *was* one angry, pissed-off bitch like Wiley said.

Screw him and his stupid club! She was finished here!

When Lisette got to her dressing room, she slammed the door and ran her hand across her dressing room table, not caring what she knocked over.

Bottles of makeup, tubes of lipstick, and cans of hair spray went flying. She kicked off her high heels, flung them across the room, and stomped barefoot and naked except for her G-string into the bathroom. She grabbed a towel and rubbed the sweat off her body in quick, angry strokes. God, she wailed silently. Did I just quit another job? How am I going to explain this one to Mo?

He wouldn't dare take Wiley's side in this, would he? She seethed as she pulled her robe over her body and tugged her G-string off, throwing it on the floor in a ball. When she stormed back into the dressing room, she threw things around until she found her cigarettes and lighter, and then she collapsed on the couch. She lit up, not caring that there was no smoking backstage. What was Wiley going to do to her about it? Fire her? She didn't work here anymore.

God damn it! she fumed. She had lost two jobs in less than a week and what was she supposed to do? Crawl back to Wiley and beg for her job back? Or call Mo for yet another favor? She was so angry she wanted to cry, but she didn't. She never cried. She hadn't cried since her mother's funeral, and she wasn't about to now. As bad as all of this was, it was nothing compared to that. She was sure of that. She lay stretched out on the couch, puffing on her cigarette, thinking of her mother. When she died, Lisette was ten, and she had slept wearing her mother's furry, white jacket for months. Even now, she'd wrap herself up in it some days to make herself feel better. It was part of her act, the fur fitting in with her Attila look, but it made her feel like her mother was with her.

"Shit!" she cried suddenly, sitting up and scanning the room. Where *was* her mother's jacket?

"Oh, God!" she cried, remembering how she'd flung it into the audience tonight – something she never did, but felt she had to tonight to keep the attention focused on her. What had she been thinking? She had to go find it. Her mother's jacket was somewhere out in the club. Her mother's! She had to get it now. She jumped up off the couch, pulled her robe tight, and yanked open the door into the hall. As she did, she lurched backwards. A man was standing there, his hand up like he was about to knock.

"You scared the shit out of me!" she said, grabbing at her chest.

The man was stunned too, so she yelled first. "This is a private dressing room and I…"

Then she noticed her furry, white jacket in his arms.

"Where did you get that?" she said, grabbing it. "How did you find it?"

"A guy was prancing around behind the club with it on," he explained. "So I took it from him. I thought you'd want it back."

"Yes, yes! It was my mom's!" Then she looked at him sideways. "I know you, don't I?" She paused and added, "You took care of that heckler for me tonight, didn't you?"

"Yeah, and I got thrown out of the club for it. But that's not why I'm here. Mind if I come in? I'd like to talk to you about your act."

Lisette bristled. "What about my act? You saw it. I don't do it for free, and I don't do it for a roll in the hay. Especially not for someone who smells as bad as you do. Jesus, you stink." She raised her hand and held her nose. "When was the last time you had a bath?"

He frowned, ignoring her question, and pressed on. "I'm interested in the historic basis for your act. You are Attila the Hunny, right?"

"Yeah. That's my stage name." She managed a smile at him and softened her voice. "Do you like it? An old boyfriend of mine thought of the act, but I designed the costumes."

"I am more familiar with Attila the *Hun*, the historical figure: king of the Huns and the most ferocious barbarian in the Roman Empire."

She didn't like the tone of his voice. "Are you trying to impress me with what you know? I know squat about it. So what? It's not about history, you jerk. I'm a stripper, for god sakes!"

"Yes, but your act captured so much of who Attila really was. You were amazing! The essence of Attila's spirit radiated from every pore of your body!"

She eyed him carefully. He was talking to her like she had a brain in her head, and she didn't trust that either. Men only said that to get into her pants.

"I have a business proposition for you," he persisted. "I have an idea that will take you out of places like this to where your talents will be appreciated." Then his voice changed as if he were talking to a child. "Do you know what a performance artist is?"

She looked at him blankly.

"I thought you wouldn't. They are..." he stumbled for words, "They have a theme, a political philosophy, a way of communicating their art through their bodies. I don't know if you can understand." He eyed her cautiously.

"Understand? I think you're an idiot!" She grabbed the door and tried to push it shut, but he had planted himself firmly in the doorway and now he threw his weight against the door. All she could do was scream and wave her hands at him.

"I want you out of here. Now!"

"No, please. Just give me a minute," he went on hurriedly. "I've been thinking about this for a long time, how to communicate the political philosophy of a genius – a barbarian, yes, but a genius – to the masses. And when I saw your picture and your stage name, well... don't you see? It's like the Jane Fonda workout tapes."

"What?" Lisette snapped. "What does Jane Fonda have to do with it?"

"Who would have ever thought those silly tapes would make her millions?" he went on. "Hell, I'd do this myself, but you're right. I'm just a smelly old fart. But you – you could do it. You're an artist, do you know that?"

Lisette looked into the old guy's face. He said the magic word. She always thought of herself as an artist, even though no one else did. Not even Mo. But did he really think a line like that would get him somewhere with her? Who was this guy? If he cleaned himself up, he might look okay, and if she tried, she'd get what he was talking about. But she was too tired and too upset about quitting her job tonight to even care.

"Hey," he finally said. "What do you have to lose? I just want to talk to you."

She looked at him again. He had talked to her for more than two minutes and not hit on her, but most of all, he had made her curious. What does a performance artist do anyway? she wondered.

"All right, old man," she said with a scowl on her face. She didn't want him to think she was going soft on him. "But if you're jerking me around, I'll squeeze your balls so hard..." Her voice dropped and she clenched her hand tightly into a fist, giving him a preview of coming attractions. When he didn't flinch, she stepped aside and waved her hand in front of her as a sign she was letting him come inside.

"My name is Lisette La Tour. And you are?"

"Ambrose August Smith." He added, "But you can call me Ambrose."

"You can call me Ms. La Tour," she said in a fancy tone of voice.

But as he stepped into the room, she sighed and added, "Oh, hell, call me Lisette. I've been called worse."

As Ambrose moved quickly into Lisette's dressing room, he was sure that he saw this whole scene very differently than she was seeing it. He could sense that she was skeptical and unsure of what he wanted from her. But he saw it as an incredible opportunity that he wanted to take advantage of before she could change her mind and throw him out of there.

She was one tough cookie, but he liked her. Sure, she could have been more grateful for him bringing back her jacket or dealing with the heckler, but she wasn't. He could see he was going to have to prove himself to her all over again and he was ready for it.

"I'm a lawyer, you know," he said, as he breezed by her and she closed the door behind him. "Of course, I haven't been inside a courtroom in years."

"You don't look like one," she said flatly, obviously not impressed.

"May I sit down?" he asked, pointing to the couch. She nodded, but as he moved toward it, there was a sharp knock at the door, followed by Wiley's voice bellowing out, "Let me in! I need to talk to you."

Lisette looked at Ambrose and hissed, "Quick! Get into the bathroom. I don't want Wiley to see you. I'm in enough trouble with him already."

Ambrose wanted to ask what difference that made, but she stopped him.

"Don't argue with me. I'll get rid of him as soon as I can."

Another yell came from the other side of the door. "Goddamn it! Let me in." Then another knock came, louder and more insistent. "What is wrong with you?"

Quickly, Ambrose got into the bathroom and left the door open a crack so he could see and hear everything. He watched Lisette tighten the belt to her robe and walk to the door. She flung it open and said, "Sorry. I was in the bath and didn't have anything on."

"For Chrissake, I'm not here to check out your tits," Wiley growled, then shoved her helmet, sword, and streamers into her hands. "Here's your stuff."

"Gee, thanks," she said, but Wiley ignored her as he pushed past her into the room. He sniffed the air. "Do you smell something rancid coming from the bathroom?"

Ambrose saw Wiley's eyes dart toward the door, and he stepped back. Lisette quickly moved in front of the door, grabbed the knob, and pulled it shut.

"I don't smell anything," she said, her voice more muffled now, but Ambrose was still able to hear her. "Unless it's my bath salts."

"No, it's not a pleasant smell." Wiley sniffed again. "It smells like that moocher Ambrose who started everything in the club tonight."

"Who? What?" Lisette asked, sounding confused.

"Never mind. It's not important. So what do you have to say for yourself?"

"Me?"

"Yes, I know things can get out of hand, but you could have handled it differently."

"*I* could've handled it differently?"

"Yeah, the first part of your act drags too much. Takes too long to get things going, and that's why the audience went crazy when you finally got there."

"Are you telling me it's all my fault because my act is too long?"

"If the shoe fits…" Wiley muttered, and Ambrose couldn't hear the rest of it.

Lisette said, "Listen, old man, I'm not changing my act for you."

"I'm just saying that you need to understand that the Pussycat is…"

"What?" she screeched. "A dirty, disgusting dive run by idiots? Fine! Let's see you jiggle your ass on that stage as the headliner for the rest of the month. Look, I know you're here to grovel because your bar tabs probably tripled tonight. I'm good, and the guys were out there chanting for me! Hell, once the word gets out about my act, the place will be packed. So don't you bullshit me!"

"All right, all right!" Wiley grunted. "Webster should've been on that stage for you tonight. But about your act – these guys are here for tits and ass, not artsy-fartsy stuff."

"It was Jerry's fault," Lisette began. "If he hadn't screwed up, I'd…"

"Jerry's out. I fired him for stealing booze. We'll rehearse your act tomorrow and get it right." When Lisette made a sound to protest, Wiley cut her off. "I'm not asking you to change it – just tighten it up a little. Get to the good part faster."

Then Wiley's voice moved toward the door. "Do we have a deal?"

"I want one more thing," she replied. "Tell your goon Webster to lay off the guy who helped me out with the heckler."

"What do you care what happens to a snake in the grass like him?"

"I don't, but he helped me out tonight when you didn't. So leave him alone."

Wiley made a sound that showed his disgust.

"Agreed?" she insisted.

"Yeah, sure," Ambrose heard Wiley say as he huffed out the door and it slammed behind him. Only then did Ambrose poke his head out of the bathroom door.

"Thanks for getting Webster off my ass," he said to Lisette.

"Yeah," she replied distractedly, and then she pouted. "You liked my act, didn't you? You heard what he said about it. Do you think it's true?"

"I love your act!" Ambrose replied, coming over to her. "You *were* Attila the Hun up there on stage for me. It's like art imitating life!"

"What does that mean?" she shot back, but her eyes were kinder now.

"It means you're doing something that says a lot about the real Attila and you could do more. I can help you. Don't you see? Assholes like Wiley only see sex when you're dancing, and that's what he's paying you for so everyone will come to see you. But you're better than that. What you're doing isn't wrong; you're just doing it in the wrong place. I can take you to places where the special something you have will be appreciated. Performance art is perfect for you. Don't you see that?"

Ambrose pressed his hand onto her shoulder and felt the heat of her flesh through her robe. He wasn't coming on to her, and she didn't brush him away, but they did connect. He could feel it. He needed her to see what he saw in the future. She shook his hand off her shoulder and eyed him.

"I'm tired. It's been a crazy night. I want to go back to my hotel and think about it. Understand?"

He nodded his head slowly.

"But," she added, her voice softer, "we could talk tomorrow after my show."

"Yes," he said eagerly. He was hanging onto her every word now.

"And we can talk about whatever it is you are talking about." Her voice trailed off, as if she was trying to hide her confusion.

"About performance art," Ambrose said. "That's what I'm talking about."

"Yeah, whatever." She waved her hands. "And one more thing – clean yourself up, would you? Wiley could smell you from across the room, for God's sakes."

Ambrose looked down at his clothes. "I don't usually let myself go so much. But I could clean up. I mean, I will." Then he backed up to the door. "You won't regret this."

"I better not," Lisette said as she opened the door. "Remember what I said before." She squeezed her hand into a fist like she had his balls in a vice grip.

Ambrose nodded as he brushed by her out into the hallway and watched the door close behind him. He got it. She had nothing to lose from talking to him, but she would make mincemeat out of his balls if he screwed up. She was tough, but he could be persistent if he wanted something. They were quite the match.

He couldn't wait for the games to begin.

CHAPTER FOUR

Among the Dead

"Tell me your dreams," Ambrose asked Lisette the following night as he sat opposite her at a table in the dim light of the bar at the Pussycat.

What a line, she thought, frowning, but he didn't seem to notice her reaction. He was nursing a glass of beer, and it was nearly two o'clock in the morning. Her second night of stripping at the club was over, and the bartender had made the last call. When Ambrose offered to buy her a drink, she told him she'd have a ginger ale with no ice. Now as she sat sipping the drink with a straw, she stared closely at the man with the steely blue eyes seated across from her. Seeing him again, she realized he was easily twice her size. She was glad that she was meeting him out here in the bar with other people around. Last night, in her dressing room, things got a little too crazy, and although she could take care of herself, she had learned never to take chances. But now he looked very different from the man who had barged in on her last night. Tonight, he wore a clean white shirt and a pair of jeans. With his beard trimmed and his long hair, fresh from a shampoo, hanging down over his shoulders, he reminded her of Willie Nelson, her favorite country-western singer.

Lisette had listened to Willie Nelson's music ever since she was a kid, and his laid-back way of crooning a tune was so soothing to her. She had always wanted to marry a nice, easygoing guy like Willie. She doubted that Ambrose was like that, but tonight he looked like a fairly normal guy. She even detected a whiff of aftershave as he leaned in closer to her now, waiting patiently for a response to his question. Lisette was surprised by it. No one had asked her about her dreams in years. She must have misunderstood him.

"You mean my sexual fantasies?" she asked him now.

"No, I mean what would you do if you had all the money you needed?"

Lisette eyed him carefully and then leaned back in her chair. "Go camping."

"Camping?" A snicker came across his face at first, and she noticed how he held back for a moment. But then he leaned in, like he was interested in knowing more and asked, "Where?"

"In Peru," she said in a flash. "Along the Inca Trail to Machu Picchu. It's an ancient city in the mountains."

Ambrose eyed her carefully. When she returned his gaze calmly and steadily, he chuckled. "You know what you're talking about, don't you?"

"Would I make that up?"

Ambrose taunted her. "Have you ever been camping?"

"No, not really, but my mother wanted to go to Machu Picchu. Never did."

"Why not?"

"She died when I was ten. She had cancer and she went fast." She wanted to say more, but she didn't want to cry in front of him. She took another sip of her drink instead.

"Isn't Machu Picchu some kind of mystical, healing place?" he asked her.

"Yes. It gives off very ancient energies. My mom had this book all about it with lots of pictures."

"So that's where you'd go if you had all the money you needed, huh?"

"Yeah. Where would you go?"

"To China. I think I lived there in a previous life."

"Really?" Lisette leaned forward and stared at him. "How do you know that?"

"I don't. I just have this feeling that if I go stand on the Great Wall and look out, I might recognize something."

"That's weird!" She laughed and sat back taking another sip of her drink.

"Why? Because you don't believe in past lives?"

"No, it's hard enough being where I am without wondering where I've been. I don't have much of a life right now." Her voice wavered a little. "Not one with a future. I've got dreams, but I haven't gotten too far with them."

"Have you ever gotten anything you've wished for?"

"That's hard to say. I got to be on my own at sixteen. That was something."

"You could go trekking in Peru too, you know. That's what I'm offering you."

"A trip to Peru?"

"No, silly. A chance to change the direction of your career. Get out of stripping and into the performance art world."

"You don't get it, do you? I don't have a career. I'm just doing what my mother did."

"That's different." He chortled. "Are you saying it's a tradition to become a stripper in your family?"

"Yeah. What's wrong with that?"

"Nothing." Ambrose backed off a little. "It's not quite what every mother wishes for her daughter, but then you're a pretty tough kid. You did threaten to squeeze my balls quite hard last night!" He clenched his fist at her in jest.

"Now you're making fun of me," she said, pouting.

"Oh, no," he said quickly. "I've never been so serious. If you don't believe me, come see these performance artists for yourself. Make up your own mind."

She considered his request. "Where do they perform?"

"Usually in clubs in New York City that cater to that kind of act. But there's a show in town this week with some of the NEA artists. They were funded by the National Endowment for the Arts, but Congress cut the money when the art got too controversial."

Lisette's eyes glazed over and she sighed. "I don't know. What good will it do?" She made a noise with her straw as she finished her drink and placed the glass on the table. "I don't know enough about Attila the Hun. You're wasting your time."

"Don't worry about that. I know all there is to know about the barbarian." He paused for a moment. "But it might be helpful if you got some historical background. I'll get a few books from the library for you to read, and then we could talk about them."

In an instant, Lisette's body went rigid and her eyes flashed at Ambrose. "I don't want to read any books. I don't even have a library card. It expired."

"Jesus," Ambrose huffed. "They're just history books." Then he backed off a bit. "I'll mark the stuff you should read, and what I pick out, even a first grader could read."

"Well, actually," she mumbled, lowering her eyes, "if you must know, I can't."

"You can't what?"

"Read," she said quietly, holding herself as steady as she could while her heart raced and her face flushed with embarrassment. *Oh, God! Why am I telling him this? What will he think of me now? That I'm stupid. A complete idiot!*

"Are you telling me you never learned to read?"

She shuddered at the disbelief in his voice. It wasn't that bad, was it?

"I can read," she blurted out, looking up at him and struggling to hold his eyes. She had to make this sound better than it was. After all, she didn't even know this guy. Why was she telling him her secret? Just because he looked like Willie Nelson?

"But not well enough to read a whole book or anything like that," she added, her voice toughening. "So you can just forget the books."

"But you said you read that book your mother had about Machu Picchu," Ambrose insisted. "What about that?"

Her head dropped to her chest. She was embarrassed. "I just looked at the pictures."

Ambrose made a noise with his mouth and she looked up to see him staring at her.

"Don't look at me like that! It's not the end of the world. So I can't read or write." Then she added, "I can write a little more than I can read. I write in my diary every chance I get."

She heard Ambrose sigh and watched him rub his hands over his broad forehead, making circles on his brow with his fingers. Finally he said, "All right, then we'll just have to teach you to read better. Raise your reading level a few grades. I'll get some books out about how to do that. It shouldn't be hard."

Lisette's voice softened. "You'd do that for me?"

"Why not? It's not a step I anticipated, but it's no big deal."

"It *is* a big deal to me. No one's ever helped me like that before. Except my mom when I was little." Lisette looked down at her hands folded in front of her on the table. "I'm just surprised. You don't seem the kind of man who'd…"

"…care about you?" He completed her sentence. "But I do. You… you," he stumbled over his words, "you really are something, you know. We could go a long way together." He reached across the table, put his hand on hers and looked into her eyes. "Hey, what do you have to lose?"

At that, Lisette pulled her hand away and gave him a hard look. "Does that line always work for you?"

"What line?" Ambrose slouched back into his chair.

"You keep saying that to me. Like I'm some kind of loser at nineteen. Just because you know my stupid dreams and that I can't read." Suddenly she was ashamed that she had opened up to him. That was so unlike her. What had made her do that?

"Hey, I never said you were a loser. You just seem a little lost. I want to help you."

Her voice turned cold. "You've never done anything like this before, have you? Managed a career for a performance artist?"

"No, not really."

"Then why do you think that I should trust you? What if it doesn't work?"

He smiled at her. "Well, then I owe you one of your dreams."

"Christ, you are a charmer, aren't you?" She laughed and shook her head. She caught him watching her long blonde hair flutter across her breasts.

"Then you'll come with me?" he asked eagerly. "There's a show Sunday afternoon, a matinee. We could go. That way you won't have to miss work."

"Right! I can't miss work. I'm the only one working around here."

"So you'll come with me?"

"Yes, but remember what I said about your balls the other night. You may be bigger than I am, but no one crosses me."

"Sure, sure, I heard you," he said breezily. "If I screw up, I'm a goner." He winced and then cackled.

"I mean it!" Lisette shot back. "No joke!" She got up and leaned down into his space, her left shoulder wedged against his. "I don't trust men, and I don't trust you."

"At least that's settled," he said lightly. "I'll pick you up on Sunday afternoon at your hotel about noon. You're staying at the Bickford, right? That's where Wiley has all his headliners stay. I know you're going to love the show."

She looked at him carefully. How could he know what she liked? And how did he know so much about what went on at the Pussycat? Could she trust him? Was there something about him that she could get to work for her? Unsure, she gave him a scowl. Maybe, but she didn't want him to think it was going to be easy.

"I'll see you on Sunday in the hotel lobby, but only if you can leave me alone for a few days. I'm exhausted. I need some time to myself. Don't follow me; don't even think about it. I'll get my own taxi home. Good night."

There, she thought, as she turned and walked away from him, not waiting for a reply. Let him think about that for a while. If he thought he was going to come waltzing into her life and take it over, he was wrong about that.

No one was in control of her life. Not anymore.

No one.

Good God! What was Lisette thinking?

Ambrose wasn't going to let her control her own life. No way! He was just like Ari. A manipulative madman! A murderer! A maniac! Can't you see? Ambrose is trouble, big trouble! Just like Sophie said about Ari.

Lacey had been in Lisette's body since Sunday night and had experienced the daily humiliation and degradation of this girl's life. She couldn't enjoy getting up on stage and taking her clothes off. What she did wasn't artistic; it was disgusting! And what Ambrose was offering her wasn't because he cared about her.

Wrong! Wrong! So wrong!

She had to get Lisette to do what she had never done. See Ambrose for what he was: a possessive, controlling man who could harm her. He was, like Ari, manipulative, treacherous, and diabolical, but fancy words wouldn't persuade Lisette. She had to do something radical, and she had to do it now. Every part of her screamed out, Get out now, Lisette, while you can! While you are still alive!

She couldn't let that happen. Lisette was in danger. By the time eight o'clock rolled around that morning, Lacey had an idea.

Let's go, Lisette. Let's go to my funeral. Get up! Let's go! she said over and over again as Lisette slept. She waited; she didn't care how long it might take. She could be patient. She wasn't going to give up.

Let's go, Lisette! Come on, let's go!

Lisette woke that Friday morning feeling like she had somewhere to go – but where?

She was exhausted. She had worked late last night at the Pussycat and afterward she met Ambrose in the bar. She had to admit that she enjoyed their talk. She liked how he paid attention to her. Besides her agent Mo, she hadn't had anyone pay that much attention to her in a long time.

Let's go! a voice in her head suddenly said. That was all. *Let's go!*

"Go? Go where?" she found herself saying back as she sat up in bed and looked bleary-eyed at her alarm clock. It was only eight o'clock. She had nowhere to go today until she worked tonight, so what was the hurry?

Let's go, the voice repeated and Lisette's mind raced ahead to Lacey Lockhart's funeral. She knew from the local TV news, which she had taken to watching since Lacey died, that Lacey would be buried today at a church down the street from her hotel. But why did she suddenly feel a strong need to go? She didn't know the girl, and she hated funerals ever since her mom's. Besides, she had nothing to wear to one except maybe for that dress, the one she had bought the day after Lacey was killed and she quit her job at the Bare Bottom. She had wandered into a classy dress shop near her hotel and found a long, simple black dress that fit her perfectly. She could wear that to the funeral. Maybe she was supposed to go after all. So she got up, got dressed, and headed for the church.

When she got there, Lisette entered the front door of the building. She felt strange being back in a church. It reminded of her mother and what they used to do some Sunday mornings when her mother would wake up and say, "We need some fire and brimstone, honey. Let's go to church. It'll be good for us." So they'd dress up in their best outfits, go to church, sing the songs, and say the prayers. That was it. Then they wouldn't go until her mom was ready again.

Now as Lisette walked up the center aisle of the church, she saw things that reminded her of those childhood visits with her mother – lots of flowers and candles, and in front there was a pulpit where Lisette imagined the preaching still went on just like when she was a kid. She looked for a place to sit near the back of the church, but it was crowded, filled with people mostly her age, probably kids who knew Lacey from school. She wandered up the main aisle until she saw a seat near the front, but only if the lady on the end of the pew would be willing to squeeze over.

"Excuse me?" Lisette asked her politely. "Is that seat taken?"

The lady stared at her for a moment, her bright red hair peeking out from under a snug purple hat, but then the younger woman sitting one seat over looked up at Lisette and answered, "Sure." Then she grabbed the arm of the older woman and said, "Move over, Gram. Make some room."

Oh, Sophie, Sophie! It's so good to see you! I've missed you so much! How are you? You and your Gram look so sad! I sent Lisette to you. Help her! Help me!

As she eased herself into the seat, Lisette felt a funny buzz in her ear, like someone was jabbering something, but she couldn't understand it.

This isn't a coincidence. I sent Lisette to your pew. I need your help!

Then the younger woman leaned over and stared at Lisette.

"Do I know you?" she asked and put her hand out to Lisette. "I'm Sophie. I was Lacey's best friend. This is my grandmother, Ruth. How do you know Lacey?"

Lisette didn't know what to say, but then she didn't have to because suddenly the church bells rang long and low, and everyone in the church stopped talking. The service was about to begin, but Lacey's casket wasn't there yet. Lisette remembered how her mother's casket was brought to church in a long black car and then carried up the aisle before the service even started. How could Lacey's be so late?

Sophie always said I'd be late for my own funeral, and she wasn't wrong!

Suddenly, there was a buzz at the back of the church, and everyone stood. Lisette turned to see a dark, polished wooden box being wheeled up the aisle and a group of people walking behind it.

Oh my God! I'm in that casket. Or at least my body is. So that's where it went. And look, there's Daddy and Jimmie walking behind it. They look so awful!

Lisette knew how Lacey's family must feel. When her mom died, it was unreal to her too – like her mother couldn't be dead. She still felt that way sometimes. So must Lacey's family, especially the young man walking behind the casket who must be Lacey's brother.

Yeah, that's Jimmie. Poor thing! I always tried to protect my little brother. He must feel terrible for not protecting me. But it wasn't your fault, Jimmie. I screwed up, not you! It was my mistake!

Lisette thought that the older man walking with him must be Lacey's father, Mr. Lockhart. His face looked tired and puffy, like he had been crying. But where was Lacey's mom, Mrs. Lockhart?

Oh, Daddy! Thank God Mommy's not here. She couldn't bear this. I'm okay. I'm here with Lisette. Look over here. We're in the long black dress, like the one you bought me for Christmas last year. I made Lisette buy it. Don't cry. It's me. I'm here.

Then others came up the aisle – Lacey's grandparents, aunts and uncles, and cousins, Lisette thought, all looking so sad, so stunned.

Oh, Grandma. You look the worst. What can I say? It's so unfair.

Lacey was dead, Lisette thought. Even the love of her family and friends hadn't saved her. In fact, someone who loved her, or thought he did, killed her.

The little bastard! Look what he's done to me! What he's done to my family!

It was all so terrible Lisette sighed as Lacey's family filed into the seats across the aisle. But why was she drawn to this dead girl, and now her family? Why? Why?

My family doesn't deserve this! It's not fair!

By now, everyone in the church was crying, and Lisette felt a deep emotion stab at her heart too as she sobbed uncontrollably.

"Are you okay?" Ruth turned to ask, her voice filled with concern.

Lisette nodded that she was, but her stomach felt like she was going to throw up; when her sobs came again, her whole body shook. She fell forward and she felt Ruth's hand grab her arm as she whispered to her. "Come sit down with me for a moment, dear. Let me help you." As Lisette let herself be pulled down into the seat, Ruth added, "Take a deep breath. Relax, relax!"

Lisette tried to breathe, but her nose was stuffed up and she gasped for breath.

"Here." Ruth pressed a tissue into her hand. Then she went on, "It's all right, my dear. Lacey is safe now. No one can hurt your friend anymore."

Lisette looked at the woman. "Did you know her?" she asked.

Ruth looked surprised. "Yes, of course. She was my grand-daughter's roommate, her very best friend. We'll miss her a lot, won't we?"

"Tell me something," Lisette asked, gripping the woman's hand. "Do I look like her? Is that why I'm here? Tell me, what is it about me that's like Lacey?"

Ruth drew back, startled. "You mean you didn't know her?"

"No. But I... I..." Lisette's voice dropped off as everyone else in the church sat down now. With Lacey's casket in place in the front of the church, the minister began by saying a few prayers at the pulpit. Then Lisette saw Lacey's father get up from his seat and join the minister. They hugged for a moment and then the minister went to sit down. Lacey's father stood there alone, and Lisette could clearly see the lines of his grief and agony over his daughter's death on his face. He pulled out a paper from his pocket, unfolded it, cleared his throat, and began.

"I'm not much of a speaker," he said, looking up from the page in front of him. "At least not like this. I never thought I'd even attend my own daughter's funeral let along speak at it. A father shouldn't have to bury a child. It's not right! It's --"

His voice trailed off for a moment, and Lisette could see he was struggling to keep his composure. When he began again, his voice had an angrier edge to it.

"Some things in life you don't have control of." He read now from the paper. "This is one of them. I wish I could change what has happened to Lacey. I wish that she was still here with us today."

I wish that too, Daddy. But I'm not there. I'm dead. I understand that now.

He looked up at the congregation for a moment and then went on reading.

"We are all trying to make sense of this cruel and insane act that took her away from us. She had so much to live for, so much more to do in this lifetime. She'll never do any of it now. It doesn't make any sense and I feel cheated out of the future we would have had together. It hurts really bad."

I know, Daddy. I feel cheated to. I'm sorry it ended this way. But this can't be all there is for me.

"I should have told her more how much I loved her when she was alive. I wanted her to know that I will miss having her in my life every day."

Tears were coming down Lisette's cheeks as Lacey's father struggle through the rest of his remarks. She felt so sorry for him.

"All I can do is hope that wherever Lacey is now, she is happy and without fear or pain. We will carry her in our hearts along with the wonderful memories that she gave us until we see her again in the next life. I believe she is there now with her mother and she is okay and safe from harm forever and ever."

I wish it was like that, but it's not. I'm still here in this church, watching all of this – and, Daddy, it's scary. I'm here with this girl who is crying her eyes out about me because it's the only way I know how to show my own grief. But Daddy, where is Mommy? You lied to me, Daddy, about how I'd see her again when I died. How could you do that? It took me so long to figure out that what you told me happened to her wasn't right. I still remember how I did that. It was a long time ago, but I still remember. Daddy, Daddy! How could you?

"My mom says kids shouldn't smoke because it'll stunt their growth," Alyssa said as she puffed madly on a cigarette in the girl's bathroom at St. Mary Magdalene's High School for Girls during the waning hours of a Friday afternoon. Then she snickered, "Can you believe that, Lacey? If she only knew."

Lacey frowned at her friend through the smoke of her own cigarette. She hated it when the girls at school talked about their mothers. She didn't know what to say.

"Here I am, smoking like a chimney," Alyssa went on, "and my boobs still keep growing. Last week at the dance, a guy from Catholic Central wanted me to go out back with him so he could touch them." She let out a squeal. "Isn't that just too much?"

Jenna, the other girl with them, snarled, "Who'd want to touch you, you big oaf?"

"*He* did," Alyssa insisted. "I swear it."

"He did not. No one's that desperate."

"Just because I'm not a slut like you doesn't mean that boys don't like me!"

"I am not a slut!" Jenna screamed back.

"You are too!"

"Am not!"

Lacey listened until she couldn't stand it anymore.

"Cut it out," she hissed. "Or someone is going to come in here and find us."

"Don't be so paranoid. No one is going to hear us." Jenna laughed. "Sister Ignatius is so deaf she doesn't even hear us sneak out of study hall. Besides, it's the last period on a Friday. Nobody's paying attention. Stop being such a scaredy-cat."

Jenna grinned and blew smoke rings out of her mouth.

"I can't afford to get ten demerits for smoking in the can," Lacey replied. "My dad will kill me if I can't go to graduation. He's already pissed off at me."

"Who cares about graduation?" Jenna said, picking a piece of tobacco out of her teeth. "Besides, you're the teachers' pet around here, Lacey. Rules don't apply to you."

Lacey grimaced. True, she was one of the best students in the school, sure to be valedictorian of her graduating class in June, now only a few months away, and she had already been accepted at several colleges. She had been smoking in the john with Alyssa and Jenna since last fall without getting caught. She hoped her luck would hold out.

Jenna took another puff of her cigarette and blew the smoke out her nose. "Why is your dad so pissed at you anyway? I thought he was a nice guy."

Lacey looked at her like she was stupid. "He's a salesman. He can make anyone think he's nice."

"What's he really like?" Jenna asked, making her voice sound dark and mysterious. "Does he ever let you drive his car, just for fun? My dad does. My mom gets really mad but then he says, 'How's the girl ever going to learn how to do anything if she doesn't get to try?' God, my mom hates it when he says that!"

"Yeah," Alyssa chimed in. "My mom hates it when my dad lets me take a swig of his beer from a bottle. She thinks girls my age shouldn't be drinking and certainly not out of a bottle. 'How uncouth,' she says. I tell her, 'I'm almost eighteen. Soon I can drink all I want.' She hates it when I remind her how old I am. That means she's an old lady."

There they go again, Lacey groaned, talking about their mothers. Would it ever stop hurting so much? Why do they rag on them? They are so lucky to have a mother!

"What about your mom, Lacey? What pisses her off the most?"

Lacey felt her throat tighten. She had been dodging the issue of her mother since she started smoking with these girls. Her other friends knew that such talk was forbidden. They knew her mother was dead and it was easier for Lacey that way.

"Come on," Jenna goaded her. "Something you do must drive your mother wild. I bet she doesn't think you're as perfect as everyone does. I bet she'd shit a brick if she found out you smoked. Is she a screamer? My mom is. She can yell and yell…"

"Shut up!" Lacey screamed. "You don't know anything about

my mother." Then her face reddened as she blurted out, "I don't even remember her anymore."

"What don't you remember?" Alyssa asked as she put her cigarette out in the sink.

"She doesn't remember her mother!" Jenna exploded. "Don't you listen, stupid?" Then she turned to Lacey, her voice softening. "It must be hard when your parents get divorced and you don't see your mom a lot."

Lacey looked at Jenna for a second. If she said nothing, Jenna would think what she wanted and leave it at that. But Jenna didn't stop.

"I was reading about women like that in a magazine the other day," she went on. "They get divorced, move to another city, and stick their ex-husbands with the kids. I know my mom would like to dump my dad, but she'd never leave us behind. Never!"

Lacey's eyes got wide at the sound of those words.

"God," Alyssa broke in. "If my mom went away, life would be so much easier."

Jenna elbowed her in the ribs. "You idiot! Don't say that. Tell her, Lacey. Tell her how hard it is not having a mom."

Lacey looked at Jenna and then back at Alyssa. She could have said, "Yes, it's terrible," and that would be that. After all, her mother did go away and she was never coming back. But something made her go on.

"It wasn't exactly like that," Lacey said, slowly.

"Then what happened?" Jenna was clearly intrigued now.

Lacey took a deep breath, not believing the words that were forming in her head. Even as she spoke them, they sounded foreign and strange.

"There was an accident, sort of, and my mom, she…" Lacey hesitated for a moment and then went on, her voice quivering. "She died. She died when I was five."

Although her heart was beating wildly, once the words were out, she felt stronger and, for some reason, more alive. She *did* have a mother and years ago, she died. Surely she could talk about her now. What was the big deal?

"Wow!" Alyssa gasped, her eyes wide and her mouth hanging open.

"Gosh," Jenna said softly. "I never knew anyone whose mother died." Then she took a deep drag on her cigarette.

Lacey smiled and wanted to say more, but she was afraid she'd cry. Alyssa looked at her and asked, "Was it a bad accident? Was your mother all smashed up?"

Jenna gave Alyssa a dirty look.

"What? What's the matter?" Alyssa shrugged. "I just wanna to know. What's wrong with that?"

"It's all right," Lacey said with a sigh. "I just don't talk about it much."

"I can see why," Jenna said sympathetically. "Some people wouldn't understand. But you can tell us. We won't tell a soul, will we?"

"No, absolutely not," Alyssa said with a gleam in her eye. "It'll be our secret."

Lacey looked at the two girls and wondered if she could trust them. But then, why not? Her mother was dead. Nothing she could say to anyone could hurt her mother now.

"She was sitting in her car," Lacey began. "It was parked in the garage and the gasoline cap fell off. She died from carbon monoxide poisoning."

The two girls were silent for moment.

Then Alyssa screwed her face up and asked, "Can a gas cap fall off like that and kill you?"

Jenna spoke more carefully. "I thought you had to put a hose on the exhaust pipe, pump the fumes into the car with the windows closed or you'd never kill yourself."

Kill yourself! Lacey almost gagged at the sound of those words. Her mother didn't kill herself. She sat in the car, listening to one of her favorite songs on the radio, and died. That's what happened, wasn't it? That's what her dad told her.

"What do you mean?" Lacey asked, narrowing her eyes at Jenna.

"I mean that you need a pretty high concentration of exhaust fumes in your lungs in order to die. I heard about that somewhere I think."

"No, not that. Are you saying my mother committed suicide?"

Jenna looked at her and Lacey felt a current cross between them. What did Jenna know that she didn't about her mother's death? Her mother couldn't have committed suicide. Or did she? Suddenly the school bell rang and Jenna looked relieved.

"Hey, what do I know, Lace, about these things?" Jenna giggled nervously, putting out her cigarette in the sink and grabbing her stack of books from the top of the towel dispenser. "Got to go. I've got a big weekend planned." Then she turned to Alyssa, who stood looking dumbfounded at the sink, her second cigarette burning down into the fingers of her hand. "Are you coming, Alyssa, or not?"

But Alyssa didn't respond. Instead she looked at Lacey and asked insistently, "But did your mom kill herself or not?"

Jenna grabbed Alyssa by the arm and pulled her toward the door. "Forget about that. Where are your books? Let's go. We've got a bus to catch, stupid."

"But Lacey…" Alyssa's voice trailed off, as Lacey felt everything in the room blur. Suddenly she was remembering what happened the day her mother died. She was at school, and her grandmother had come to get her, telling the principal that there was a family emergency and her granddaughter had to come home with her right away. As they left school, Lacey asked her grandmother if something had happened to her grandfather. Her grandmother said no. Then she took Lacey to her house until her father came and told her the story about the accident with the car in the garage that killed her mother. When they got back to their own house, Lacey was forbidden to go into the garage. It was all locked up with a chain and a big padlock that stayed there until they moved out several months later. She never saw her mother's old car again either.

Now Lacey wondered what had been in that garage that her father didn't want her to see. Why didn't she go out there and find out for herself what happened to her mother? At least she would've known, and Jenna wouldn't have had to figure it out for her. How could she have been so stupid to believe whatever her father told her about it?

Suddenly, she felt a tug on her sleeve and she heard Alyssa saying her name. "Lacey? Jenna and I are leaving now. Are you all right? You look as white as a ghost."

Lacey stared into Alyssa's face and wanted to cry. Cry about her mother, about not knowing, about being so incredibly stupid. Instead, she said, "Yeah, I'm okay."

Alyssa looked at her with big, sad eyes. "I'm really sorry about your mom."

Lacey nodded, and as Alyssa went out the door, Lacey stood by the sink, looking in the mirror at her face drained of color, and stunned by the force of her realization. Of course, her mother didn't die from sitting in a car that had no gas cap! Why had her father told her that? That bastard! And why would her mother want to leave her and Jimmie alone without a mother forever? Lacey's brain was spinning with the possibilities. Maybe Jenna was wrong. Maybe it happened just like her dad said. After all, hadn't she learned in religion class that the souls of people who take their own lives don't get to go to heaven? Was her mother burning in hell for all eternity? That couldn't be. She loved her mother so much. It just couldn't be. But only her father knew for sure. She had to ask him. He'd have to tell her the truth. Did her mother kill herself or not?

She had to know.

CHAPTER FIVE

Sins of the Father

Lacey couldn't believe it.

Right there, in the middle of her own funeral, she was remembering the tiniest details of her life with her father. How she sat on the blue-striped couch in the large living room of their two-story house that day when she was still in high school and waited for her father to come home from work.

She wanted to tell him what she had learned at school about her mother's death. Only two hours ago, she was sure she had died accidentally in her car in the garage. But now, after talking with Jenna and Alyssa in the girls' john, she was just as sure everything that she knew about her mother's death was a lie. So many questions raced through Lacey's mind that day, she wished she had her notebook so she could write them all down. She was determined to ask her father every one of them. She'd grill him until he told her the truth, the whole truth, and nothing but the truth about her mother.

What would make her mother want to commit suicide? Was she that mad at her father? Did he do something to make her want to kill herself? That thought made her furious – and to think that her father hadn't told her the truth about any of this! Did he think she'd never figure it out? Jenna did. It was a no-brainer for her. Why wouldn't she?

Then there were more questions. If her mother did kill herself, is that why she wasn't buried in the same Catholic cemetery as her grandfather? Because you can't be buried on sacred ground if you kill yourself, right? Isn't that what the nuns had taught her? And what if committing suicide runs in the family? Would she try to kill herself someday too? Or maybe Jimmie?

She was so absorbed in these questions that she didn't hear her father's car in the driveway until the automatic garage door started to grind open. She felt her stomach tighten up and her hands get sweaty, she was so nervous. It wasn't going to be easy talking to her father about her mother. The topic had been off limits with him for years. Thank God, Jimmie was away at military school. Her father has sent him there even though he was only nine years old. That meant that she and her father would be alone there in the house and Jimmie wouldn't hear any of this conversation.

Soon she heard her father coming into the house through the door leading from the garage to the kitchen, and suddenly something else dawned on her. When they had moved into this house after her mother died, her father had insisted upon having an attached garage. In their old house, the garage was separate and you couldn't hear what was going on out there from inside. You couldn't tell if, for instance, someone was committing suicide out there! "The bastard!" she mumbled under her breath. He had never told her the real reason he had wanted an attached garage. He had lied to her about that, too.

"Lacey, I'm home." Her father's voice echoed through the empty house and demanded a response, but Lacey sat silently stewing on the couch.

When she was a little girl, she remembered how she used to run and hug her dad the moment he came through the door in the evening. But tonight, she wasn't about to seek out the man who had lied to her about so much.

"Lacey, where are you?" Her father's voice grew nearer and more insistent. When he appeared in the living room doorway, he sighed. "There you are." She could hear the relief in his voice. "You're so quiet. I didn't realize you were in here."

He walked over to the dining room table, took off his suit coat and threw it over the back of a chair. Then he loosened his tie and picked up the mail she left there for him on the table. This was his daily routine and she knew it well.

"How was school?" he asked her absentmindedly as he flipped through the bills and catalogs, discarding what he didn't want back on the table.

Still not responding, she fixed her eyes on her hands folded in her lap and waited. She knew it would take him a while to notice that her silence had some significance. Soon she heard her father throw the rest of the mail on the table and step back into the living room.

"Lacey, are you all right?" He looked at her carefully for the first time. "You haven't said a word."

She looked up and stared at him for a moment. Funny how his face looked the same as it did this morning when she didn't think he was a liar.

"What's with the silent treatment?" he quizzed her. "Is it going to last all night?"

"It depends," she said in a coarse, low voice.

"It depends on what?"

"If all subjects are open for discussion."

"Sure," he said with a smug grin, and then he went on as if he knew what this was all about. "We can talk about the car, but you're still not getting it until graduation. You have to wait three more months."

But the car, a bone of contention between them lately, was the last thing on Lacey's mind. "I want to talk about my mother," she blurted out. She held her breath, watching her father's face, ready to pounce on his response. But he was more surprised than she expected.

"Oh!" was all he said at first, and that came out of his mouth like a sound, not a word. His face went pale and he sank down into the armchair next to the couch. "What about your mother?" he finally managed to say, barely able to look at her.

"I want to know how she died."

These words seemed to stun him even more. He tried to look away from her, but she held his eyes and commanded his attention. He squirmed in his seat, took a deep breath, and then let it out slowly. His voice was low and tight when he said at last, "I told you a long time ago. It was an accident. She died in the car from carbon monoxide poisoning."

She glared at him. "Not that old story about the gas cap falling off, Daddy! I want the real story. Or did you think I was so stupid that I'd never figure it out?"

She meant her words to provoke him, but he didn't take the bait. Instead, he gave her a blank look and stared at a spot on the wall behind her. God! How she hated it when he did that to her. Behind those eyes, she knew his mind was working. He was very cleverly trying to figure out his next move, like this was a game. Goddamn it! Couldn't he see how important this was to her?

In a flash, she went for the jugular, blurting out before he could blink again, "Why didn't you tell me my mother killed herself?"

With those words, Lacey watched her father's eyes dart back to hers and all the color drain out of his face. Then his shoulders slumped forward, and his body deflated like a punctured balloon.

For a moment, the question hung between them, like a gulf she expected to be filled with an answer. Her father's face twitched as though he was going to say something, but instead he seemed to be calculating his options.

Finally, her father sighed, drew a hand through his thick black hair, and then let it drop wearily back down into his lap. "She didn't kill herself," he said in a shaky, muffled voice. "It was an accident."

"You expect me to believe that?"

"You can believe what you want. I can't tell you anymore than that."

His voice was steadier now, and that infuriated Lacey even more.

"You can't, or you won't tell me!" she bellowed. "I want to know how she died. Don't lie to me, Daddy!"

Her father thrust himself forward in his chair. "I've never lied to you," he insisted. "Your mother's death was a terrible accident. There is nothing else to say." He stopped talking but then added quickly, as an afterthought, "I'm sorry."

"Sorry? Is that all you can say?" she screamed, and her voice went shrill. "All these years I thought Mommy's death was my fault. 'What did I do wrong that God took my mommy away from me?' Now I find out that something else might have happened, something that would make me feel less guilty, and I have to know how my mother died. I have to know and you have to tell me!"

Her father looked at her as if he hadn't thought of it that way. But then his eyes glazed over, and he responded in a stiff, tinny voice.

"Life has a very slippery edge, Lacey. What difference does it make how your mother died? She's dead. She wouldn't want you going over and over this. Life is hard enough, and it will only get harder as you get older. But there are wonderful things about life, too, things that you can only imagine but can't possess right now."

She couldn't believe his gibberish.

"You drove her to do it, didn't you, Daddy?" she said in a low voice that slowly began to rise. She could feel herself going over the top with him, but she didn't care. She was desperate. "It was you," she finally screamed. "You killed my mother, didn't you?" It was an outrageous accusation and she knew it, but it was all she had left. She had to provoke him into telling her what she had to know.

"You did!" she went on uncontrollably, grabbing one of the pillows next to her and lunging at him over the arm of the couch. She hit him over and over again with the pillow as she screamed, "You did! You did! You killed my mother!"

Each blow punctuated her words; her eyes were wild and her hair flew in all directions. Rage was coming out of every pore of her body, but still he didn't react. He sat there like a lump, shielding his face with his hands and taking the blows as if he was a human punching bag.

How dare he not care about me, my pain and my incredible loss? she thought wildly as she hit him repeatedly until, slowly, spent and exhausted, she stopped and sank back down on the couch. By then, tears were streaming down her face, and she brushed them away with tight, closed fists. Still her father showed no emotion, nothing that could make her think that anything she had done had made any difference at all.

They both sat there for a moment in silence, thinking their own thoughts. She was at a loss as to how to reach him, and he acted as though he deserved what he had gotten from her. Then he shifted slowly in his chair and stood up, moving to a spot right behind her on the couch as she turned to look up at him, towering above her, his face set in a stone-cold expression. Whatever emotions he had about all of this, he was holding them deep inside, hidden away from her.

He touched her shoulder lightly, leaned down, and whispered in her ear, "Your mother is gone. When you die, you'll see her again. She'll be waiting for you. Remember that. Everything else is just not important."

She sat there stunned, feeling him move away from her. She heard him walk down the hall to his room. The bastard! He wasn't going to tell her anything! He didn't love her enough. He didn't care how much she hurt. He was a mean, cruel, heartless coward, and she'd never forgive him for this.

Never!

When Lacey's father finished speaking at the funeral, his last heartbreaking words still echoing through the silent church, Lisette watched him fold up the paper he had read from, put it in his pocket, and step down from the pulpit. He walked slowly back to his seat in the front, nearly across the aisle from her, pulled out his handkerchief, and wiped the tears from his face.

He was pale and drawn, and Lisette felt sorry for him. What he had said about Lacey was so wonderful that it had made her cry all over again. She didn't know how he could even read all those things without breaking down completely. He was a very brave man, she decided, to say aloud how much he loved his daughter and how much he would miss her. Her father would never say anything like that at her funeral. He probably wouldn't even come. He hadn't been at her mother's service. He was such a coward! He was the last person on earth she could ever admire.

But Lacey's father was different. To her, he seemed like the best dad in the whole world, but then she knew no one was perfect. She wondered what Lacey thought about her father. What would she say if she was in the church right now?

He's such a liar!

The words, so loud and clear, startled Lisette. It was as if someone right next to her had spoken them out loud, and she instantly turned to Ruth at her side.

"What did you say?" she blurted out.

Ruth gave her a perplexed look and replied, "I didn't say anything."

"Sorry," Lisette muttered, sinking back into her seat. She must not be hearing right. No one in the church would call Lacey's father a liar. Not in the middle of his daughter's funeral service. But then the voice came to her again.

Don't pretend you didn't hear me! I said my father is a liar. He lied to me about my mother.

"Your mother?" Lisette blurted out, unable to stop herself from speaking aloud.

This time, both Ruth and Sophie turned and looked at her.

"Sorry," Lisette muttered again. She sank lower into her seat. Was she making all this up, or was she really hearing that damn voice in her head again? What was it saying about someone's mother?

You heard me. My father lied about how my mother died. That's what I was saying. And, if you don't believe me, just ask Sophie. Ask her about my mother. She'll tell you. I told her all about my mother. Go ahead – ask her!

The voice was getting louder and more insistent, and Lisette just wanted it to go away. She put her hands over her ears and sputtered, "Would you shut up and leave me be!"

At that outburst, both Ruth and Sophie turned to look at her. "What did you say?"

"Nothing," Lisette mumbled, but then something made her go on. "Tell me, would you?" she almost hissed at Sophie. "Is Lacey's mother really dead?"

"Oh, yes," Sophie said. "She died years ago. Lacey told me all about it."

See, I told you. Now ask her how she died. Let's see what she says.

"What happened to her?" Lisette went on without missing a beat.

The look in Sophie's eyes softened. "She died in a car accident. It was so sad. But Lacey is with her now."

Told you! He lied. He's lied to everyone. They all think that I'm with her, but I'm not. He's such a liar, that bastard!

"I don't get it," Lisette groaned and then squirmed in her seat, so upset and confused now that she could hardly sit still.

Of course you get it. Weren't you ever so mad at your father that you…"

That was all Lisette needed to hear about her father. Suddenly, she jumped out of her seat and headed down that wide, empty aisle to the back of the church. Lots of people noticed her, possibly even Lacey's father, but she didn't care. Being at this funeral was bad enough, but to have to think about what happened between her and her own father was making her sick. What did he have to do with any of this? Was he the voice in her head? How could that be?

Horrified at that thought, Lisette rushed past the last pew, pushed open the doors, and fled outside into the warm spring day. Once there, she bent over and gasped for air. She stayed that way for a moment, taking in big gulps and trying to calm herself down. But just as she straightened up, she heard the voice again. This time it was angry and shrill.

We can't leave now. I'm not through in there yet.

"What do you mean, 'we'?" Lisette yelled out loud. "Who the hell are you? What do you want from me?"

The voice ignored her anger. It replied in a light, snippy tone. *I thought you would have figured out by now who I am. I know who you are.*

"Cut the bullshit," Lisette growled. "I don't have time for a guessing game. Tell me who you are or I'll… " She spun around, her fist raised up over her head like she was going to hit someone or something, but there was nothing there.

The voice let out a laugh. *Christ! You are really pissed at your father. When I said something about him, it set you off enough that my voice finally broke through. I've been talking to you for an hour and you haven't heard anything. What is it with you and your father, anyway?*

"Leave my father out of this," Lisette snarled, enraged as she paced across the church steps, waving her arms. "I want you out of my head. Do you understand? Go away!"

Sorry, I can't do that.

"What do you mean you can't?"

Exactly what I said. I'm stuck here with you until I can get somewhere else. If you haven't noticed, dummy, I don't have a body anymore. It's in that casket in church.

"Don't call me a dummy!" Lisette screamed wildly, but then her voice changed as she realized what body and what casket the voice was talking about.

"Lacey? Is that you?" Lisette's voice quivered with amazement. "Are you the one who's talking to me?"

Of course it's me, the voice said, more somberly now. *Look, I'm sorry I upset you, but there was no other way to tell you. Not that I understand much of it myself. Being dead is so confusing. It's my first time, you know. It ought to come with an instruction manual!*

Lisette had to smile. This was Lacey, she thought. She always knew that, besides being beautiful and smart, Lacey would be a very funny girl.

It's not fun being stuck in your body, as you know. It must be cold dancing up on that stage with no clothes on. It feels cold to me! How do you do that every night, anyway?

"You're in my body?" Lisette felt a chill go through her. "Where?" she demanded as she whirled around, frantically touching her arms, shoulders, and head. "Where are you in my body? This is way too weird. I'm out of here."

She flew down the church steps as the voice continued to yell.

Go ahead, run away. But wherever you go right now, I go too. That's the way it is. You can't get away from me. We're in this together. Don't you get it?

Lisette stopped suddenly at the bottom of the steps and heaved a sigh. "Please, just go away. You're scaring me." Lisette felt another shiver go through her.

The voice came again, calmer and more understanding. *I'm as scared as you are. I wish I could go away, but I can't. There must be something I can do, but I don't know what it is. Hopefully I'll figure it out soon or else…"*

"Or else what?" Lisette felt herself panic. "What do you know that I don't know?"

Calm down. I won't be here forever. It just changes things.

"What things?" Lisette asked nervously.

You know, things. I mean, since I died, haven't things been different for you?

"Yeah! My life's a wreck right now. I keep losing jobs." Lisette thought for a moment and went on. "Are you saying that's your doing? Are you trying to ruin my life?"

Me? Ruin your life? the voice quipped. *How much lower can you go than a stripper, for God's sake? I do like your Attila the Hunny act, though. I can see why Ambrose likes it so much. In fact, he's quite taken with you. And you like him too. Well, to each his own. He's a little too – what did he say about himself? Oh, yes, too farty and smelly for my taste."*

"But he cleans up really well, don't you think?" Lisette replied quickly, and then stopped when she realized what she was doing. She was talking about Ambrose to the voice of a dead girl in her head. What was she nuts?

Then it hit her. "My God, you know everything, don't you? What I hear and feel and think." Suddenly her head spun with all the things that Lacey knew about her. How she feels when she dances and the secrets about her life that she told Ambrose last night.

"You can't know all that about me," Lisette fumed. "That's not right!"

Hey! the voice broke in. *I'm not trying to be a voyeur here or anything like that.*

"What do you mean a 'voyeur'?" She hated it when people used words she didn't understand.

It's like a Peeping Tom. Someone who's spying on you. But that's not what this is about. I think it's more about something I have to do before I can move on.

"And what's that?" Lisette was really agitated now.

Hey, if I knew that, I'd be God. And you know how they say that when you die you get to see God? Well, I haven't seen anyone who even comes close to magnificent yet, so God isn't in the picture, and neither is my mother. Come to think of it, I only see what you see. And your life is pretty crazy, if you ask me."

Lisette ignored that remark. "Hey! Wait a minute," she said as an afterthought. "If you haven't seen God, then how do you know your mother isn't with him?"

Lacey's voice was silent for a moment. Had Lisette really said something that made Lacey think? Was she was on to something important here?

You're right. I haven't seen or talked to anyone except you. Maybe I'm not doing this death thing right.

Suddenly the word "forgiveness" popped into Lisette's mind, and she blurted out, "Maybe you're supposed to forgive your father…. Oh, God," she moaned. "Where did that come from? Don't you hate it when people say that all we have to do is forgive someone who treats us like dirt and we'll be okay? What did he do to you anyway?"

That's a long story, but basically he lied to me about how my mom died. So you're saying if I can forgive him for that, I can move on. But how am I going to tell my father that now? The voice stopped for a moment and then added, maybe you could help me.

"Me? You're the one who came into my body. Why do I have to help you out?"

I don't see anyone else around who's volunteering. Unless you want to go back inside and ask Sophie. Of course, you'd have to explain to her about this voice you're hearing inside your head first. She'll have a good laugh with that.

"Are you nuts? She already thinks I'm crazy, coming to someone's funeral who I don't even know and then running out of the church in the middle of the service."

All right, then. I guess you're it. Believe me, if I could do it myself, I would. And if I could have chosen the body I'd get stuck in, it wouldn't have been yours.

"Thanks a lot! What's the matter? My body is not good enough for you?"

Are you kidding? I'd do anything to still have a body like yours. It's just that you're being so pigheaded about all of this.

"I am not. You're the one being bossy."

If I'm going to get out of here, someone's got to take charge. Are you going to help me or argue about it?

Lisette heaved a big sigh. "What do I have to do? It's not anything too weird, is it? All of this is too weird already."

All you have to do is find my dad and tell him that I forgive him. That's it.

"Just like that?" Lisette had to laugh. "Walk right up to him and say, 'Oh, by the way, I was just talking to your dead daughter and she forgives you.' You've got to be kidding! He'll never believe me in a million years."

Then you've got to convince him, or else this might not work. If he doesn't believe that I really forgive him, I could be stuck here forever.

"Oh, no!" Lisette protested. "You've got to go. It's got to work!"

We won't know until we try. So, are you going to talk to my dad or not?

Lisette sighed and shrugged her shoulders. "Do I have a choice?" Then she added, with desperation in her voice, "I want you out of my body!"

Now who's making me feel like I'm not good enough for you, the voice teased.

"Sorry," Lisette whimpered. "It's just that…"

That's okay. I know this can't be fun for you either. But it will be over soon.

Just then Lisette heard the organ music inside the church swell. "How much longer are they going to be inside there anyway?"

Not too long now. You can make your move when the service ends. I'll know when they get to the final hymn because it's going to be one of my favorites!

Swell, Lisette thought sarcastically, as she plopped herself down on the bottom step to wait. Here she was, trying to get through this craziness, and Lacey was playing disk jockey at her own funeral.

How weird was that?

When the music of the hymn "Amazing Grace" came wafting out of the church, Lisette sat up with a start from her seat on the bottom of the front steps.

Pain stabbed at her heart as she remembered that she and her mother had sung that song together a long time ago. Except it felt more hopeful to Lisette then, not so sad like today. Was this Lacey's favorite hymn? Did that mean that the service was finally over? Lisette asked Lacey but there was no reply.

"Lacey, are you there?' Lisette stood up and spun around. "Where did you go?"

Instead, Lisette heard the doors swing open at the top of the church steps and the singing got louder and stronger. This had to be the end of the service, Lisette thought, as she raced back up the steps and peered into the church. Sure enough, the casket with Lacey's body inside it was being wheeled slowly back down the center aisle of the church and it was heading in her direction. She watched it come out the door, carried down the steps, and placed into the long, black car parked in front of the church. Soon, everyone was filing out behind it, including the man Lisette recognized as Lacey's father.

"There he is, Lacey," Lisette said to the voice in her head. She watched him walk slowly down the steps and then be surrounded by a whole group of people when he got to the bottom. "You've got to help me, Lacey," she insisted. "What do I say to him, and how do I get him alone?"

But the voice still wouldn't answer. Lisette stood there for a moment, watching until the group of people slowly drifted off and Lacey's father walked alone toward the black limo parked behind the funeral car. This was it, her moment, she thought. Her one chance to get him alone before someone else came along, or he got into the car and drove away. But she felt so stupid. This was such a bad idea. The poor man just lost his daughter. Why couldn't she leave him alone? But she had to get Lacey out of her body. She had no choice.

She raced down the stairs and pushed her way through the crowd, wishing that she knew how she was going to explain all this to Lacey's father. When she got near him, she blurted out, "Excuse me, sir? Mr. Lockhart? Could I talk to you?"

That wasn't enough to get his attention. He was standing against the car, staring off into the crowd, looking pale and distracted, as if he was hoping that Lacey was still alive and hanging out with the young people there. She'd have to try harder to get his attention, and do it fast.

"Shit, Lacey!" she mumbled under her breath. "What's your father's first name?"

But the voice still wouldn't speak to her.

"Where the hell are you, Lacey? Could you help me here, please?"

Then it came to her. His name was Howie. She frowned. What

kind of a name was that for a grown man? But since the only other surefire way she knew to get a man's attention was to take her clothes off, she went for it.

"Excuse me, Howie," she asked, this time raising her voice a little louder. "Could I talk to you?"

At that, he turned and looked at her as though he'd just seen a ghost. But it did the trick. This time, he heard her. Without waiting for a reply, she went on nervously, "Look, I'm really sorry about your daughter. It's a terrible thing. But I need to..."

"You called me Howie," he broke in. "Only my wife called me that. Do I know you?"

"No, but..."

He gaped at her, like he was still trying to figure out who she was and what she knew about him.

"I know this sounds a little weird," she continued, "but Lacey has something she wants me to tell you."

He looked stunned for a moment and then blinked his eyes.

She took it as a sign to go on. "You're probably wondering how I know Lacey. I can't explain that to you exactly, but I can tell you she's fine and she wants you to know that she's sorry. She forgives you for lying to her about how her mother died, and if she were here, she'd tell you how sorry – how very, very sorry – she is."

"I never lied about her mother!" Howie suddenly exploded. Then he glared at her. "You can't know about that. How could you?"

"I'm only telling you what she told me, Howie," Lisette whimpered. "You have to believe me."

"If this is some kind of sick joke, I'll have you..."

"Oh, no, no!" she insisted. "It's no joke. If you could just understand..."

"I understand that you're a very sick person." His mouth twitched, and his face went flush. "And I won't stand here and listen to this."

He moved toward the back door of the car, but Lisette grabbed his arm.

"But you don't understand. Lacey's here, but she can't talk to you, so I have to…"

He pulled his arm away from her and sputtered, "If you knew Lacey, you'd know she'd never play a hairbrained trick like this on me. Not me, not her father. She loved me, and now she's gone." His voice cracked as he continued. "Lacey's dead. She's not talking to you, and you're not talking to me anymore."

He moved away from her again, but this time Lisette grabbed the edge of his suit coat and yanked him back. She was desperate and losing her patience. She couldn't let him get away. "Listen, you sorry son-of-a-bitch," she whispered hoarsely. "Why else would I know to call you Howie if Lacey hadn't told me?"

He looked at her as if he was actually considering what she had just said.

"And what I said about her mother," she went on. "That's true and you know it. So let's cut the crap. Lacey's sorry. She forgives you. There, I delivered the message. Do you think I like having dead people talk to me? Or that I have to talk to pigheaded idiots like you?"

"You're crazy!" he screamed at her, his face turning a deep red.

"Me, crazy?" she yelled back. "It's your daughter who's making me crazy."

"You leave Lacey out of this. Do you hear me? You're a lunatic!"

In one quick motion, he yanked his coat out of her hand, opened the back door of the limo, and jumped in. As the door slammed shut, Lisette lunged for him.

"No, wait, Howie," she wailed. "Mr. Lockhart! Please wait!"

But it was too late. Howie was already in the car, and she now heard the automatic lock click. In desperation, she pressed her face against the car's dark-tinted glass window.

"Please, I'm sorry I upset you. But Lacey's stuck in my body, and she won't go away. If you don't forgive her, she'll never go!"

She was too busy yelling and pounding her fists on the window to see the crowd of people quickly gathering around her. Then two men in dark suits came up behind her, grabbed her by the shoulders, and pulled her off the car.

"What the hell do you think you're doing?" one of them shouted at her. "Can't you leave the poor man alone? He just lost his daughter."

"I know that, you asshole," Lisette snapped back. "That's why I'm here. Lacey sent me. I'm telling you, I've talked to Lacey."

Just then, the limo pulled away from the curb, and Lisette broke away from the two men. She ran down the street after it, yelling, "What do I have to do to convince you that Lacey is sorry! Please, Howie, please come back!"

She kept yelling and running as fast as she could, her purse flipping about on a long chain that hung from her shoulder. But in her high heels and long, tight black dress, it wasn't easy to keep up. Soon she couldn't see the limo anymore. She kept going anyway, not caring how she looked or what people thought. She weaved in and out of the cars in the funeral procession until she slipped, breaking the heel of her shoe.

"Damn it!" she muttered, as she stumbled to the ground, right into the path of one of the cars.

"Hey!" the guy behind the wheel of the car yelled out his window as he slammed on his brakes, narrowly missing her. "Get out of the street! Do you want to get killed?"

That made her laugh. At this point, getting killed wasn't such a bad idea. She'd go find someone's body, just like Lacey had found hers, and drive them crazy too.

Out of breath and unable to run anymore, she felt lost and alone, limping along, half in the street and half on the curb, until a hand grabbed her from behind and spun her around.

"Lisette?" a man's voice said. "Is that you? What are you doing here?"

It took her a moment to recognize the voice. It was Erick, the bouncer from the Bare Bottom Dance Club. She gaped at him. His face was dripping with sweat and his breath was coming in gasps. "I was coming out of class a few blocks back," he added, "and I saw you running down the street. Didn't you hear me yelling at you? I've been chasing after you forever!"

Lisette stared at him blankly. Yes, he had told her that awful night he walked her home from the Bare Bottom that he was taking classes at the college, but she didn't care about that right now. She shifted her weight back and forth from one foot to the other, trying to get her balance, but it didn't work. She kept falling over, and Erick had to catch her.

"I tried to tell Howie," she said, her words garbled and her body swaying even with Erick's hands firmly on her shoulders. "He didn't understand."

"Who's Howie?" Erick asked, bending down and looking into her face.

Lisette glared at him like he was an idiot. "Lacey's father. You know, the girl who was killed."

"What girl?" Erick asked again; he still wasn't getting it. "Who are you talking about?"

"The girl at the college," she said woozily. "The one who got killed." She wanted to explain all about Lacey and her father to him. She really did, but the words were caught in her throat. Suddenly everything was fuzzy and she felt herself falling.

"Oh God! I don't feel so good," she said, putting her hand up to her forehead.

But before she could say or do anything more, everything went black.

CHAPTER SIX

Nothing's Forever

"Lacey, is that you?" Lisette asked. She felt the blackness around her thicken, and then finally she experienced the lightness that always came to her when Lacey was around. Only moments ago, she had been standing on the street talking to Erick, but now she didn't know where she was.

At least Lacey was there with her.

"Lacey?" she repeated. "I know you're there."

Yeah. It's me, Lacey's voice said, sounding tired and pissed off.

"Where have you been? I was worried about you. Why did you stop talking to me when I went to see your dad?"

I don't know. Suddenly I froze. It was too hard to see him standing there.

"Did you love the look on his face when I called him Howie? Did your mother really call him that?"

Yes, and he called her "Poopsie."

"You're kidding," Lisette laughed. "Howie and Poopsie! What a couple!"

You did good, Lisette. At least you tried. My dad can be very stubborn.

"Do you think it worked?"

I don't know. I'm still here.

"You are, aren't you? I thought when you weren't talking to me for a while that you might have gotten out. So me telling your father that you forgive him didn't work, huh? What are we going to do now?"

Think of something else, I guess. Damned if I know what.

"Look, could you do me a big favor and do this by yourself for a while? You're really making me crazy. I don't know where you end and I begin. If you come up with something, I'll try to help, but I've got Ambrose to deal with, and once I come out of this fog, I've got to get Erick calmed down. He thinks I'm crazy too."

I like Erick. He's a nice guy. Why don't you like him?

"Guys like him want too much. I don't have time for all that."

You have time to hang out with Ambrose, the old smelly, farty one?

"Ambrose isn't that bad," Lisette protested. "He cleans up nice. We're going to a show tomorrow. Maybe then I'll know what he's talking about for this new act for me."

He reminds me of Ari.

"The guy who killed you?"

Lisette was shocked that Lacey mentioned his name. She never had before.

Yes, he knew how to manipulate me to get me to do what he wanted me to do. Just like Ambrose is doing to you now.

"He is not," Lisette insisted. "Ari was a killer. Ambrose is not like that."

How do you know? I didn't think Ari was a murderer either.

"You're scaring me, Lacey. You've got to cut this out. Just leave me alone."

Sure, but I want to show you something first.

"What?"

But she got no answer. Instead, she felt the blackness around her fade and another whole scene appeared before her eyes.

What is this? she wondered. But there was no one to ask. Lacey's voice was gone, and a man's voice was saying something.

Suddenly, she was there seeing him, watching what was around him as thought it were a movie. No, she thought, a dream.

And then when she realized what it was, she knew it was a nightmare. She didn't want to watch; she didn't need to see this.

"Lacey!" she screamed. "Why are you doing this to me? Why?"

But Lacey was gone. All Lisette could do was watch and listen until it was done.

"You're *so* beautiful," Ari said breathlessly, stroking Lacey's long blonde hair and gazing intently into her eyes. Lacey was lying naked facing him on the bed in his dorm room as he paused in the middle of their lovemaking to admire her.

In the five months since she had met Ari, he would tell her often how beautiful she was, but still it made her uncomfortable to hear it.

"You're my angel," he went on. She tried to hold his eyes, but it was hard. She felt self-conscious, lying there naked with nothing to cover her. Ari was different. He was full of brash and bravado, so comfortable with his own naked body. She knew he wouldn't understand why she, under his intense, albeit admiring, scrutiny, wanted to leap out of bed and run out of the room, leaving him there unsatisfied and unnerved.

"Your hair shimmers in the light, did you know that?" he said in a soft voice, as he played with tendrils of her long hair, raising them up and letting them fall back down over her soft, full breasts. "It flows like wings off your shoulders," he added in a whisper. "Just like an angel."

"That tickles," she giggled and wrapped her arms around her chest as though she could hide something from him now. She tried to move away, but he leaned into her and drew his face closer to hers.

"You have the most wonderful hair," he continued with that same softness in his voice that made her melt. Then he sniffed it. "It smells like… like…"

"…lavender," she cooed, still trying to take in his words of admiration.

She knew what he was saying. That she was beautiful. But she couldn't see it herself. In her mind's eye, she was still the plain, fat girl she had been in grade school, the ugly duckling who apparently had turned into a swan so that at nineteen, slimmed down, tall and stately, she had no trouble attracting men. But she wanted more, so much more than that. She wanted for a man to be close to her, so intimate with every part of her body that she'd be certain she was beautiful inside and out. That she was indeed lovable and loved.

"It's lavender from my shampoo," she went on, allowing her eyes to move slowly down his body now, taking in his broad shoulders, smooth chest, and slim waist. He was beautiful too, she thought, although she couldn't say those words to him out loud like he had just said them to her.

He moved closer to her now and held her tight. She could feel him hard and swollen against her and she liked that. What would people think if they knew how she thought constantly about Ari making love to her and how much she wanted him to be inside her right now? What kind of a girl would they think she was?

Ari's voice pulled her back into the moment.

"Lavender?" he asked inquisitively. "I don't know lavender. We don't have it in my country."

"Yes, you do!" Lacey squealed, jabbing him in the stomach in mock reproach. "And what's this 'my-country' shit? You've been living here since you were a kid. You're as American as I am, silly."

"No, no. Don't say that," he replied hastily. "My father doesn't even know that I'm dating an American girl."

"What is his problem? This isn't the sixteenth century, you know. If he's living in America, he's got to get used to it."

"Get used to it?" Ari snorted. "I don't think so. He wants me to have one of those arranged marriages."

"Ugh!" Lacey yelped, flinging herself dramatically over onto her side with her back to him now. "How could anyone do that to another human being? It's so barbaric."

Ari threw his arm around her and pulled her closer. "You don't understand," he whispered into her ear. "That's what my family wants."

She turned back and looked at him. "And what do you want?"

"I want you," he gushed without hesitation. Then he grabbed her shoulder and pushed her onto her back. He climbed on top of her and put his face so close to hers that every delicate feature of it – his dark brown eyes, slender nose, and full-bodied lips – was totally focused on her.

"I'll always want you," he said in a low, hushed voice filled with so much emotion that Lacey couldn't keep her eyes off him now. "I loved you the first moment I saw you," he went on. "You're my angel."

Then he kissed her gently on the lips and ran his hands up and down the curves of her body. She shivered at the lightness of his touch, and when his kisses grew in intensity, she matched them. As his tongue probed and filled her mouth, she let herself feel how much he wanted her.

Sex had never been like this for her before. Sure, she had done it with some boys while she was in high school, but they had pawed and groped at her because they didn't know what they were doing. She had panted and groaned her way through it so she wouldn't appear stupid or inexperienced. But with Ari, it was different. He was a college man, a year older than she was, and he knew how to please a woman. He made her feel special and she liked that. She liked that a lot. He wasn't afraid to show her how he felt about her.

After one more long, deep kiss, Lacey sighed, opened her eyes, and looked up at Ari. "I'm no angel," she teased. "Just ask my dad."

She watched his eyes grow soft and hazy, and as he replied, his voice was once again full of emotion. "Then he doesn't know the Lacey I see. You *are* my angel."

He planted soft, wispy kisses on her neck that made her giggle. Then he moaned, "Oh, baby, baby. You *are* beautiful! *So* beautiful."

From her neck, he moved slowly down her body until he nuzzled his face in her breasts and moved his tongue lightly around the tips of her nipples. As she moaned and gasped with pleasure, he slid his tongue further down, licking the skin on her belly, then inside her navel, and finally between her legs.

"Oh, Ari, Ari," she cried out, grabbing at his head and rubbing her hands wildly through his hair. How did he know where her magic spot was? She never knew she had one until she made love with him for the first time. Somehow he knew where it was and how to make her feel good down there.

"Oh, Ari! Ari!" she repeated, moaning.

He looked up at her. "You like that, don't you, my angel?"

"Oh, yes. Yes! Please don't stop."

She let herself feel the ecstasy of his tongue flickering all over her. She moaned and thought whatever else he wanted to do was all right with her.

Slowly he inched his way back up to her neck and lowered his body on top of hers. She could feel his hardness pressed into the space between her legs, and she arched her back up to meet him as he pushed himself into her.

"See how much you want me," he crowed as he drove himself deep inside her with long, hard thrusts.

Yes, yes, she thought as she moved her body rhythmically up and down with his. This is what she wanted. This was wonderful! She opened her eyes for a moment and saw the pleasure on his face, flushed and red now, as he pushed into her over and over again.

"Tell me you're mine!" he howled. "You're mine, mine forever!"

"Oh, oh," was all that she could say, however, and Ari gasped and repeated himself. "Tell me you're mine!"

Then he shouted, "Oh, God, God!" to no particular deity and came in the same moment that Lacey felt her entire body go into spasms.

"Oh, yes, Ari. Yes!" she cried out as she came too.

Then he collapsed on top of her, and they lay there for a moment, totally spent, their hearts pumping wildly together and her arms wrapped around Ari's back. Her head felt light while her insides throbbed, and she thought wonderful, happy thoughts until Ari jerked his head up off her chest.

"What's the matter with you?" he yelled. His voice was desperate, his eyes afire. "I just screwed your brains out and you can't even say you're mine forever?"

"Jesus, Ari," she croaked, making a joke of it. "Nothing's forever!"

But he didn't laugh. Instead, he pressed his hands against her shoulders and pinned her down on the bed. Then with the full weight of his body on hers, he pushed harder and harder down on her chest until she sputtered and gasped for breath.

"Ari, you're hurting me!" she cried out, beating on his back with her hands. "Get off me now!"

Ari stopped suddenly and threw himself off her and onto the bed.

She sat up like a bolt of lightning had hit her and tossed her hair off her face.

"What is it with you? You're scaring me!"

He continued to lie facedown for a moment, his body still. Then he lifted his head up and looked at her.

"Forget it," he said gruffly, rolling over on his back. Then his voice softened and he sounded more like the Ari she knew. "I'm sorry." Then he grinned and took her hand and kissed it. "You know I love you. You're my angel."

"Yeah, sure; I love you too. But what is it with you and this 'forever' shit?"

"Nothing," he muttered. "I just want to be close to you."

Then he flashed her another smile, snuggled up next to her, and closed his eyes. She sat there, watching his breathing slow down and his eyelids flutter. Only then did she sigh with relief. A few minutes ago, she thought, he was a maniac demanding an answer from her. Now he was like a little boy cuddled up next to his favorite teddy bear.

She had to smile as she leaned over his motionless body and ran her fingers gently through the dark hair right above his ear.

"Nothing is forever, Ari," she whispered. "Nothing."

She was only nineteen. She wasn't looking for forever. Why did he have this sudden obsession to push their relationship forward? What had brought that on?

She wanted to know, but when he stirred for a moment and then quieted down, she knew he was out for the night. She'd have to wait until tomorrow morning to ask that question. So she reached down, drew the blanket up over them and turned off the light on the nightstand next to her. As she slid down under the covers, she repeated softly to herself the truth of what she knew as she drifted off to sleep.

Nothing is forever.

Hadn't her mother's death taught her that? Why did Ari think she could promise him something that wasn't even possible?

Why didn't he get it?

"Oh, God, Lacey! Why didn't you see? He means forever in hell with him!"

Lisette screamed as she suddenly woke up and the blackness lifted. She struggled to open her eyes, and when she did, the first thing she saw was Erick's face.

She was never so happy to see anyone.

"Oh, God!" she cried out and threw her arms around his neck. "It's you. Thank God, it's you. Where am I?"

"You're here with me. You fainted. Are you all right? You hit the ground pretty hard."

She felt okay. Nothing hurt now that she could feel her body again.

"I'm fine," she muttered as she clung to Erick and she felt him lift her up and carried her away. She rested her head against his shoulder as she drifted off to where she had been before, in the blackness. She saw two people there, smiling and happy at first and then fighting, angry, and upset. She wasn't sure what she was seeing, but it didn't last long. Where had she gone, she wondered, between the time she felt faint on the street until now when Erick was carrying her in his arms? Had she been with Lacey? Was Lacey one of those people she saw? Soon she couldn't remember anything she had seen. It was just blank space that she couldn't fill in. No sounds, no thoughts, no voices.

Now she felt Erick putting her down on something and asking her again if she was all right. She opened her eyes and saw that she was sitting on a bench near the park, and Erick was there next to her.

"You had me scared," he said. "One moment you were talking to me, and the next thing I knew, you were down on the ground. You went out like a light!"

Then he reached over and brushed her hair away from her face with a light touch.

"Are you sure you're all right?"

She thought she was, but she wasn't sure. Her body was shaking, and she leaned into Erick, feeling weak and frightened. He put his arm around her, and they sat there for a while without talking.

Finally Erick spoke in a soft voice. "What's going on, Lisette? Are you in some kind of trouble?"

She looked up at him but didn't know what to say. How could she tell him what was going on with Lacey when she didn't even understand it herself? He'd think she was crazy, and she didn't need that. Erick must have seen the scared look on her face because he quickly backed off, "It's okay. You don't have to tell me."

"It's so stupid," she hedged. "You're going to laugh."

"Try me," Erick said, looking into her eyes intently.

She took a deep breath and let it out.

"I had a message from Lacey for her father," she said carefully. "I tried to deliver it to him at the funeral."

"Lacey?" Erick flinched at that. "Isn't that the girl who was killed at the college? How could you have a message from her?"

"I hear her voice inside my head. She's been talking to me since that night at the Bare Bottom. I didn't know it was her until today."

Erick looked shocked. "Why didn't you tell me this before?"

"I… I don't know," she stammered. "I guess because you'd think I was a lunatic."

Erick took a deep breath. "You should talk to someone about this."

"I am. I'm talking to you."

"No, I mean a professional, someone who can help you more than I can."

"You've already helped me, once when you walked me to my hotel after that terrible night at the Bare Bottom and again just now. I don't know what I would've done without you."

"No," he insisted. "Don't you see? You're projecting this girl's pain onto yourself. That's why you think you hear her voice in your head."

"You mean I'm making it up?" she said with an edge in her voice. How could he think that of her? But she could see she had gone too far in telling him all this, so she switched gears and changed the tone of her voice.

"It's all right," she said lightly. "It's all over with. I'm sure what I said to her father did the trick."

"What do you mean?"

"The voice is gone. Lacey hasn't said a word to me since the funeral."

"This is crazy," Erick protested. "You have to talk to someone."

"No, we're going to forget about it," she said firmly. "I know that's hard for you because you're studying about crazy people in school."

"You mean that I told you I'm studying psychology and want to be a psychologist some day?" Erick asked.

"Yeah, that's right? But I don't need any of that mumbo jumbo here. I'm over it. I'm going back to my hotel."

She stood up from the bench, but her legs wobbled and she grabbed Erick's knee to steady herself.

"You can't go like this," he said firmly. "You're dizzy, and the heel on your shoe has broken off. I'll get my car and drive you. We can talk some more. You need help."

But suddenly Lisette didn't want Erick's help anymore.

"No, I'm fine. I know where I'm going," she repeated, smoothing her wrinkled dress down her body and running her hands through her hair. Then she reached down and took both shoes off her feet. "There. I'll walk home barefoot. See, no problem!"

He looked at her with big, sad eyes and pleaded, "Lisette, let me help you."

"No, I'm all right." she said, as she turned unsteadily and walked away.

"Hey! Don't forget your purse," Erick said, coming after her and handing her the small black bag with the long shoulder strap on it.

She snatched the purse from him, flung it over her shoulder and waved back at him as she walked toward the park.

"See you around," she called. "You don't have to rescue me anymore."

"It's no problem," Erick yelled after her, but she kept walking. When she got into the park, she stopped and rummaged in her purse for a cigarette and lighter.

As she stood there taking her first drag, she heaved a sigh of relief and then felt guilty. That was rude, she thought. She hadn't even thanked Erick. Why was she so mean to him? Why was he always so nice to her? Did he want something from her? What was his game?

She sighed again and walked slowly through the park. Why did everyone want something from her? Ambrose wanted her to do that performance art thing, and Erick wanted her to get some help. And Lacey, ah, Lacey! She was the hardest to understand, but now the voice in her head had stopped, Lisette wasn't going to think anymore about what Lacey had wanted from her. It was over. Now she would go back to her hotel, take a hot bath, and then a long nap. Her life would be normal again. She was letting Lacey go.

What was that prayer her mother had taught her when she was a kid?

"May the souls of the faithfully departed, through the mercy of God, rest in peace, Amen."

"Yes, Lacey," Lisette prayed now. "Rest in peace, Amen."

CHAPTER SEVEN

Tight, Dark Places

By early Sunday afternoon, after two days of rest, Lisette was feeling much more like herself.

Lacey was gone and Ambrose had actually left her alone for a few days. Today, she was looking forward to going with him to the performance art show, and when he met her in the lobby of her hotel, she was surprised by how good he looked.

His long, graying hair had been washed and was neatly combed back into a tail that hung fashionably over the collar of a dark blue double-breasted blazer. He wore a pair of dark jeans and a white shirt opened at the collar. Even his boots were clean and buffed up. But the biggest change of all was that Ambrose had completely shaved off his beard.

"Oh," she said in an almost seductive tone of voice, reaching up and grazing his clean-shaven face with the back of her hand. "I like you without the beard. You even smell good. If I would've known that you clean up this good, I would've asked you out first."

He gave her a big grin, and then took her hand from his face and squeezed it tight before he let it go. "And if I would've known it would get such a big reaction, I would have done it earlier."

"Where did you get the blazer?" she asked.

"I stole it," he said with all seriousness.

"Did you really?" She giggled, not sure if he was pulling her leg or not. "From whom?" she added, testing him.

"Someone who didn't need it anymore," he replied with a big smile.

Then she laughed, because suddenly she was having fun and it felt good. So good that when he helped her on with her jacket and they walked out of her room and down the hall to the hotel elevators, she put her arm in his so that they looked like a couple.

She liked that, even if it wasn't true, because, for the first time in a long time, it made her feel happy, so very, very happy.

Lacey couldn't believe how bored she was getting – and angry too.

After all, she had spent the last few days sitting quietly in Lisette's body not doing or saying anything, and yet where was all this being nice getting her?

How could she feel one minute as if she were still alive and living through Lisette and the next plunged into this great unknown? She hated it. It was like being in a deep, dark cave where every so often someone would shine a light, but she could only see and do what Lisette did and nothing more. Right now, that was so boring and stupid that it was turning her into a lunatic.

She wanted to scream, "What about me? Doesn't anyone care about me anymore?" But she didn't. Instead, she waited quietly in the deep, dark recesses of Lisette's body and tried to be patient.

Alone and dejected, her thoughts drifted to her father. Howie, the jerk, the liar, she thought. The father who knew too little, the father who knew too much. The father who wouldn't tell her what she wanted to know.

Why was she thinking about her father? she wondered. And why were some of the thoughts hers, some of them her father's? How did that work? It was as if she was playing around in her father's head, being pulled into his thoughts in a way she couldn't resist. His thoughts were so heavy. He was complaining about why so much death and destruction had been visited upon him. First, his wife, Marge, had died in a mysterious way, then his daughter was murdered. Now with only Jimmie left, he was so terrified that his son would be taken away from him, too.

It was all his fault, his thoughts went on. He was being punished. But then they could've had more kids. It was all her fault that they didn't. It was her moods, her depression that kept him away from her.

"What's the big deal about having another kid?" he remembered screaming at her during a fight about having another child after Lacey. After all, he wanted a son. He deserved one. Someone to carry on his name. Someone who was just like him. How could Marge not know that about him?

When she finally had his son, how was he supposed to know that Marge would do what she did? How could anyone have imagined that?

But what had her mother done? Lacey had to know. What? What? she wanted to scream, but Howie's thoughts didn't go there. Instead he went on.

It wasn't his fault. He wasn't a psychiatrist. He couldn't have known what she was capable of. No, it was all her fault. He was sure of that now.

Capable of what? What? Lacey wanted to know everything. Suddenly a whoosh went through her, and in a flash, she was jerked away from her father's thoughts and thrust back into her own. A great silence came upon her then and she felt light and unburdened by her father's overbearing thoughts.

What was happening? she wondered as she felt herself traveling, floating, going faster and faster into a world that had no definition, no physicality. It was like an out-of-body experience, the kind she had read about in books. She had told herself that at her moment of death she'd be very conscious of what was happening to her and record her every thought and feeling.

But Ari had spoiled all that. It had happened so fast with the gun and all that blood. Red, red blood that soaked through everything she was wearing and created a stain in the carpet the size of a watermelon that only got bigger and bigger. It was her blood draining out of her. Going, going, gone.

No, she stopped herself quickly. No, no, she repeated. Don't go there. Control what you think about. You can do it. Think about something else. Suddenly she was pulled back into her father's thoughts by a force that she couldn't see or explain but only feel in a weird, surreal way. How did she get there, down in the basement of their house? What was he doing behind the stairs in the crawl space, the crawl space she had always hated?

She hated tight, dark places, and it freaked her out when her thoughts shifted for a second to how her own physical body was in a tight, dark place called a coffin, buried deep underground.

No, no, she told herself firmly. Don't go there either. Stay here with your father, you idiot. And find out what the hell he's doing crawling around in the dark.

She focused on him. She had no choice but to hover close so that his thoughts were hers now. Except that those thoughts were mostly grumblings about crawling around with all the goddamn spiders, until he stepped back out into the light, dragging behind him a large, dark wooden trunk. Lacey recognized it immediately. It was the cedar chest her mother called her "hope chest." Lacey hadn't seen it since her mother had died.

What was he doing with it here in the basement? When she had asked about it, he had told her that her grandmother, Marge's mother, had taken it and he told her never to ask about it again.

But now she knew he had lied to her. The chest, with all her mother's precious things inside, had sat all these years in the basement crawl space, hidden in a place that he knew neither she nor her brother would ever go. What a goddamn liar he was! Not that she was surprised. He had lied to her about so many things that were important to her. But suddenly she realized that all she had to do was hover and listen to his thoughts, and she'd find out all she ever wanted to know. It was perfect, she thought with smug satisfaction. A perfect revenge on him!

She listened now as his thoughts moved from complaining about the spiders and how goddamn heavy the chest was to thoughts that were soft and tender. A surge of these emotions flooded his head as he unlocked the chest, opened the lid, and undid the soft folds of her mother's wedding gown lying across the top wrapped in tissue paper, just the way Lacey remembered it.

This shift in her father's thoughts was quite remarkable. Suddenly he was an emotional wreck, all mushy and vulnerable, with tears coming to his eyes as he lifted the gown, still looking white and luxurious, to his face and took in its smell. Lacy knew that, by now, it must smell mostly of the scent of cedar from the chest, but he looked as if he could smell something totally different. Like he was remembering the day his wife wore that dress so many years ago.

Lacey couldn't believe it. Was this her father? Was he really standing down here in the basement, blubbering like a baby over her mother's wedding gown? This was the warm, sweet side of her father that he hardly ever revealed. As a kid, she remembered him showing it when they opened their Christmas presents – or that time he had bought her and Jimmie an ice-cream cone and when he laughed and joked with them, saying, "Are you saving that drop of ice cream on your shirt for later?" That father of hers was usually locked tightly away, but today, he was in full view.

The mean, nasty part of her father was easier to recall. There were the arguments, loud and long at night. She remembered how he screamed and called her mother every ugly name in the book while her mother begged him to quiet down or the neighbors would call the police.

"Let them call the goddamn police," her father yelled. "Let them come over here, and I'll tell them what a goddamn lousy wife you are!"

At first, she was terrified of what might happen next, but she learned to tune it out. Still, the fights never stopped upsetting her. She wanted her mother to stand up just once, call her father a lousy, goddamn so-and-so and say she was leaving him. "I'm taking the kids," Lacey wanted her to say, "and you can't do a goddamn thing about it."

Instead, her mother whimpered, moaned, and begged. "Please, Howie! Someone will hear. What will they think? Please, Howie, no. Just come to bed."

Her father would throw something across the room at her, and she'd beg him again. "No, Howie, no! I'll do anything you want. Anything! Just come to bed."

A few minutes later, it would be quiet upstairs, and she imagined she heard the sounds of her parents kissing and making up, right there in that big, wide bed she loved to crawl into on Saturday and Sunday mornings, when everyone got to sleep in late. Her mother would be so cheerful then, even after one of the bigger fights, and her father all warm and cuddly. He'd tease and poke at her mother until she'd let out a giggle and say, "Oh, Howie, you say the sweetest things."

But the man who stood weeping into the folds of her mother's wedding dress was remembering the good times. How he was smitten with her the first moment he saw her, and how her father hated him but how her mother took to him right away. It helped that whenever he brought flowers for his date, he'd also have a gift of candy or sweets for his future mother-in-law.

Yes, her father could be so charming, Lacey thought, so good at appearances. At this very moment, he was making her think that he really missed his wife, that he was sorry for the way he had treated her and wanted to be forgiven. Lacey didn't doubt that it was genuine emotion, but if he had known that she was listening to his thoughts, he would have been different. Admitting how he really felt was just too scary for him. And yet, if he could have shared all this good stuff with her when she was still alive, it would have made a real difference in their father-daughter relationship, the one she alternately dreaded and cherished.

Suddenly, the door at the top of the stairs leading to the basement jerked open, and Lacey heard Jimmie's voice. "Dad, are you down there? It's getting late. If you're going to drive me to the station, we have to leave right now." Then her brother stuck his head down the steps a bit. "Dad, did you hear me? I've got to go."

His father jerked his body up quickly and wiped his hand over his face while he responded, his voice trembling around the edges. "Yeah, I'll be there in a minute. Just keep your goddamn pants on. I'm coming."

Lacey noticed that his gruff tone with Jimmie belied the tender care he took in laying her mother's gown in the chest and gently closing the lid. Then he shoved the chest into the front of the crawl space and quickly closed and latched the door shut. As he trudged up the stairs, he wiped the dirt off his hands onto his jeans and pulled out his handkerchief to wipe his eyes and blow his nose.

"I'm coming," he grumbled again. "Just give me one more goddamn minute. I'm coming."

Lacey couldn't believe the sudden transformation of this man. One moment he was weeping tenderly over his wife's wedding gown; the next, he was a grouchy father coldly begrudging his son, the last living member of his family, a ride to the train station. How could that be? And what made him go find her mother's chest at that particular moment? In less than an hour Jimmie would have been on the train back to military school, and Howie could have gone down into the basement and blubbered all he wanted.

Howie, her father – what a strange bird he was! But she wasn't through with him yet. Oh, no! Before her time was up, she'd know all her father's deep dark secrets, the ones he had never wanted to reveal to her. He had no choice now. She was in his thoughts, and she could muck around in them all she wanted until she had what she needed.

Until she had the truth.

The truth at last.

Walking down the street with Lisette, Ambrose felt lightheaded, almost giddy.

He couldn't believe it. Just a few days ago, he was lying drunk in a gutter, and today he was escorting an incredible-looking woman to the theater. She was a delight. Now she was telling him what she had been doing since he last saw her after her Thursday night show. That was the night she had told him about her dreams.

"You did *what* on Friday?" he asked her, not sure he had heard her right.

"I went to a funeral," she repeated, but her voice was stiff, as if she was unsure she should be telling him this.

"Whose funeral?"

Lisette frowned at him. "What does it matter? Just some girl I knew."

"But you don't know anyone here in town. You just got here. Unless it was someone at work."

"No, no one at work." She sniffed, and he could feel her shutting down.

So he added, "Did it help you? I find funerals a waste of time. Crying over someone who's dead doesn't make a lot of sense. They're gone; they're not coming back. The sooner you get used to it, the better off you are."

Lisette looked at him carefully. "But what if someone is dead but not gone? What do you think of that?"

"Dead is dead," Ambrose replied with a snarl.

"But what if," Lisette persisted, "someone dies and gets stuck and they have to go into someone else's body until they get unstuck? What do you think of that?"

"Do you think a dead person is in your body?"

"Oh, no! This is not about me," she said quickly. "I had a friend once and that happened to her. She kept hearing someone talking to her inside her head."

"Shit!" Ambrose said with a laugh. "I hear voices in my head all the time, and trust me, no one but me is inside here." He thumped two fingers against his chest and then went on with a grin. "Some days I wish someone else would step in and give it a rest, though!"

"So you hear voices?" she asked curiously.

"Sure. Especially when I'm drunk, but I've learned to live with it. Sometimes the voices can be amusing."

Lisette was quiet for a moment.

"Look," he continued. "If I were you, I wouldn't worry about the voices. Just think about something else."

"But what?" she said with a sudden urgency in her voice. "What?"

"How about your new performance art act?" he suggested, trying not to sound too eager about that.

She looked at him as if an act like that was something she had never considered, and it threw him. Was doing a performance art act with him not something she was thinking about? And why was she worrying about some dead person anyway?

But before Ambrose could panic about any of this, they arrived at the theater and entered the lobby, where their conversation turned to more mundane things. He picked up the tickets he had reserved at the box office for them, and they found their seats.

Did she realize how much trouble he had gone through to take her to this performance? he wondered. It had taken him days to rustle up enough money to pay for the tickets and get his hair shampooed and beard shaved off at a nearby barbershop. Then he had to find the clothes he was wearing – and, no, he hadn't stolen the blazer. It was one he had worn to court years ago and had stashed away at a friend's place. He got it from him and took it back to the men's homeless shelter where he had been staying for the last few nights so he could take a shower and shave.

But if all this had been a lot of work, he realized he had a much more work ahead of him as they sat down in their seats right up near the stage, waiting for the performance to begin. God, he thought, as he watched her sit with her mouth hanging open and her eyes staring at everything around her. She was like a little kid at the zoo for the first time. Everything was as foreign to her as a Himalayan panda or an orangutan from Borneo.

"Jesus, I can't believe the classy people here," Lisette whispered in a nervous, excited voice as well-dressed, well-coifed men and women took their seats in the small theater. "These folks would never come see my act!" She giggled into her hand like a school-girl. "Well, some of the men might. On a business trip, *without* their wives." As lights went down and the show began, Lisette leaned forward in her seat and fixed her eyes on the stage.

He watched her and was mesmerized by her own transformation. She wore a simple black jersey dress that clung to the well-endowed parts of her body in an understated, attractive way. Her long blonde hair was pulled back and tied with a smart, black ribbon. Without all her stage makeup, Ambrose could see her natural good looks.

But as sophisticated and grown-up as she looked, she took in everything that whirled around on the stage through the eyes of a kid. He had seen that look in his own children years ago, but Lisette's gaze seemed oddly haunted. Since he only knew snippets of her life story so far – the fact that her mother had died when she was ten and not even a mention of her father yet – Ambrose could only imagine how it felt to be a fragile, abandoned child inside and one tough cookie on the outside. Perhaps that's why Lisette came across as so feisty. She hid her loneliness and deep grief very well, he mused.

Suddenly Ambrose felt ashamed of what he was doing. She really was like an innocent child, despite what she did up on that stage night after night. And he was no better than a street dealer pushing drugs on her, trying to entice her into the decadent, bizarre world of performance art. His only solace was that stripping wasn't as highbrow, and yet he was hardly a shining example of moral strength. He was a hustler, a drunk, and a connoisseur of kinky sex shows. A shower, a shave and a change of clothes couldn't change that, and her mingling with this crowd wouldn't raise her up into this world either. Suddenly, Ambrose felt as if they were fugitives from two other lives who were quickly being drawn into a third.

And this new world was amazing. The first performance artist, a young woman probably in her early thirties, came out onto the stage nude and stood in front of the audience, talking without a hint of self-consciousness. She spoke quietly at first, but then her voice got louder as she went on about the state of her life as a female member of the human species on this planet.

"Women are misunderstood, oppressed, and enslaved by men," she said angrily. Tonight, she explained, she was going to show the audience exactly how all this tyranny at the hands of men felt on a woman's body.

She walked over to a table covered with bowls and dipped her hands into the largest one. She brought up a fistful of dark, thick liquid that looked like melted chocolate and smeared it all over her body.

Lisette gasped along with the rest of the audience as the performer put handful after handful of the stuff on her body. All the while, she explained that the dark liquid represented the mask of male oppression, but to Ambrose, it looked like her body now had a candy-coated shell.

"Oh, gross!" Lisette squealed and grabbed his arm. Then she whispered, "Is that really chocolate she's smearing all over her body?"

"I think so," Ambrose nodded.

"Thank God stripping is not that messy!"

By then, the woman grabbed handfuls of things from the other bowls on the table, throwing them on her body. Each one, she said, represented another aspect of the domination of women by men.

Alfalfa sprouts, for example, she noted, were a symbol of male sperm. There was popcorn, followed by wood chips, and by then, Ambrose wasn't listening. He was fascinated at how each new thing attached itself to her nude body until it seemed to be wearing a gown shimmering with her political and emotional rage toward men.

In the end, she stood triumphantly proclaiming herself a woman "scorned but invincible" and the audience clapped enthusiastically as the lights went up for intermission.

"God, wasn't she amazing?" Lisette exclaimed, grabbing Ambrose's arm again and thrusting her program at him.

"Read to me about this lady, the one we just saw," she demanded. "I'd try, but it would take me forever."

"Are you sure you don't want to go into the lobby and stretch your legs?" he asked, almost teasing her, just to test her resolve.

"No, read!" she insisted.

So he opened the program and read the woman's biography and a discussion of the political philosophy of her act. Lisette listened intently, periodically asking Ambrose what some of the words meant. After they had gone through the program twice and the audience was seated again for the second act, the lights went down, and Lisette linked her arm in Ambrose's. He smiled and wrapped his hand around hers and squeezed it gently.

The second performer invited the men in the audience to come onto the stage with her. Several men came up, and before they knew it, they were being asked to look up the performer's crotch with a flashlight.

"Jesus!" Lisette snickered and giggled. "I could never do that in my act!" She put her hands over her mouth and giggled some more.

Ambrose couldn't believe that a stripper could be embarrassed by anything to do with the nude body, but Lisette was. He smiled and patted her hand as she watched intently how the performer interacted with the male volunteers from the audience.

Each grew bolder in their exploration of what was between her legs, and the performer tied each man's actions to something that had actually happened to her in her life, like being rejected by a man or abandoned by a loved one. Lisette seemed to relate to it all, nodding her head at time in approval.

As the show ended, Lisette jumped up out of her seat and joined in the standing ovation. She put her fingers in her mouth and let out a loud whistle. After the audience stomped and clapped through one more curtain call, Lisette smiled broadly as she walked out of the theater with Ambrose.

"I loved that!" She laughed, then added excitedly. "I can't believe she did it, but what she did was awesome. I'm so glad you invited me here. Could we go somewhere and talk about this some more?"

Ambrose had to smile. "Of course. Whatever you want," he said nonchalantly as he steered them down the street toward a bar, but inside Ambrose was jumping for joy. She liked the show. He was going to convince her to do an act with him. Everything he had ever dreamed of would finally come true.

What a stroke of genius he had had with Attila the Hunny!

He was brilliant and she was beautiful. What a team they'd make!

CHAPTER EIGHT

Poking at the Truth

Lacey didn't stay in her father's thoughts very long after he climbed the stairs into the kitchen and got ready to take Jimmie to the train station that Sunday afternoon. Soon she heard that same whooshing sound, and she was thrust back into silence, alone in Lisette's body with nothing to do or say but what Lisette had to do or say. Not sure how she had gotten into her father's world and when she might be invited back, she occupied herself by imagining Jimmie and her father together on that half-hour ride to the station.

Jimmie, soon to be fourteen, had been in military school since he was seven years old and then went to a boarding school when he turned twelve. He seemed to like all the structure, Lacey thought. For Jimmie, school was an oasis, a place where he could escape the battles that she and her father had had after her mother died. There were no happy times back then, as she remembered it.

Jimmie was only six weeks old when their mother died. Her father hired several women to take care of Jimmie, but Lacey, even though she was only five years old, would hear nothing of it. She was adamant that her mother wasn't going to be replaced so easily; the only person she would let near Jimmie was her grandmother. Quickly mastering from her everything she needed to know about taking care of Jimmie, Lacey took over. She threw away her dolls, and played mommy with Jimmie. She was sure she could make it all better.

At first, her father protested. "You're just a little girl. You should be out playing with the other kids."

"I don't care about them," Lacey insisted. "I care about Jimmie. But you don't, do you, Daddy?" she taunted him. "Like you never cared about Mommy."

Soon her father let it go, and she was in control. She was determined to be everything to Jimmie – his mother, his big sister, his playmate, and his companion. Her father thought Lacey would grow out of it, but she didn't. It wasn't until Jimmie entered public school and became such a handful that things changed. Her father Howie took the advice of Jimmie's teachers that perhaps the discipline of a military elementary school was the answer.

Lacey couldn't believe that her father would do that to Jimmie, or that Jimmie would go so readily. But he marched off without a whimper at age seven and then he went off to boarding school when he was twelve years old, he only came home for holidays and summer vacations. Lacey missed him so much! She cried herself to sleep, lying in his bed with all his toys and stuffed animals around her. She had lost her mother, now her brother, she wailed. When would it end? All she had left was her father, and he was nothing to her. Nothing!

Her father, on the other hand, Lacey reckoned, would be quiet and detached on the ride to the station, one that he had made many times over the last few years. This man whom she came to despise had never let her or Jimmie grieve their mother's death, so why would it be any different with her own death? And yet this was the same man whom she had just seen weeping over her mother's things in the basement. How could she explain it? What was going on in her father's head anyway?

As if her wish was a command, suddenly she heard the whoosh-ing sound in her head again, and she was back in her father's thoughts. He was at the station now, watching his son get out of the car and gather up his things.

"Are you okay?" her father asked Jimmie gently, while Lacey could hear the thoughts in his head racing on desperately. Oh, God! What am I doing? He's all I have left. I can't just let him go like this. He's just helped me bury his sister. His *murdered* sister. Oh, God! He's so young. He's suffered so much in his life. He doesn't even remember his mother. He doesn't know what she tried to do.

Lacey was amazed. Her father's thoughts were coming in loud and clear again, but all this gushing over his son was unusual, very strange. Her father being gushy over Jimmie? That almost seemed impossible. And why was it that she only tuned into his thoughts when he was like that?

"Sure, Dad. I'm okay," Jimmie said with an easy smile. "It's you I'm worried about. What are you going to do tonight when you get home?"

Lacey sighed. Wasn't that just like Jimmie? The little soldier with a kind heart. Jimmie, Jimmie, she wanted to wail. I wish I could be there to take care of you now.

"I thought I'd go over to your grandmother's and see how she is," he said in a voice that sounded tight and constrained. He was struggling to control his emotions in front of Jimmie, Lacey could tell. He was afraid to let out the torrent of feelings he was holding inside.

"She's having a hard time," he went on. "Lacey was always her... her...." He stumbled over his words.

"Favorite," Jimmie broke in with a grimace.

"Oh, no!" he came back. "I wasn't going to say that. She loves you both exactly the same. It's just that Lacey was her first grandchild, and she spent a lot of time with us after your mother died. I don't know what I would have done without your grandmother."

His voice cracked again and Lacey couldn't believe it. Was he really saying kind things about her grandmother? What had gotten into him?

"It's okay, Dad," Jimmie said, smiling broadly. "Lacey was her favorite. That doesn't mean she doesn't like me. She just understood Lacey better."

"Do you think so?" her father asked quickly. "I, for one, never understood your sister – or ever tried to. I can see that now. I wish I had…." His voice trailed off slowly, his thoughts full of guilt now.

"Dad," Jimmie said firmly, grabbing his father's arm. "You can't go on beating yourself up about Lacey. She's okay. I know. I had a dream about her last night."

"You did?" He looked at his son blankly for a minute and then blurted out, "How can she be okay? She was murdered, for God's sake, by that kid. I knew I shouldn't have trusted him. The little bastard! I wish he was here right now so I could kill him myself with my bare hands."

"Dad," Jimmie said in a low, calm voice. "People get killed every day. The wages of war are the innocent people who get killed. Lacey didn't deserve to die, but she's okay. I'm sure of it."

His father looked stunned again. "I'm not sure of anything, and yet you are. How can that be?"

"You're taking this way too personally, Dad. Lacey didn't die to punish you. She died, well, just because she died. And now that she's dead, you have to move on."

Lacey couldn't believe the words that were coming out of her little brother's mouth – or the thoughts that were whirling through her father's head. What had he done to his son? He sounded like a general reviewing the troops before they all march off to battle, ready to die. Chin up; forget the loss; onward and upward!

Lacey could feel the chill that ran through her father's body. Had that school been brainwashing his son? Or were they simply teaching him a way of coping with the world that he wasn't able to wrap his thoughts around yet? Move on... that seemed so impossible to him. It was what he had to do after Marge's death, but that only was because of Lacey and Jimmie. He had to be strong for them and not let them know what really happened. He couldn't let them know how horrible and dishonorable it really was.

Horrible? Dishonorable? Lacey picked up on those words right away. What was so dishonorable about her mother's death? That she killed herself? Did she dishonor her family? And what was horrible about it? How did she really die?

With these questions filling her thoughts now, she egged her father on. Go on, think more about your wife. Tell me more about what happened to her. Tell me!

But instead, she felt his thoughts slowly fading away from her again. Not as suddenly as before, but she could feel the soft, mushy Howie being replaced by the rigid, detached man she knew so well. This was the Howie who had to be strong, had to be in control. The one who couldn't let his son upstage him.

"Hey," her father said now with bravado in his voice. "Don't think that your old man is getting soft or anything here. Of course we'll move on. We'll put this behind us. Just like we did with your mother's death. Hey, buddy, do you have everything you need? When will I see you next? Don't forget to call your grandmother."

With him running off at the mouth like that, Lacey knew it was time for her to lose contact, and she wondered when she'd pick up Howie's signal again. That's what it felt like – as though she were dialing his thoughts in and out on a radio frequency whenever he got vulnerable and unable to cope. It looked like she'd have to wait for his next wave of guilt or self-pity. And that could take a long time.

But then, what was time to her? What was any of this to her anyway? She wasn't a part of this life anymore. Why couldn't she let it go? Why was she still hanging on? What did she expect to happen? And what difference would it make now if she knew how her mother died?

Not much, except she'd know *why* she hadn't seen her mother yet and *if* she might ever see her again.

This dying was a strange business. Almost as weird as living with her father.

Almost.

Once Ambrose had a Scotch in his hand and Lisette sat across from him with a ginger ale in hers at a bar near the theater, he asked her the big question.

"So what do you think?" He edged slowly into it. "Could you do something like that?"

"Me?" Lisette gulped. "I don't think so. These women were talking about their lives up there. I could never be myself up on stage! When I dance, I have to pretend that I'm someone else, otherwise…"

"…it would be too self-revealing?" Ambrose broke in.

Lisette frowned. "What does 'self-revealing' mean?"

"Just what it sounds like: these performers revealed – or told you – something very personal about themselves, so it was self-revealing. They used art to communicate a personal, but universal, political message to the audience. It struck a chord with you because it's something you've felt too, and you connect with them on a very deep level."

"But I don't want to connect with anyone in my audience. They're all jerks and idiots."

"I'm talking about when you're a performance artist."

"Yeah, but I don't get this stuff." Lisette whined.

"Of course you do. Look, it's simple. Take the woman who had the guy look up into her cervix. According to the program I read you, she's worked in a massage parlor and been a prostitute and an actress in pornographic movies most of her life. Suddenly, she gets sick of doing that, and now she wants people to know how it made her feel when men used her body for their own sexual gratification. You know, to get themselves off on her. So in her act, she demystifies…" Ambrose hesitated, searching for a simpler word to use "…she exposes a part of her body that is involved in having sex, but she does so in such a way that the audience will see it as just another body part. Like she's saying to this guy who has a flashlight up her crotch, 'Look, you jerk. My cervix is just like my arm or a leg. No big deal.'"

"And do you think he gets it?" Lisette asked incredulously. "I wouldn't let any of the horny old geezers in my audience get a peek up inside me, no matter how demystifying, or whatever that word is, it might be for them."

"But that's the whole point! You react that way because you think that your body belongs to those creeps who pay money to come in and watch you take it off on stage. She, on the other hand, is saying: 'I'm in control of my body and my cervix and I'm going to tell you how to think about it!' I mean…" Suddenly, his voice turned inquisitive. "What *do* you think about when you're up there, anyway?"

"*Me?* What do I think about?"

"Yeah. When you go out there and those men are hooting and hollering at you, wanting you – no, screaming at you – to take it all off, how does it make you feel?"

Lisette squirmed a little in her chair and scratched her head.

"That they don't pay me enough money to do it," she said with a smile.

"That's right," Ambrose said, egging her on. "And how does it make you feel when one of those guys assumes that just because you took your clothes off in front of him on stage, he has the right to have sex with you?"

"Like my father did when he used… when he…" Her voice trailed off and Ambrose watched her body go rigid. Suddenly she sat upright in her chair and crossed her arms tightly across her chest. Her eyes stared at the space in front of her as if she were in a trance.

"Lisette?" he asked her carefully. "What about your father?"

She bit her lip and pressed her shoulders against the back of the chair.

"Lisette, what about your father?" he repeated.

When she didn't respond, he reached across the table and gently put his hand on her arm and waited for something else to happen. He didn't know what. Maybe he had pushed her too hard.

Suddenly, she came back into motion, and she reached down and pulled a tissue from her purse. Was she crying? He couldn't tell. As she dabbed at her eyes, he leaned down and whispered in her ear.

"I'm sorry. I'm not trying to pry. There might be something about your father that we could make into a political statement for the act," Ambrose explained. "You could do it just like those women did. Do you understand?"

Lisette looked up at him for a moment and then said in a hoarse voice. "I never talk about or even think about my father. I don't know where that came from."

"But what do you mean?" Ambrose jumped in. "How did your father use you?"

"My father wasn't a very nice man," she said in a whisper. "After my mother died, she wasn't there to protect me."

"Did he sexually abuse you?" Ambrose asked quickly.

Lisette lowered her head and spoke so quietly this time that

Ambrose had to lean down toward her in order to hear. "He didn't abuse me like that," she said bitterly. Then she tossed her head back and added, "I can't say that he didn't want to, but he found a way to make it work for him."

The girl was talking in riddles, trying desperately to avoid telling him what he really wanted to know. After years of cross-examining witnesses in the courtroom, he could have gotten her to spill her guts, but he held back. He sensed that now was not the time to push. He might shut her down forever, and he didn't want that.

"Oh, I see," he said matter-of-factly, leaning back in his seat and quickly changing the topic of conversation. "What time is it, anyway?" he asked. "I should get you back to your hotel soon. You've got a show tonight, right?"

She nodded and gave him a weak smile. She was still lost in some memory of her father. Then she looked up at him, her deep blue eyes clouded over as she spoke in a little girl voice, "You're coming to see my show tonight, aren't you?"

"Sure," he replied with a big grin. "I wouldn't miss it for the world." Then he got up, came around behind her and put her furry white jacket over her shoulders. He felt like she needed her mother, and the closest thing to her was the jacket. He realized that it might be of some comfort to her. He threw some bills on the table to cover their tab, gathered up Lisette, and steered her out of the bar and into the street, keeping a tight grip on her arm. They walked in silence for a few blocks until they got to her hotel. Ambrose stopped and leaned down to ask her, "What do you say we go to the library tomorrow?"

She gave him a confused, almost terrified look.

"Don't be frightened," he went on, with a tenderness in his voice that surprised him. "We can get you some books on Attila the Hun and read them together. Would you like that?"

"Oh, yes," she said, so sweetly that he suddenly felt her come back to life. "I'd like that very much," she added with enthusiasm.

"Then I'll pick you up about ten o'clock tomorrow, okay?" He moved away from her, but she clung to his arm. "Are you all right?" he asked gently.

"I'll be seeing a lot of you from now on, won't I?" she said.

"If you want to. Would you like that?"

"Oh, yes!" she said eagerly and then dropped his arm.

"Then I'll see you tonight at the Pussycat."

She smiled and waved and then disappeared into the hotel lobby. He stood there for a moment watching her go. Damn, he thought. That wasn't bad for a few days of work.

Just imagine where he could be in a week.

This girl was gold, and he was on a roll.

Lacey's father drove home from the train station, feeling lost and alone and thinking about Lacey.

Lacey could feel that now as suddenly she was thrust back into his thoughts. He was getting gushy again, and she knew what that meant. The reception would come in loud and clear.

Jesus, he thought, was Lacey really okay? Was Jimmie's dream right? Was it possible to know those things before your own death? He always thought he'd have to wait until he died to find out if the people he loved were okay. But he knew the truth. He could feel the need to confess all he knew about what had really happened to Marge that day in the garage. But such a confession, even to a priest, would have complicated every-thing. Too many things had been said or not said that couldn't be undone or shouldn't be undone now, he thought. And he had promised himself that he would take his wife's secret with him to the grave.

He may not have always been the best husband to Marge or a good father to Lacey and Jimmie, but keeping this secret was his way of showing them how very, very much he loved them.

Oh, God! He wanted to scream out that secret within the confines of this car so that at last it would be out there. But he couldn't. Instead, Lacey heard his thoughts as he struggled to hold it all inside.

Please forgive me! Forgive me for not being the kind of man who could have prevented what happened. The man I wanted to be. The man I could have been. Then you and your mother would still be alive. We'd all be a family again. There'd be no more lies, no more secrets.

He knew that at the core of all the arguments he had had with Lacey was her need to know the truth about her mother's death. He wasn't stupid. He remembered when she came home that day when she was still in high school and demanded to know if her mother had committed suicide. She was a smart girl. He knew she wouldn't buy the story that her mother's death was an accident.

But still he couldn't tell her the truth. He couldn't risk how she might react, what she might think of her mother and him. And yet she couldn't see how much he sacrificed to keep the truth from her. He didn't want her to hate him, but he couldn't tell her what she wanted to know. He was as sure of it then as he was now.

But I'm not sure! Lacey bellowed in her own thoughts. *Stop all this bellyaching and tell me the story. You can do it. You can remember it now. Just close your eyes and remember. How hard can that be?*

He wanted to remember, but it was too painful. I can't do this, he whimpered in his thoughts. I can't go back there and not drive this car off the road.

Then pull the goddamn car off the road, Lacey commanded him in his thoughts. *Just do it. Do it now.*

Without knowing why, he suddenly slammed on the brakes, pulled the car over to the side of the road, and turned off the engine. He put his head into his hands and wept as he began to remember. As he went back to that day fourteen years ago when Marge had changed their lives forever, Lacey was right there in his thoughts with him. She had waited for this moment for so long. She had wanted to know the truth. Now all she had to do was listen as her father remembered the story. But that didn't happen. Suddenly, he screamed and beat his hands against the steering wheel. "No, I won't remember it. It's too hard. It's too much. Let me alone. Just leave me alone."

Then he gritted his teeth, thought about last Sunday's basketball game, and started up the engine.

What is wrong with you? Lacey shouted back. How could he leave her hanging like that? What was wrong with this man?

What the hell was wrong with her father?

CHAPTER NINE

Secrets and Signs

On Monday morning, Ambrose and Lisette took the city bus to the main library near the state capitol and walked up the long white steps of the building. It was a great building, Lisette thought. It had big white columns that stuck out in the front and huge wooden doors that looked almost too heavy for her to open.

But that didn't matter, because Ambrose got to the entrance first and held the door open for her. When she stepped into the large, open lobby of the library which was full of people, she felt as if something wonderful and exciting was going to happen to her here – something that hadn't happened to her since her mother was alive.

She looked up at Ambrose, and he smiled at her, a big, warm smile that seemed to say, "Stick with me, kid. Things are always exciting in my world."

Then he said in a hushed voice, "The children's section is downstairs." He steered her down a set of wide stone stairs to the lower level. They went through a set of double doors and into a big room where the walls were brightly decorated with pictures and lined with shelves of books. "We'll start off with some easy books," Ambrose was saying. "That way we can see what your reading level is."

Lisette hardly heard what he said, though, as she gaped around the room, watching all the moms with their kids picking out books, just like her mom used to do with her. She didn't have a clue what a reading level was, but she followed him to a row of tables and chairs right in the middle of the room.

"We'll try the card catalog first," he said, sitting down in front of a computer on one of the tables. He hit a few keys until a screen popped up.

Lisette gazed at the screen, totally confused.

"What happened to that big cabinet with all those little cards in it?" she asked.

Ambrose looked up at her and grinned. "It's all on the computer now."

"You mean kids come in here and use a computer to find their books?"

"Hell, yes. Even four-year-olds know how to use these things now. It's really easy." He pointed at the screen in front of them. "First, I'll type in 'Attila the Hun,' and we'll do a search on that. It's really fast."

Lisette watched as he let the computer whirl for a moment and then turned to ask her, "When was the last time you were in a library?"

Her voice went soft. "When I was a kid. I even had my own library card. It's expired now, but I still have it. Do you want to see it?" Without waiting for an answer, Lisette rifled through her purse and found her wallet. "It's here somewhere," she said as she went through a bunch of papers and cards stuffed in between the dollar bills.

"Goddamn it!" she said exasperated, still rummaging. "I can't find it. But here's a picture of me and my mom." She held up a small piece of paper with frayed edges. "Do you want to see it?"

Ambrose leaned over and took the photograph from her, looking at it very carefully.

"How old is your mom in this picture?" he asked.

"Let's see," Lisette sighed. "She had me when she was nineteen so I was probably two, three years old. That makes my mom in her early twenties."

"God! You look just like her," Ambrose said, amazement in his voice.

"Nah, I don't," Lisette insisted. "My mom was way prettier."

"No," he said, holding up the photo so she could see it again. "Don't you see it? You stand like her, and your smile is the same. You're a spitting image of her."

Lisette grabbed the photo from his hand. "Yeah, so what?" she grumbled, roughly stuffing the photo back into her wallet. "So I get to die like she did. I can hardly wait," she said in a mean, sarcastic voice.

"Don't be like that," Ambrose said. "Just take the compliment. You're as beautiful as your mother."

"Yeah, well," Lisette snapped, "I don't see the resemblance."

"Fine, then don't," Ambrose said with a sigh, shaking his head as if he had more important things to do than argue with her. Instead, he went back to the computer screen and pushed a few more buttons on the keyboard. Then he pointed at the screen. "These two books look the best. One is a biography about Attila. The other is about the Roman Empire."

"What's a biography?" Lisette asked with renewed interest.

"It's your life story but written by someone else. If you write it yourself, then it's an autobiography. But Attila couldn't do that because the Huns didn't have a written language."

"They didn't write anything down? That's amazing. I don't know what I'd do if I couldn't write in my diary."

"I don't get that," Ambrose interjected. "You can't read but you can write. How does that work exactly?"

"I have my own way of writing," she said shyly.

"You mean phonetically?"

"What's that mean?"

"That's when you spell the words the way they sound."

"Yeah. It's sort of like that."

"That's one way to keep your diary secret." He grinned.

"It's not like that. My mom wrote something in my diary, you know. About how much she loved me and how I should always have my dreams."

"Sounds like she was a good mother," Ambrose said softly.

"Yeah. I guess you don't appreciate what you have until it's gone."

"Yeah," Ambrose said, in a haunted kind of way.

"If I knew I'd end up with my father when my mother died, I would've appreciated her a lot more."

"What about your dad?"

"I don't want to talk about him."

"I know. You were pretty definite about that the other night."

"If that means that I don't want to talk about him, then I don't." She frowned again.

Ambrose went back to the computer and hit another button. In a flash, a piece of paper came through the machine next to them.

Ambrose grabbed the sheet and said, "Here's the list of the books we need. Let's go find them, and you can read them to me."

"Me, read?" Suddenly, Lisette felt her whole body shudder at the thought of reading in front of someone. She hadn't done that in years. "Right here, right now?"

"Yeah, in the reading room over there." Ambrose pointed to a glassed-in room in the back.

"Yeah, but…" she whimpered, then added, "You'll help me with the words, won't you?"

"Sure. That's why I'm here."

Ambrose stood up from his chair, and she followed him as he went from one bookshelf to another. Eventually though, she wandered off by herself and was looking at some books when Ambrose came up behind her and asked, "What did you find?"

"Look," she said excitedly, waving several books in his face. "*The Cat in the Hat* and *Green Eggs and Ham*. My mother used to read these to me. This is so amazing. They're still in the library."

"I read those to my kids, too. All kids love those books."

"You have kids?" Lisette stared at him in amazement.

Ambrose looked away from her and down at his shoes. "I don't like to talk about them," he snarled. "Just like you don't like to talk about your father."

"You have kids, and you didn't tell me? How many? How old are they? Where are they?"

"Look, we came here to read books, not jabber away. If you want to take out those books, fine, but let's get on with this, okay?"

"I guess it's definite then," she said with a sly grin. "You don't want to talk about your kids."

Ambrose glared at her.

"You get to ask questions but I don't? Is that it?"

"I was asking you about your father for a reason."

"Remind me again." She stood with her hand on her hip.

"All I want from you and your past is a way into your new act."

"And what if I don't want a new act?"

"Fine. If you don't want to work with me, fine. I have better things to do than hang around here. I've done my time in the reading room upstairs just to keep warm. I even lied about where I lived in order to get a damned library card. So don't work with me. Fine!" Ambrose slammed the books down on the top of the bookshelf in front of him and turned to walk away. "I thought you'd be different."

Lisette grabbed his arm and held his eyes for a moment. "Who said I'm not?"

Ambrose turned back to look at her.

She gave him a slow, sweet smile. "Stay here with me. I want to read about Attila the Hun." She paused for a second, and then went on. "You need to take it a little slower. I'm not stupid, but I need you to go slow. Can you do that?"

"Sure," Ambrose said with a grin. "I can do that."

She grinned back at him and put the Dr. Seuss books back on the shelf.

"No, take those with you," Ambrose said quickly. "I'll check them out later."

"I don't know why I want to read these again. I practically memorized them when I was a kid. I read them over and over out loud to my mom."

Ambrose smiled at her again, this time as if he knew what she was talking about. Maybe his kids had done the same to him. She wanted to ask him, but she was afraid he might blow up again and spoil everything. Instead, she followed him to the reading room, and they sat together on the kiddie-sized table and chairs.

"I hope this will hold me," he said, rocking back and forth on the chair for a moment. Then he looked up at her. "Where do you want to start?" He spread the books on the table in front of her.

Lisette's eyes went to a slim, bright red book that had a picture on the front of a man on a white horse. He had his mouth wide open as if he was yelling at someone and a wild, crazy look on his face. He had a long spear in one hand and a shield in the other. A large, furry black hat sat on his head. He looked fierce and danger-ous, she thought. Even his horse looked scary. "Is that what Attila looked like?" she asked.

"As best as historians can tell. There were no pictures of him drawn while he was alive, but several people who met him described him in their writings."

"He looks pretty mean," she said with a slight shiver. Lisette opened the book to the first page and read aloud. "Attila was born in a..." She turned to Ambrose. "What's this word?"

Ambrose looked over her shoulder. "Chariot," he said. "Do you know what a chariot is?"

"Is it like a wagon?" she asked.

"Yeah. The Romans used chariots with horses to get from one place to another. But the Huns used them as their homes."

Lisette started again. "'Attila was born in a chariot as his family roomed...'"

Ambrose interrupted her. "I don't think that's right." He looked at the book again. "That's 'roamed. The family 'roamed' around the wilderness because they were nomads. That means they didn't have any permanent home. The warriors were always on their horses looking for food and fighting. Their women and children followed behind them."

"In their chariots?" Lisette asked.

"Yeah. Go ahead." Ambrose continued looking over her shoulder.

Lisette corrected herself. "'Roamed the plains of....'"

"Hungary," Ambrose interjected.

"'Hungary near the...'"

"Danube," he said patiently. She went on, sounding out the words, slowly and carefully, syllable by syllable.

"...Danube River on the site of the present-day city of..." She faltered again.

"Budapest."

"Budapest," she repeated, and then glumly looked up from the book.

"Damn. This is going to take me forever," she said, thrusting the book at him. "Maybe you should just read it to me."

"No," he insisted, pushing the book back at her. "I want you to read. It'll get easier, you'll see."

"I'm so dumb! I should know how to read!"

"And I should know how to strip!" he quipped. "It's okay. Just take your time."

"We'll be here all night if I keep this up."

"Look, there's no rush, and I wouldn't be here if I thought you were stupid."

Lisette screwed up her face. "You wouldn't?"

"No, I wouldn't. So let's start again. 'Attila was born…'"

She looked down at the book and had to smile. Ambrose was right. They had all the time in the world, and she liked reading again. She liked reading with Ambrose.

She liked it very much.

Lisette woke up Tuesday morning with a weird feeling in her head.

She looked quickly around her hotel room and then yelled, "All right, Lacey. Come on out."

At first, there was silence, but Lisette went on, "Cut the bullshit, Lacey! I know you're there. What was our deal? I asked you to leave me alone, right?"

Lisette waited for a moment, hardly able to breathe, and then she felt something stir behind her. She turned around quickly and saw a soft, shadowy figure that wasn't there before. It looked like the pictures of Lacey she had seen on TV the day after she was killed.

"Lacey, is that you?"

The wispy figure stood there for a moment, silent, while Lisette stared at it. Then it spoke, hesitantly at first. "Kind of. It's more your vision of me. But this way we can talk and you won't feel so schizophrenic."

"Schizo what?" Lisette asked, frowning at another word she didn't understand.

"It's like you're split in two. And the two different personalities are at war inside you."

Then Lacey's image came closer and Lisette felt it sit down on the bed next to her.

"This is too weird," Lisette said, her voice quivering as she put her hand out to touch the shadowy figure's face. When she did, her fingers went right through it, and she pulled them back with a gasp. "Oh my God! You're a ghost."

"Actually, I'm not. But that's probably the easiest way for you to think about it."

"Thank God you're here. I thought you got stuck in hell with Ari for all eternity."

"No," Lacey said sadly. "I'm stuck here with you for now." Then, with more spunk in her voice, she added, "Hey, how did you like the dream I gave you?"

"What dream?"

"You know, when you were out cold after my funeral."

"I don't remember anything about that."

"You don't? And I gave you a really good dream about me and Ari."

"I don't know that I want to know about that."

"I had to do something. Watching you with that Ambrose character has been making me crazy! I might've been clueless about what Ari was doing, but you have to see that Ambrose is doing the same thing to you. You've got to watch out for him. I'm telling you, he's not what he seems."

Lisette looked incredulous. "Ambrose? He's a teddy bear. I can handle him."

"That's what I thought about Ari. But Ari was out to control me just the way Ambrose is trying to do to you."

"No, he's not." Lisette laughed. "He wants me to do this performance art thing with him, but I think that's kind of sweet."

"Right," Lacey's voice growled back sarcastically. "Ari was sweet like that with me at the beginning too. But men like Ari and Ambrose always have something up their sleeves."

"But Ambrose is nothing like Ari," Lisette protested.

"Are you sure?" Lacey gave her a cold, hard stare.

"You mean like he's going to kill me?" Lisette had to laugh out loud. "Don't you think you're a little over the top here?" Lisette could feel Lacey's eyes staring at her so intensely that she had to add, "I don't even know what really happened between you and Ari. So how can I tell if Ambrose is anything like Ari?"

"There *is* more to the story. I could tell you and you can decide for yourself."

"I don't know," Lisette murmured. "I don't have time right now. Ambrose is coming to pick me up. We're going to the library to read books. I've got to get dressed."

"It will only take a minute," Lacey's voice insisted. "I promise. Lay back down and close your eyes."

Lisette frowned but slowly slid back down on her bed. "Will you be here when I wake up?" she asked. "The thought of dreaming about Ari gives me the creeps."

Lacey's shadowy hand came near Lisette's face and she felt a sudden, comforting warmth all over her body.

"Don't worry," Lacey assured her. "I'm not going anywhere."

Lisette shut her eyes and she let herself drift off to another time and place. She was going into Lacey's world, where she knew she would see everything through Lacey's eyes and feel everything Lacey felt. It was just like when Lacey was in Lisette's body. Now Lisette would be in hers.

As the scene unfolded before her eyes, Lisette wasn't sure what the point of it was, but she was curious.

Suddenly she wanted to know what really happened between Lacey and Ari – and she wanted to know it now.

When Lacey woke up that morning, Ari was already up and out of bed. She could hear him singing in the shower. How could he be so damn happy so early in the morning? But then he was a morning person and she wasn't.

Not ready to face anything or anyone yet, Lacey rolled over and covered her head with the blanket and laid there until she felt a cold hand come up under the covers and jab her in the side.

"Hey, babe! Time to get up," Ari said playfully. "It's Friday. Last day of school before the weekend. And what a weekend we're going to have."

"Friday?" Lacey asked sleepily as she turned over and saw Ari standing over her, dressed in a towel robe and fresh from the shower.

Then her eyes popped open and she gasped, "Oh my God, it's Friday!"

Ari looked at her with a big grin. "Yeah, and we have the room to ourselves for the whole weekend. Scott won't be back until Sunday. At the last minute, he had to go out of town with the team for an exhibition game. They're raising money for some charity."

"Oh, no!" she cried out. "I promised Sophie I'd go to The Keg tonight with her and the other girls. I totally forgot about it. I've got to go."

"What about *our* plans?" Ari's voice shot up in volume, and instantly Lacey bristled at its sharp, angry tone. It made her strike back when she might otherwise have understood how he felt. True, she was ruining their plans to spend the whole weekend together but, goddamn it, she didn't have to change her plans just because Scott decided to go home for the weekend at the last minute.

Almost without thinking, she yelled at him, "And what's wrong with me going out and having some fun with my friends?"

"Not on my time you can't!"

"Do you think you own me?"

"No, but I'm your boyfriend and you should want to be with me." Lacey could hear the rage in his voice ratcheting up. That pissed her off even more.

"You can't tell me what I should or shouldn't do!" She jumped out of bed, grabbing her clothes and putting them on in a fury. "I can't help it if you don't have any friends to hang out with," she added gruffly.

"I have friends. But I'd rather be with you."

"And you want me to have no friends at all?"

"That's not a bad idea," he muttered, his voice hedging as if he was trying to see how she would react. But she wanted no part of it.

"I *will* have friends, and I *will* go out with them tonight! And that's final."

Then she looked down at her watch. "Shit! I'm going to be late for class. I have history first hour. Professor Morris has a fit if you're late."

"So what your teacher wants is important to you but not what I want," Ari dropped himself down on the bed with a dramatic plop. Then he hissed, "Why can't you ever see things my way?"

She glared down at him. "Stop being such a baby. It's only one night."

"Yeah, but how often do we have *two* nights in a row when we can sleep together without Scott being around? Why are you doing this to me?"

"I'm not doing anything to you. Why is everything always about you?"

"You're just pissed about last night, aren't you?" Ari looked at her warily. "Because I pushed you about loving me forever. It's just an expression, you know." Then he blurted out, "Besides, you can't keep punishing me just because you think everyone who will ever love you is going to die."

"What do you know about love?" she sputtered. "It's all about sex to you."

"For Chrissakes, Lacey, give me a break." Then his voice got more accusatory. "Every time we get really close, like the other night, you get scared and back off. Well, I get scared too, and I need to know you're really mine. That you're with me all the way."

She swallowed hard and her mind raced. Was that true? Is that what she was doing to him? She stood there dumbstruck.

"Look, if you want to go to The Keg tonight with your friends, fine." His voice was quieter now but even more strained. "But don't act like making me happy isn't important to you anymore. I couldn't stand it if you stopped loving me. I wouldn't want to go on. Life wouldn't be worth living." Then his voice cracked and trailed off as if he were too upset to continue. Something in his voice scared Lacey.

"Don't say that," she said in a rush, moving toward him, putting her hands on his shoulders to shake him. "Don't ever talk like that, do you hear?" Then her voice got calmer, and she sat down on the bed next to him. "Of course I love you," she went on. "But I get so confused. It's all going too fast. I don't know what you want from me, and I can't keep up with what I feel and what it all means."

That was true, wasn't it? she thought quickly. Maybe he was right. She loved her mom, and she died. Maybe she was afraid to love him and that was screwing up their relationship.

"Oh God, Ari, I'm so sorry!"

She took his face in her hands and kissed him long and hard. They fell back onto the bed, kissing and holding each other, until she finally whispered in his ear, "I won't go to the bar tonight. I want to be with you."

"No, go. You promised Sophie. You'll just owe me one." He looked at her now with a lopsided grin.

"Are you sure?"

"I've got plenty of studying to do tonight while you're gone." Then he went on carefully, "But I could drive you and the other girls to The Keg if you like."

At that, Lacey winced. There was one strict rule about girls' night out. No boyfriends were allowed.

"I've got Scott's van. He took the bus with the team and left the keys. He said I could use it. I'll drop you off, and you can call me when you're ready to be picked up."

Lacey pulled away from him, sat up on one elbow, and eyed him for a moment. That might work. Scott's van was bigger than Sophie's car, and if Ari drove them, they could drink as much as they liked.

"But you can't stay and hang out with us at the bar," she warned him.

"I know," Ari said easily. "I'll come back here and hang with Tom. We both have a paper due on Monday. I need someone to help me out."

"I'll think about it," Lacey told Ari now, even though she was pretty sure she'd let him drive them. But she needed to ask Sophie if it was all right before she gave him a final answer. She saw how his eyes narrowed and his mouth twitched when she didn't say yes right away.

"Look, I'll think about it," she repeated. "Don't worry. I'm not going to The Keg to pick up guys. It's good for me to kick back with my girlfriends sometimes." Then she leaned down toward him on the bed and touched his cheek with the back of her hand. "I'll miss you," she cooed. "I'll be so hot for you tonight!"

"How about being hot for me right now?" he shot back as he grabbed her around the waist and pulled her down onto the bed beside him with one quick motion.

"No, Ari, no," she cried out, but he ignored her protest and climbed up on top of her. His towel parted as he did and she felt the cool, clean skin of his naked body against hers and his hardness against her leg.

"Why do you want to spend time with those silly girlfriends of yours?" He glared down into her face now. "You could have me instead, all straight and tall just for you, any time you want."

"Stop it!" she yelled, struggling to pull herself out from underneath him. "I've got to go to class. Sophie is waiting for me. I can't be late."

"Goddamn it, Lacey! Sophie can wait. I want you now, and I can't wait."

Then, before she could stop him, he reached down and pulled at the waistband of her jeans. He undid the button with one jerk of his hand and yanked open the zipper. In the next second, he had her jeans down off her hips and one hand up under her blouse.

"Oh, baby, baby!" He crooned in her ear, as his other hand moved down her body. "You feel so good."

She let out a low, deep moan and then cried out, "Oh, Ari!"

"You like that don't you, my angel?" he said. His voice was high and full of excitement.

"Yes," she cried out again. "Yes."

Then she arched her back and closed her eyes as jolts of pure ecstasy radiated through her whole body. All she could think of now was Ari and how good, how very good he was making her feel. Screw history class, she thought. And let Sophie wait. Nothing could drag her away from this bed now.

Besides, Sophie was her roommate and best friend.

She'd understand. She always did.

CHAPTER TEN

The Power of Control

"I don't get it," Sophie called out to Lacey as the two of them stood shivering in the cool April night later that evening in the parking lot outside their dorm. "Tell me again, why do we have to wait for Ari to drive us to The Keg? It's freezing out here!"

Lacey turned around and frowned at Sophie. She could see Sophie's body trembling underneath a skimpy, hip-length coat that barely covered her body.

"I told you to wear something warmer," Lacey admonished her, purposefully changing the subject. "It's not August anymore."

She had already told Sophie why Ari was driving them tonight, but Lacey could tell by the tone in her voice that Sophie was fishing for something more. She wasn't about to let Sophie make her feel stupid for letting Ari have his way. So Lacey gave Sophie another sour look and added, "Why don't you wait inside the building with Laura and the rest of the girls? It's warmer in there. I'll let you know when Ari comes."

"But you said he'd be here twenty minutes ago," Sophie said, barely able to stop her teeth from chattering.

"He'll be here when he gets here," Lacey said with irritation creeping into her voice. "Go inside. You don't have to wait here with me."

"But that's what I don't get," Sophie insisted. "We're standing out here in the cold when my car is right over there. We could be at The Keg already. Why are we waiting for Ari?"

"Because it's complicated! That's why."

"What's so complicated about saying no to this guy?" Sophie shot back. "You say, 'No, Ari! You don't need to drive me and my girlfriends to The Keg tonight. We can get there all by ourselves. That's what women in this country do. Go places by themselves and have fun.' That's it, Lacey. Sound pretty simple to me."

"That's enough, Sophie. I thought you of all people would understand."

"Oh, I understand. This guy has got his hooks into you and you don't even know how deep."

Lacey glared at Sophie.

"You don't believe the story he gave you about going to fill up Scott's van with gas before we can leave, do you? Don't you see that he's doing everything in his power so that we never get to The Keg tonight?"

"But the van does need gas," Lacey protested. "And it's only nine o'clock," she added, looking at her watch. "We still have plenty of time to party tonight."

Sophie eyed her carefully. "I think he's making us stand out in the cold so you'll just give up and stay home. Jesus, can't you see how he's trying to keep you away from your friends?"

"He is not," Lacey insisted, but even as she did, she was remembering how Ari had said something this morning about not wanting her to have any friends.

"I hate to be the one to tell you this," Sophie continued solemnly, "but I think he's crazy."

"Sure, he's crazy," Lacey said with a laugh. "He's crazy about me."

"No," Sophie went on. "It's crazy how he needs to have you with him or know where you are every minute of the day. Like he doesn't trust you. Like you can't have a life of your own. That's not right. There's something wrong with him."

"You're wrong, so wrong, about this." Lacey's face flushed with anger and her eyes burned into Sophie's. "You talk like Ari's evil or something, and he's not."

"How do you know he's not? How else can you explain his obsession with you?"

"He's not obsessed with me. He loves me."

Before Sophie could reply, a squeal went up as Laura and the other girls came running out of the building behind them. Lacey looked up to see that Ari had arrived, stopping in front of them in the parking lot.

"See, he's here," Lacey said in triumph, standing back with Sophie as the other girls opened the back door and piled into the van. "Look, I know what I'm doing here. Everything's cool with Ari. Honest it is."

Sophie gave her a look that said she wasn't so sure about that, but Ari's voice interrupted them, calling out from inside the van. "Are you girls coming or not?"

"Yeah, get inside, will you?" Laura cried out from the back seat. "You're letting all the hot air out. Ari's got it all nice and cozy inside here for us."

Sophie sighed resignedly and then climbed up into the van and closed the door.

Lacey got into the front seat next to Ari and acted, for Sophie's sake, like she was upset with him. As he rolled out of the parking lot and mumbled something about being sorry for taking so long, she looked at him but didn't respond. She could have said it was all right, even though it wasn't, to appease him, but she didn't. She'd show Sophie he didn't control her every thought and action.

Instead she ignored him and focused her attention on what was going on in the backseat where everyone, except for Sophie who sat there with a sullen look on her face, was in pretty high spirits.

Jennifer was teasing Laura, the drop-dead gorgeous one of the group. "I can't believe you cut off all of your hair this afternoon. What were you thinking?"

Lacey pictured Laura's long, frizzy black hair and thought about how she looked like a pixie now, cute but not so beautiful. As if he read her thoughts, Ari said in a low voice that only Lacey could hear. "I love your hair long, baby. Don't ever cut it, will you? You're so beautiful."

Then he reached over and squeezed her hand. At any other time she would have squeezed it back, but Sophie's words burned in her ears. She'd show her she could stand up to him.

Lacey turned around and yelled into the backseat, "I've thought of cutting my hair. I'd do it in a minute, but I know I would feel so naked without it!"

As soon as those words were out of her mouth, Lacey felt Ari jerk his hand away from hers. When she looked back at him, he was scowling, both hands gripped tightly on the steering wheel.

Laura chirped from the backseat. "That's what I always said. But you can't believe how freeing it is to not have all that hair on your back all the time." Then she giggled. "My boyfriend, Ray, likes it clipped short. He says it's like my pubic hair now!"

A howl went up from the van, and Lacey turned around and let out a whoop with the rest of the girls. She heard Ari groan in disapproval, but this time she didn't even look at him. She knew that in his culture women were demure and invisible and never talked dirty. Well, not here in this country, she wanted to shout at him. Women are free here and so was she. If he didn't like what she did and with whom she did it, then screw him.

She was going to enjoy herself tonight. She'd show Sophie that Ari wasn't running her life. She would do whatever she felt like.

Drink, pick up some guys, and dance the night away. She didn't care what Ari thought about it.

No, she thought, screw him!

Tonight, she was with her friends and she was going to have a great time, the best time of her life!

Lacey sat alone at a table at The Keg with the loud music and noise of the college bar on a Friday night swirling around her. Her head felt light from the beers she had been drinking one after another since she and the other girls had arrived a few hours ago.

Everyone but Lacey was out on the floor now. No one noticed that she had come back to the table by herself after only a few dances. She told herself that the music sucked and she was tired, but all she wanted to do was drink and stop the wild thoughts that were making her head throb. With each bottle of beer she downed she felt some relief. Pretty soon, she figured, her head would be totally numb and she'd stop thinking about how right Sophie had been about Ar

The more she thought about it, the angrier she got. Why did Ari have to be so pigheaded about driving her and picking her up tonight? Didn't he trust her? Did he think he could have her all to himself? Things between them were getting too serious, too fast. She wasn't ready to settle down with anyone – and certainly not Ari.

Suddenly Sophie's voice, yelling over the music, pulled her out of her thoughts. "What are you doing? It's not like you to sit in the corner and drink all by yourself. Why aren't you dancing?"

"I don't feel like it," Lacey muttered. "Go have a good time. Don't worry about me."

Sophie looked at her with a glint in her eye. "There's this cute guy up at the bar asking about you. He's in our history class. He's got a great smile."

Lacey gave her a disinterested look, but Sophie pushed on. "Why don't you go ask him to dance? His name is Jack."

Lacey scowled at her, and Sophie leaned in closer. "This is what he wants, you know, for you to mope around and not have fun. Stop stewing about Ari. He's not worth it."

Lacey wanted to argue that she wasn't doing that, but Sophie gave her a look that said it was useless to try. So Lacey looked over at the bar and saw a guy with closely cropped blonde hair and a nice, easy smile looking at her.

"You say his name is Jack?" Lacey asked as she slowly got up from the table, trying to hold herself steady.

"Yup," Sophie said with a smile. "Jack Howe, and he's a cutie."

"Thanks," Lacey said, putting one foot carefully in front of the other as she headed toward the bar. Halfway there, she realized that Jack was watching her and she liked that, so she slowed her walk down to a slink and stuck out her chest. She had forgotten that there were other men out there besides Ari who found her attractive. Jack evidently was one of them by the way he was looking at her.

When she got to the bar, she flashed Jack a smile and motioned with her index finger for him to come closer. "Would you like to dance?" she whispered into his ear in a husky, sexy voice.

"Sure," he said, taking her hand and leading her to the dance floor.

She felt his fingers warm and tight around hers, and as they walked she checked him out. He was dressed in khaki pants and a blue shirt like most of the guys at school, but he looked really good in them. He had broad shoulders and a narrow waist, and she could see how tight his ass was as he walked. She thought he carried himself like someone who could take charge, but in a quiet, easy way.

He was so unlike Ari, and she liked that too. When they got on the floor, the music slowed down and Jack took her into his arms.

She put her hand on his shoulder and felt the muscles under his shirt. When he pulled her into an embrace, she felt his body hard against hers, and she allowed herself to relax.

The music that was playing was an old tune, "In the Midnight Hour," by Wilson Pickett that made Lacey feel sexy. Lacey's father had played that song a lot when she was a kid and she liked its slow, sultry beat.

As they moved to the music, Jack pulled her body even closer to him. Lacey was used to dancing slow and suggestively like this at The Keg, but she didn't expect to respond to Jack the way she did. With his hand on the small of her back and his body moving into her, she felt a spark pass between them. It was as if he was igniting her magic spot without even touching it.

Wow! Lacey thought. She closed her eyes, threw her head back, and let her body roll forward each time Jack pressed his body into hers. She imagined him getting excited by her body, and she wanted to kiss him so bad. Nobody had ever made her feel so wonderful just by dancing with her.

With their bodies swaying and moving in unison now, it seemed that their two separate existences had melted into one, like molten steel, and they were floating away as light as air. She couldn't explain it, but dancing with Jack made her feel as though she could fly. With her eyes shut tightly, everything but the music faded away. Jack's hands were moving slowly up and down her body now, and she wanted more. That was until another hand gripped her shoulder and spun her around, away from Jack.

"We're leaving now!" a gruff voice yelled coarsely in her ear.

Startled, her eyes flew open, and she saw Ari.

"What are you doing here?"

"I'm here to take you home. That was the deal."

"No, that's not the deal!" she yelled back. "And I'm not ready to go home yet."

Jack stepped toward Ari. "What's the problem? If she's here by herself, she can leave all by herself."

"You don't understand, asshole. She happens to be my girl-friend," Ari puffed himself up against Jack as though he was as tall and strong as Jack was, but Lacey knew there was no way. "You're dancing with my girl, and I don't like it."

"If she's your girlfriend," Jack fired back, "then why is she here with me and not you?"

Lacey could see that the two men were squaring off, so she stepped between them and put her hand on Jack's chest to hold him back.

"Please, Jack," she begged. "I have to go. I enjoyed our dance." She smiled at him, but her lips were quivering and her legs felt shaky. She didn't want to leave, but she could feel the heat of Ari's hand on her arm and his anger coming right through it. She wasn't sure that she could get Ari out of there without wanting him to fight it out with Jack, and that would be disastrous. She didn't want to see either one of them get hurt, and Ari was her problem, not Jack's.

"You don't have to go anywhere with him," Jack insisted.

She looked at him and pled her case silently. I don't want to go, she tried to tell him, but it's easier if I go. I'll explain it later. There will be a later. I promise you. Instead, she simply repeated, "I have to go."

He grabbed her arm and held it tight. "Are you sure?"

"Yes," she said with as much resolve as she could muster.

"Will you be all right?" Jack seemed to think that if he kept talking to her, she wouldn't have to go anywhere.

"Of course she'll be all right," Ari shouted now into Jack face. "She's with me. Remember, that's who I am, the boyfriend. You're the asshole."

Jack glared at Ari and Lacey saw his nostrils flare for a moment, but then he backed off and released his hold on Lacey's arm.

"Until next time," Jack said, bending down and whispering in her ear so Ari wouldn't hear.

Ari tugged at her arm. "Let's go. The van's out front."

By now, Lacey could see Sophie rushing toward her from across the room, but she lost track of her as Ari pulled her through the crowd. She was relieved to hear Sophie's voice right behind them as they got near the front door.

"What the hell happened?" Sophie asked, grabbing Lacey's arm and spinning her around away from Ari. Then she hissed at him, "And what the hell are you doing here?"

Before either of them could respond, Sophie pushed Lacey toward the ladies' room door only a few feet away from them. "You're coming with me!"

"And you!" She pointed at Ari. "You stay right there. Do you hear me? One more stunt like the one you pulled on the dance floor and I'll flatten you. Don't think that I won't."

With that, Sophie pulled Lacey into the ladies' room and closed the door.

The nice, cool blue-and-white tile on the bathroom walls and ceiling at The Keg made Lacey feel better. Funny, she had never noticed that tile before, but now the simple pattern – blue and white, blue and white – gave her something to focus on when everything else around her was so fuzzy.

As she leaned back against the bathroom wall, she could hear Sophie's voice yelling at her. Most of it was about Ari, but not much of it registered in her head. All she could think about was Jack. Jack holding her in his arms. Jack dancing with her. Jack standing up to Ari.

How stupid of her, she thought, to leave Jack on the dance floor like that. What gave Ari the right to boss her around anyway? He didn't own her. She was never going to be his "forever" girl. Didn't he understand that by now?

Suddenly another voice interrupted Sophie's and Lacey looked up to see Laura's head poking through the ladies' room door.

"Is it true we're going, Sophie?" Laura asked excitedly. "Ari says we are."

Sophie looked at her stunned. "He told you that?"

"Yeah, he came over and said we had to go now."

"But isn't he right out there in the hallway?" Sophie was howling now.

"No," Laura said, looking back over her shoulder. "He's not."

"Goddamn it!" Sophie snarled. "I told that son of a bitch to stay put until I got Lacey calmed down."

Flustered now, Sophie grabbed Lacey's arm and handed her over to Laura. "Here, you stay with Lacey, and I'm going to go find us a ride. There's no way we're going home with that little shit!"

"But I don't want to go yet," Laura whined.

"The party's over," Sophie said somberly. "We need to get Lacey out of here." Then Sophie moved toward the door. "Just stay here and I'll be right back."

Lacey watched Sophie charge out of the ladies' room and heard Laura ask her in a tense, shaky voice, "Are you all right?"

Lacey managed to nod in response, but in fact her head was throbbing with angry thoughts about Ari. Where had he gone? Did he go after Jack? Were they fighting out in the parking lot? What a mess! She groaned to herself. She would never forgive herself if Jack got hurt.

Then she heard Laura again. "Good. If you're all right, then I'm going to go pee. You stand right there, and we'll go as soon as Sophie gets back."

Lacey nodded again and watched Laura go into a stall. She stood by the sink, steadying herself by gripping the cool, white bowl in front of her with both her hands as she stared at herself in the mirror. God, I look awful, she thought as she pulled one of her hands through the tangled mess of her hair. She gazed at her face, red and blotchy, and wanted to cry. It's all too much, she moaned to herself. The adrenaline she had been pumping ever since Ari had showed up, and the alcohol she had been pouring into her body all evening were making her brain muddled. She couldn't believe how puffy she looked. She wanted to believe she was glowing from the incredible sexual charge of dancing with Jack, but it just wasn't true.

The night was a shambles, and it was all her fault. Jack would never want to see her again. Not with Ari in the picture. What am I going to do about Ari? she thought desperately. What? He was acting so crazy!

Suddenly the door to the ladies' room banged open again, and a group of girls came in, giggling and joking.

Lacey avoided their gaze but one looked over at her and asked, "Are you Lacey?"

"Yes," Lacey croaked, turning away from the mirror.

"A guy outside, says his name is Jack. He wants to talk to you."

Jack? Lacey repeated to herself. He wants to talk to me?

"Thanks!" Lacey said, heading for the door. Jack wants to talk to her and she wants to talk to Jack. She was out the door in a flash!

CHAPTER ELEVEN

Screwing Up

Lacey came out of the ladies' room and practically fell over Ari standing in the hallway. His arms were folded across his chest and his back was pressed against the wall. At the sight of her, he jumped forward and blocked her with his body.

"What are you doing here?" Lacey asked indignantly as she looked around frantically for Jack.

"You were expecting someone else?" Ari replied coolly but with a sneer on his face that made her afraid to say Jack's name, let alone tell Ari that she was looking for him.

"Obviously not you," she snapped back.

"Too bad. I'm here to take you home." He grabbed Lacey's arm and asked, "Where's your purse? Didn't you have a coat?"

His questions threw her for a second and made her look down at her hands like she was missing something. Then she mumbled, "I think they're at the table."

"All right. Don't worry. Sophie probably has them."

"Sophie?" Lacey said dizzily, confused now and unable to focus. "Is she here?"

"She's out in the parking lot waiting for us. Let's go!" He grabbed her arm and pushed her toward the front door of the bar. "Do you want my jacket? It's cold out there."

Lacey shook her head, but regretted it the moment she stepped outside. The cold night air hit her like a slap across the face, and she regained her senses enough to realize that Sophie was nowhere in sight.

"Hey!" she demanded. "Where's Sophie?"

"The van's over there," Ari said, ignoring her question and pointing toward the darkened parking lot. "Come on. I'm taking you home." He gripped her arm more tightly and yanked it so that she'd come along.

"Ow! You're hurting me," she yelped and pulled herself away from him, planting her feet firmly on the ground. "I'm not going anywhere without Sophie."

"And what do you expect me to do?" Ari bellowed at her. "Stand out here in the cold until your stupid girlfriend decides to show up? She's probably in there dancing like a slut, just like you were with that guy, Jack. Jack the asshole! Lacey the slut!"

She glared at him. "Go ahead, call me a slut. I don't even care anymore. You're such a jerk!"

"And you're a tease like all those bar sluts in there," he fired back. "You already have a man, but you want more. How do you think that makes me feel? I can't even satisfy my own girlfriend!"

"For Chrissakes, Ari," she wailed. "This isn't about you! It's about *me, my* life. You can't tell me what I can or can't do."

But Ari wasn't listening.

"Go ahead," he ranted on. "Make me feel like a piece of shit!" His voice boomed, and his face turned red as he backed her up against the paned-glass window of the bar's front door. "Just like my dad always does! Hey, let's all treat Ari like a worthless piece of shit!"

Then he raised his fist and jerked it back to hit her. As she ducked and recoiled from him, she heard the sound of breaking glass and realized that Ari's hand had gone through one of the panes of glass in the door behind her.

"Shit! Shit! Shit!" he yelled, as shards of glass flew in all directions.

"Are you crazy?" Lacey screamed, as he pulled his hand out of the broken window and thrust it up in the air at her.

"Look what you made me do, you bitch!" Then he spun around and grabbed her arm with his bloody hand. "Are you satisfied now?"

She felt the blood from Ari's hand on her skin, wet and sticky, and she wanted to run. She had to get away from this crazy bastard! "Let me go!" she screamed as she struggled, but that only made Ari tighten his grip on her arm, so she screamed again. "Let go of me!"

Then a man's voice, deep and husky, yelled from behind them, "Let go of her, you son of a bitch!"

Lacey turned to see one of the bar's bouncers coming toward Ari with his two huge hands out in front of him. At the sight of him, Ari dropped her arm and tried to move away but not before the bouncer grabbed him around the shoulders and throttled him up against the door with a thud.

"When the girl says let go, you let go!" the bouncer bellowed. "This isn't a sideshow so your girlfriend can see how pissed you are at her." Then he reached down, grabbed Ari's bloody arm. "Or is this a sissy way of offing yourself?"

He threw Ari against the door again. With the bouncer outweighing him, Ari was pinned and begging for mercy.

"It was an accident," Ari managed to croak, wincing in pain. "It wasn't my fault."

"Bullshit," the bouncer fired back. "I've been watching you from across the way. I don't care what's going on between you and her. I want you out of here before you scare off the paying customers." Then the bouncer released Ari and looked over at Lacey. "Go, before my boss comes out and makes the two of you pay for the window."

"But my friends are in there," Lacey protested. "I have to wait for them."

"I said, get your boyfriend out of here now. I'm doing you a favor – or should I call the cops and have him arrested for destruction of property?"

"No, no! Don't do that," Lacey protested and then added, not realizing what she was saying, "But he's not my boyfriend. Not anymore."

"I don't care who he is to you," the bouncer growled. "What part of 'get-out-of-here-while-the-getting-is-good' don't you get?"

Lacey scowled at Ari and put out her hand. "Give me the keys," she muttered.

Without a word of protest, Ari took them out of his pocket and handed them to Lacey.

"Show me where the van is," she demanded. Ari pointed to an aisle on the far right, and they moved quickly toward it.

Once inside the van, Lacey pulled out of the parking lot into the street with Ari in the passenger seat holding a wad of tissues she had found in her purse pressed on his bloody hand. "Did you mean what you said just now? That I'm not your boyfriend anymore? You're not going to leave me, are you?" he whimpered. "I'm sorry, Lacey. Really I am. I don't know what made me do that. Just don't leave me. Please!"

Lacey looked at him, sitting next to her crying like a baby, and sighed with disgust. What had she ever seen in him? she wondered. Sophie was right. This guy was crazy. She'd take him to the hospital tonight, but that was it. Whatever they had between them was over.

"Grow up, would you?" she growled back at him. "And keep the pressure on that hand or you'll get blood all over the goddamn place."

What a night! she muttered to herself. All she needed was a cop to stop her and ask for her license when her purse was back at the bar with Sophie.

Sophie. Poor Sophie! She had every right to be pissed at her. Since this morning, Sophie had borne the brunt of every bad decision Lacey had made. She was so ashamed of herself.

This was all her fault. She had really screwed up tonight with Ari.

Could Sophie ever forgive her hooking up with such an incredible jerk?

Lisette's eyes fluttered open. It seemed like only a minute ago that she had put her head down on the pillow and shut her eyes. The shadowy figure that was Lacey was gone, but she could still feel her presence in the room.

"My God!" Lisette exclaimed. "Why didn't you tell me what a lunatic Ari was?"

Lacey's voice groaned. *Is that all you got out of that? He was more than that. He was a killer!*

"That's easy for you to see now," Lisette shot back. "But at the time, neither you nor Sophie could've known."

That doesn't matter anymore. What you have to see is that Ambrose is just as dangerous as Ari. He's trying to control you, just like Ari controlled me.

"There you go again," Lisette cried out, flinging the blankets off and jumping out of bed as her robe streamed behind her. "Ambrose is nothing like Ari. He's interested in me and my career. That's it."

My ass that's all it is. He wants what he wants, and he's not going to stop until he gets it. Just like Ari. You'll see. There is more to my story. It only gets worse.

"Oh, God! I haven't got time for more. Ambrose is going to be here any minute. We're going back to the library to read books."

See! That's what I'm talking about. You think he's being nice to you because he lets you read to him, but he's only doing that to suck you in. They all do that, act sweet and charming until they lower the boom. If you don't believe me, ask Sophie. She'll tell you. She knows.

"Look," Lisette said impatiently. "Ambrose is my friend. That's all I need to know."

Your friend! You don't know anything about this guy! Who is he, where is he from, and what does he really want from you? Hell, you know more about me than you do about him.

"That's because you're in my body, driving me crazy!"

Suddenly, the bell to Lisette's hotel room buzzed.

"Damn it!" she cried out. "I told you this was going to happen."

I can't help it if the asshole's early.

"He's not. He's right on time. I'm the one who's late. And he's not an asshole."

Suit yourself. I know an asshole when I see one. Trust me.

Lisette rushed to the door but stopped before she opened it and yelled at Lacey, "I want you out of here. Do you hear me? Go away!"

I'll go away if you promise to go see Sophie. Let her tell you about Ari.

Lisette flung open the door and found Ambrose standing there with a shopping bag in his hand and a concerned look on his face.

"Hey, is everything okay in here?" he asked.

"Yeah," Lisette snarled. "Come on in."

He stepped into the room. "I thought I heard you yelling at someone."

Lisette was confused for a minute and then realized that he must have heard her yelling out loud to Lacey.

"Oh, that," Lisette said nervously. "That was me on the phone. I was talking to the… the…" She stammered for a moment, and then continued, "… to the desk clerk downstairs. The toilet in my room hasn't worked right since I got here."

"What's wrong with it?" Ambrose closed the door behind him. "I could take a look at it, if you like. It might be something simple."

"No, no," Lisette said quickly. "You don't have to do that."

"I brought you some peaches." He held out the shopping bag in his hand. "This guy at the farmer's market gave them to me." He grinned at her. "Hope you like them."

Oh, isn't that nice of Ambrose? Bringing you peaches. Wonder who he stole them from?

Lisette frowned. Goddamn it, Lacey! Why hadn't she gone away like she told her to? She didn't need any of her nastiness right now.

"What's the matter?" Ambrose asked forlornly. "Don't you like peaches?"

"Oh, no! I love peaches." Lisette took the bag from him and set it down on the chair. "I'm running late. I've still got to take a shower. You don't mind waiting for me, do you?"

Oh, he doesn't mind waiting. Not Ambrose. He's a nice guy. You could invite him to take a shower with you. Maybe that's what he wants, to get his hands all over your body!

This time Lisette shouted out loud, "That's enough!"

"Excuse me?" Ambrose asked, his voice slowly rising.

"It's nothing." Lisette stormed off toward the bathroom, leaving Ambrose standing there. "I'll be ready in a minute."

You can't do anything to me. I'm only a voice in your head. But Ambrose? He's a real problem. Watch out for him. He's dangerous. Do you hear me?

Lisette stopped short of the bathroom and said, "Will you just shut up and leave me alone?" She was so furious at Lacey that she forgot Ambrose was there.

"What?" he said, as he spun her around and grabbed her by the shoulders. She winced in pain as he tightened his hands on her.

"Hey, you're hurting me!" she cried out, but he didn't respond. He was staring at her as if she were someone else, someone he really hated.

"Let go of me!" she screamed again, trying to wriggle out of his hold on her. "I wasn't talking to you. I was talking to... to..." She stopped in mid-sentence, aware that she couldn't tell him about Lacey.

"There's no one else in the room but me," he bellowed.

Lisette gave him a look that contained all the pain and bewilderment she felt, and for some reason he backed off. She felt his hands relax and drop away from her.

"Sorry," he muttered as he stepped away, looking sheepish and ashamed of his behavior.

"No, no. It was my fault." She saw the sad, worried look in his eyes and went on in spite of herself. "I was talking to this voice in my head. It won't go away. You must think I'm crazy, but..."

"No – I hear voices, too. Remember I told you about that the other night. But I thought you said a friend of yours was hearing voices, not you. Which is it?"

Lisette was silent. She didn't know how to respond.

"When I was a kid," Ambrose went on, "I used to hear Attila the Hun's voice all the time. Once, when I was about twelve, he told me to kill the cat."

"And did you?"

"Of course! No one disobeys a direct order from the great Attila and lives to tell about it," Ambrose said with a grin. "I got into a lot of trouble for that, but I don't know what I would have done without Attila in my life at that time."

"So the voice went away?"

"Oh, no," Ambrose said almost happily. "It's still around. I heard it just the other day when I saw your publicity poster outside the Pussycat. Attila told me you were someone I had to get to know."

"He did?" Lisette looked at him incredulously. "Did he say why?"

"Because you were going to make me come alive."

"Alive?" Lisette said with a laugh. "What are you – dead, too?"

"No, but I haven't had this much energy in years. I can't stop thinking about your new act. I woke up this morning with a great idea. Your mother is a symbol of abandonment for you. Everyone is abandoned by someone at some point in life. That's an emotion that reflects the universality of the human condition. It would be great to build the act around your relationship with your mother."

Lisette felt her anger rising. "There's no way I want my mother in my act."

"Not your mother, but what she represents in your life," Ambrose countered. "Your mother is a metaphor."

"A what?" Lisette screeched. There Ambrose went again, talking about things she didn't understand.

He's saying your mother stands for something else. She's a symbol, you idiot!

"What's a symbol?" Lisette asked Lacey. "And don't call me an idiot!"

"Huh?" Ambrose asked, and then his face lit up. "Yes, a symbol. That's a good way to describe it."

Lisette frowned and turned away in embarrassment.

Ambrose stared at her. "Oh I see. That part about the symbol came from the voice in your head again, didn't it?"

"How did you know?" Then she sputtered, "Never mind. There's no voice. I just made it up."

Ambrose watched her carefully for a moment, as if considering whether to believe her or not, and then he muttered, almost breezily, "Okay, whatever."

Lisette rolled her eyes. This was getting to be too much for her. "I'm taking my shower now." She turned and left Ambrose standing there mumbling to himself. But as she walked into the bathroom, Lacey's voice came back for the last word.

So you didn't tell him about me. Good for you. And you walked away from him. That's great. Taking some control here is a good thing.

"Don't get all excited," Lisette said in a huff, closing the bathroom door so Ambrose couldn't hear her. "I didn't tell him about you because it would take too long, and I don't want to spend the whole day all focused on you. You aren't the center of the universe, you know."

I am the center of your universe as long as I'm in your body. I thought you were going to help me get out, not hang around with this guy all the time.

"What's the big deal? We're going to the library." She took off her robe and stepped into the shower. "Now, can I please have some peace and quiet?"

Fine. Just remember. I warned you.

"Yes, you warned me."

Sophie tried to warn me about Ari, but I ignored her. Look where it got me. You've got to talk to Sophie. She'll tell you.

"Goddamn it," Lisette said. "Stop it about Sophie. Just leave me alone!"

Then there was silence. Lisette couldn't believe it. But maybe the sound of the water pounding on her head drowned out whatever else Lacey had to say.

Thank God we're going to the library, she thought. At least it's quiet there. No loud voices allowed there, inside or outside my head!

By the time she and Ambrose got off the city bus and walked up the long, white steps to the library, Lisette was exhausted.

Her morning of fighting with the voice of Lacey in her head

had been too much, and now Ambrose was talking away at her. He hadn't stopped since they had left her hotel room. At this point, he was talking excitedly about what books she should read next.

"Let's see if we can get you some adult books," he said as he took the steps up to the library two at a time in front of her. "I don't mean hard ones, but something that will expand the scope of your reading. I'd like to see you take on the whole Roman Empire thing. That'll give you an idea of what it was like to be a barbarian in those days."

Lisette tried to listen to him, but her mind wandered off until he got to the top of the stairs ahead of her and stood waiting for her with a big, goofy grin on his face.

Ah, she thought with a smile, Ambrose wasn't so dangerous. Why was Lacey trying to tell me that he was? He still looked like Willie Nelson to her – maybe not as laid back as Willie, but Ambrose was not a killer like Ari. She could handle him, and she liked how he paid attention to her. She hurried up the stairs now, eager to be with him, but when she got there, she saw his eyes shift away from her to something or someone further down the stairs. Before she could turn around to see what it was, she heard a voice from below calling, "Jeffrey?"

It was a woman's voice, loud and throaty. "Is that you, Jeffrey?"

At this, Ambrose's eyes bugged out and his whole body stiffened. But instead of responding, he turned and walked quickly toward the doors of the library as though he had heard nothing. Who was he kidding? she thought. The woman was there and her voice rang out again, closer now and growing nasty.

"Jeffrey, I know that's you. Don't you walk away from me!"

When Lisette turned around to look at the woman, she was rushing up the stairs toward them. She was old enough to be someone's grandmother and was dressed in a loose white sweatshirt and black stretch pants that didn't flatter any part of her over-weight body. Her large breasts flopped up and down underneath the sweatshirt and her fat thighs bulged out from her pants. Her hair was dyed a hideous bright red color and the skin on her face was baggy and wrinkled.

"I saw you way back there," she said to Ambrose, wagging her finger at him. "You heard me calling you. I know you did. But you didn't stop." She heaved a sigh and demanded, "I want a word with you, Jeffrey, and I want it now."

As if this old lady wasn't enough, right behind her Lisette saw an old guy who looked even more decrepit. With his back hunched over and his bald head shriveled up like a prune, he looked like a corpse. He was panting and wheezing as he came up the steps, waving his cane and yelling at the old woman.

"Abigail, what are you doing? Don't you start up with him!" The old man looked in Ambrose's direction and scowled. "He's not worth it."

"For God's sakes, Irving! Go back to the car before you have a spasm and need oxygen. I'll take care of this."

"What's the use?" he sputtered back. "He'll never change!" The man collapsed on a step, grabbing his chest and gasping for breath. That made it easier for the woman to ignore him, and she turned back to Ambrose.

"I know you went to Mark's school. I can have you arrested for that, you know. You have no right to see him, and I won't have you upsetting him."

At the mention of Mark's name, Lisette could see Ambrose's eyes narrow and his face turn red. The woman had hit another nerve, but Lisette didn't get it. Who was this Jeffrey? And Mark? Was Mark Jeffrey's kid?

"What the hell is going on here?" she demanded of Ambrose. "Who is Jeffrey?"

But Ambrose ignored her questions and snarled, "Let's get out of here."

Before they could go anywhere though, the woman grabbed Ambrose's arm and pulled him toward her. "Don't play games with me, Jeffrey. We have too much bad blood between us already."

His eyes glared at her. He was so much bigger than the woman and he was so angry that Lisette was sure he was going to hit her. Instead he pushed her aside, saying, "Get out of here, you bitch, and leave us alone."

But the woman wasn't going anywhere. She stood there, her head cocked to one side as though she was trying to figure something out. She suddenly looked at Lisette.

"Oh, I get it," she sneered. "He doesn't want you to know who he really is, does he, dearie? He's trying to pretend that he's not Jeffrey in front of you."

"But I don't know any Jeffreys," Lisette said weakly.

"You know this one, all right. He's a conniver and a bastard and he's Jeffrey. If you knew what he did to his family, you'd cry yourself sick. That's what I've been doing for years, but I'm done with it now." She turned back to Ambrose. "You're going to take responsibility for what you've done or I'll…"

"You'll do what?" Ambrose shot back. "Why don't you and that old bag-of-bones husband of yours leave me and Mark alone?" He turned quickly and pulled Lisette toward the library door. "Come on," he hissed insistently at her. "I've had enough of this old harpy."

"So you do know Mark!" Lisette gasped. "My God, what is going on?"

"I'll tell you," the woman broke in. "He'll say it was an accident. But it was no accident. He killed his wife – my daughter – and my granddaughter. She was only three and never did a bad thing in her life."

Lisette's mind reeled as she whirled around to glare at Ambrose. "Is that true? Did you kill someone?"

Lisette knew all about families. Sometimes you wanted to kill them. Sometimes you even tried – but to kill your own kid! How could he?

Suddenly she was afraid that he might hurt her too and she pulled away from him, but Ambrose yanked at her arm and pushed her toward the doors.

"We're going inside. Don't listen to her! She's crazy!" He dragged Lisette alongside him like a dog on a leash. "Just get inside!"

"No! I'm not going anywhere with you. Let me *go!*"

But he didn't. Instead, he dug his fingers even deeper into her arm, and Lisette could feel his rage through his fingertips. But she was angry now, too.

"Goddamn it," she exploded. "Let *go* of me!"

Suddenly, as if on command, Ambrose let go of her arm and dropped back behind her. At last, she thought. He was getting that she wasn't going anywhere with him until she found out what this crazy old woman was talking about. But Lisette's feeling of relief didn't last long. Suddenly she felt his hands grab her around her waist as he lifted her from the ground and carried her off under one of his arms.

"You're coming with me!" Ambrose shouted, headed toward the library doors.

Lisette fought him, pounding her fists into his legs and kicking her legs, but it was no use. He was bigger and stronger than she was and she couldn't stop him.

"Put her down!" Lisette heard the woman screaming behind her. The old man yelled, "Let him go, Abigail. He's not worth it!"

Ambrose pushed them both into the library, and Lisette felt a blast of cold air from the air-conditioning as he put her down. Like a glass of ice-cold water thrown at her face, it cleared her head and she was even more furious at him. Who did he think he was, treating her like this?

"No one touches me unless I say so," she screamed.

"Quiet," he shot back. "We're in a library! Keep your voice down."

"I don't care if we're in a gas station," Lisette said, but her words were drowned out by the shushing sound of a woman behind the counter across the way. Lisette glared at the librarian for a moment and then lowered her voice. "What the hell is going on? Is your name Jeffrey? And who is this Mark? Did you kill your daughter?"

But Ambrose didn't respond. He stood there looking at her.

"Either you explain all this, or I'm out of here."

"Don't believe what she says," he muttered. "She's a crabby, loudmouthed bitch."

"Fine, so she's a bitch. But what's this 'accident' she's talking about?"

"It's nothing," Ambrose muttered again.

"Nothing? You think it's nothing when some crazy old woman comes up to you, calls you by some other name, and says you killed two people? Why did you haul me in here if it was nothing?" She sighed with exasperation. "Oh, forget it. I'm out of here."

Lisette turned to walk past him.

"Wait," he said, grabbing her arm.

"Hey! What did I tell you about touching me?"

"Shh!" The librarian across the way demanded.

He snatched his hand from her arm. "I'm sorry. I didn't mean to…" His voice trailed off. "Look," he began again. "I needed to get you away from her. She hates my guts. She'll say anything to make me look bad."

"Is there anything true in what she said?"

"It depends on how you tell the story."

"What story?"

Ambrose didn't respond.

"I mean it," Lisette went on. "Tell me, or I walk out of here and you'll never see me again."

"Okay, okay," he said hastily. "I'll tell you. The truth. I promise."

"So you *are* Jeffrey?" she asked.

He nodded sheepishly.

"You had a wife, kids, and a job, I'd guess."

"Yeah," he muttered. "I had it all."

"So what happened? Tell me and don't leave anything out."

"I will, Scout's honor," Ambrose said, raising a hand to his forehead in a mock salute.

"Don't make fun of me," Lisette said, her eyes flashing. "I'll leave your life so fast…"

"No, please," he begged. "Don't go."

"Shh! Shh!" The librarian sounded like a broken record.

"We can't talk here. That old biddy will shush us to death. Is there somewhere we can go and talk?"

He nodded. "There's a place downstairs. We can get some coffee. Come on."

By the time they got downstairs to the coffee shop in the library, Ambrose was like a wild man inside. He couldn't hold back any more. Abigail had yelled out his real name in front of Lisette, and that made him furious.

Jeffrey. Jeffrey Alexander.

God! How he despised that name, and how he hated Abigail for yelling it out loud. His past life couldn't pop up now, just when he was getting somewhere with Lisette. He had gotten her to trust him, and now this. How was he going to explain it all to her?

Damn Abigail! Why was she torturing him like this? Hadn't he been through enough? Maybe he should get rid of her and that stupid husband of hers. But what was he talking about? Then he'd never get Mark back.

"Ambrose, are you listening to me?" Lisette's voice broke into his dark thoughts.

He looked up at her, full of rage. He didn't see how it was possible for him to sit there at this table and quietly spill his guts to her. He was like a caged animal, ready to kill or be killed. But Lisette wasn't his enemy. She was his salvation.

He felt her yank at his sleeve, and he looked at her.

"Hello, hello! Is anyone at home in there?" She thumped her finger on his chest and let out a little giggle.

He pulled away and glared at her. Does she think this is funny? What part of his pain and misery didn't she get?

He hated her.

He loved her.

God! She was beautiful! Suddenly he couldn't take his eyes off her. If he could just convince her to do the act, he'd have a job as her manager and the judge would have to let him have Mark back. Mark was everything to him, and right now Abigail had him and he didn't. He couldn't stand that. He had to get him back.

"You promised me you'd tell me about the accident," Lisette persisted.

"What?" he muttered. "Do you believe her? That I did all those things she said?"

"Who, Abigail?" Lisette sounded confused. "Is that who you're talking about? You haven't even told me about Mark. Is he your son or not?"

"Mark?" Ambrose said. "He's ten. It was his birthday last week. I went to go see him but it went badly, very badly...." His voice trailed off. How could he explain about Mark? How could a son hate his father, the only family member he had left?

Then he blurted out, "I didn't kill anyone!" He grabbed her hand and squeezed it tight. "You have to believe me."

"Hey, you're hurting me!" she cried out. "What did I tell you about touching me?"

"Oh!" he said, jerking his hand away. "I'm sorry."

Then she gave him a look that suggested she might understand, so he kept on talking. "It was an accident. Only Mark and I survived."

"But why did you change your name?"

It was so hard to explain. He had to try.

"Haven't you ever had something to hide?" he began, his voice low and mysterious. "Something bad that you didn't want anyone to know?"

"I… I…" she stammered, squirming in her seat and turning her eyes away from him.

"So you know what I'm talking about," he said quickly. "I changed my name to distance myself from everything."

"But what happened? I still don't get it."

He leaned closer to her across the table and let out an exasperated sigh. "It was all Betsy's fault. She's the one to blame."

"I don't care who's to blame," Lisette shot back. "I want to know the truth."

"Oh ho, the truth!" he spat out sarcastically. "Is *that* what you want?"

"Yes," she said firmly. "Friends always tell each other the truth."

That made him smile. So she thought of him as her friend. That was good to hear. He hadn't lost her yet, but if she found out something she didn't like about him, she'd be gone like everyone else. Gone, lost, never found. Like he had lost Betsy, long before the accident. Beautiful, stupid, dead Betsy. What an idiot he had been to ever fall for her!

"What's so funny?" Lisette demanded. "What's going on in that head of yours?"

Ambrose ignored her. "Betsy was a cow," he howled. "Moo!"

He saw her cringe, and he enjoyed her reaction.

"You mean Betsy, your wife?" Lisette asked.

"Yes, my Betsy was a Moo, Moo!" Ambrose went on, enjoying being silly and mysterious as he lowered his voice and repeated, "She was a real cow."

"I don't get it. Weren't you two happy?"

He laughed, "Do you think any one lives happily ever after?"

"No," she said. "But I asked you a question first."

"I should have been happy with Betsy. She was the most beautiful girl I had ever seen. We met in history class during my sophomore year of college, and she was wearing this incredible green sweater. It was so tight across her chest that I sat there thinking how I'd sell my soul to the devil if I could touch one of her breasts." Then he stopped for a moment. "Ha! I ended up married to the devil herself."

"So you weren't happy?"

"How could anyone be happy being married to a cow?"

"Stop calling her that!"

Ambrose looked at her for a moment and then laughed. "You're jealous of her, aren't you?" He hadn't considered that. Women, even the beautiful ones, could be jealous of other women. He savored that thought for a moment and waited for Lisette to react. But she didn't. She sat there, her arms folded across her chest, looking at him as though he were stupid and not worth talking to anymore. That infuriated him even more.

"What's the matter? Cat got your tongue?"

Finally Lisette muttered, "What about your kids? Did you love them?"

"Jeanine," Ambrose said with a grin and a lilt in his voice, "I called her Pumpkin. She had this funny way of looking at me that made me want to give her everything she'd ever want to have. All at once. Just like that." He snapped his fingers and smiled broadly.

"And Mark. Smart as a whip. Nothing went by him. Nothing."

"So what happened? What went wrong?"

He leaned across the table and hissed at her in a low, deep voice full of anger. "I'll tell you what happened. I was teaching Betsy how to drive a car with a stick shift, but she was an idiot, too stupid to learn something so simple."

He sat back in his chair for a moment, pleased with himself that what he said would get a rise out of her – but it didn't. So he went on. "We were out on the back roads by the airport where there weren't many cars. She pulled out onto a paved road, and I told her to let the clutch out slow, really slow, but, of course she didn't. So the back wheels of our car sprayed the car behind us with a bunch of rocks."

Ambrose leaned forward. "Can you imagine that? The car behind us was worth a fortune, and I'd be pissed too if someone did something like that. But Betsy didn't get it. She whined about how she was sorry, but there was too much to remember. Put the clutch in, let it out, step on the gas. And then she complained about not wanting to learn to drive a stick shift in the first place, which took us back to an old argument we'd been having for days. Betsy couldn't drive our new car because I needed it for work, so if she wanted a car to haul the kids around in, it had to be the old one with the stick shift."

"Why didn't Betsy go to one of those driving schools to learn?" Lisette asked.

"Those things are a waste of money! How hard could it be to teach someone?"

"I don't know," Lisette said warily. "But you could've avoided an accident."

"No, you don't understand," Ambrose snapped back. "The kids were acting up in the backseat. The minute Betsy had her eyes on the road and wasn't looking in the rearview mirror at them, Mark and Jeanine would start up."

"About what?"

"You know how kids are – Mark was six and Jeanine almost three, and they were always fighting to get her attention."

Then something triggered a memory so vivid that Ambrose fell into silence. Suddenly he could hear exactly what Betsy had yelled into the back seat that day.

"Mark, what did I tell you about hitting your sister while Mommy is driving? I'm going to get into an accident, and it's going to be all your fault if you don't stop it. So stop it right now."

Ambrose's face went pale and a lump came into his throat. Had Betsy really said that? No wonder Mark was so messed up. If Ambrose had realized that at the time, everything between them would have been different. He wouldn't have lost his patience with Mark when he couldn't stop whining and crying for his mommy. He and Mark would be together right now.

"So what did you do?"

Lisette's voice pulled Ambrose out of his thoughts.

"About what?" he muttered. He couldn't stop thinking about Mark.

"About your kids fighting while Betsy was driving?"

"I told Mark to stop it," Ambrose said curtly, still lost in thought.

"And did he?"

Ambrose looked at Lisette. "Of course not. Mark wasn't like that. He never gave up."

Oh, God! he thought suddenly. Mark had kept fighting with Jeanine that day because he didn't want to lose any ground with his sister. But Ambrose should have known something bad might happen. Did Mark mean to cause an accident? Did he think it would solve something in his life? What had Ambrose missed? What the hell was going on with Mark? Suddenly he didn't care if Lisette heard the rest of his story. It flashed before his eyes now like a motion picture, and he was mesmerized by it. He closed his eyes and saw Mark take one more swipe at his sister while Ambrose's voice exploded into the backseat, "What did I tell you?"

He twisted his body around, grabbed Mark by the collar and shook him.

"When I say don't hit her, it doesn't mean to hit her one more time before you stop. It means stop right now."

"Ouch! You're hurting me," Mark wailed, and Ambrose immediately let him go.

"And put your seat belt on, Mark! Why don't you have it on?"

But Mark ignored his father and instead poked his finger into Jeanine's arm and shouted, "It's her fault. She started it. You said I could sit by that window but she won't let me."

Ambrose turned to his daughter and tried to cajole her. "Pumpkin, let your brother sit by the window so he can watch the airplanes go by and we'll get ice-cream cones later."

"No," Jeanine said firmly. "It's my turn to sit behind Mommy while she drives."

Ambrose sighed and was about to respond when Betsy said something to him from the front seat.

"Those boys are behind us." Her voice was tense. "What should I do? They won't try to pass me in this no-passing zone, will they?"

"What boys?"

"You know, the ones in that sports car."

Ambrose looked out the back window. Betsy was right. The low, sleek red sports car was behind them on the two-lane country road. He could see the driver and his buddy. They were young, virile, unruly, and thoroughly pissed off.

"Stay calm," he said to Betsy, but his heart was pounding as the sports car came up alongside them on the left. The kid in the passenger seat hung out the window and gave Betsy the finger.

"You bitch!" he yelled. "If you don't know how to drive, get off the road."

Then Mark got up from his seat and plopped down on top of his sister. "Ow!" Jeanine let out a bloodcurdling scream. "You're hurting me!"

"Move over, you cow," Mark yelled at her. "It's my turn to sit by that window."

"Stop it, both of you!" Ambrose swatted at them blindly. His eyes were glued to the sports car which was moving dangerously into their lane.

Jesus, Ambrose swore under his breath. Were these kids going to force them off the road? What the hell was the matter with them?

"Slow down!" Ambrose yelled at Betsy. "You can't outrun them. SLOW DOWN!"

He watched Betsy, waiting for her reaction, but instead of slowing down, her foot jammed down on the gas pedal, her eyes fixed on the road ahead of her and her hands tight on the steering wheel.

"There's a car coming the other way!" she screamed. "I've got to get ahead of these kids. It's the only way!"

Ambrose looked up and saw a blue van headed right for the sports car which was still traveling in the passing lane.

"Slow down!" Ambrose repeated, clutching Betsy's arm so that she'd do what he would do by instinct after years of driving. "Let them get in front of you. They've got to get out of the way of that van, or else..."

But Betsy wasn't listening to him, so he yelled, "Stop the car! Step on the brake. Now!"

With that, Betsy obeyed his command and slammed on the brake – except she forgot to put in the clutch, and suddenly the car went into convulsions. It shuddered and shook and then careened sideways off the road toward a ditch.

"Oh my God!" Betsy cried out and, in her panic, turned the wheel into the direction of the spin rather than away from it, causing the car to go flying faster to the right.

"NO!" Ambrose screamed, grabbing the wheel away from her and turning it to the left to bring the car back, but it was no use. As the car headed toward the ditch, Ambrose looked over his shoulder to see the sports car speed past them and back into the right lane before the oncoming van reached them. The driver of the van blared his horn at both cars as he whizzed by and went safely on to his destination.

Ambrose heard the sound of the horn blaring mixed with the screams of Mark and Jeanine from the backseat and Betsy screeching next to him, "Oh, God. Oh, God. Oh, God, no!" This horrific cacophony of sounds continued as their car sailed out of control, bouncing first on the edge of the ditch and then over it toward a large tree in the middle of a sun-filled cornfield. He remembered his single, simple thought right before he closed his eyes and braced himself for the impact. Oh, God! We're all going to die!

With that moment of terror playing over in his head, his eyes flew open and without a word he got up from his chair and bolted out of the cafeteria.

"Wait!" he heard Lisette yelling after him as he headed back upstairs to the lobby of the library.

But he didn't stop. He ran, taking the steps two at a time until he got up to the reading room on the second floor and headed for his spot way back in the stacks. It was where he always went when things got to be too much. He could bury himself in the books he loved and forget what was real.

But being there today didn't stop the story from going on inside his head. Oh, God! he groaned to himself, as he hunkered down in the large, stuffed chair in the stacks. Did he have to remember more?

This was the part he hated the most.

He closed his eyes and let himself remember.

He didn't have any choice.

When Ambrose came to in the middle of the cornfield, he didn't open his eyes right away. He didn't want to see or know what had happened.

Instead he sat there, his body lodged in the front seat, slowly breathing in and out. He hoped that if he did that, everyone in the car would breathe along with him, and soon they'd climb out of the wreck and thank their lucky stars that no one was hurt.

But then he wiggled his left foot and it wouldn't move. His chest hurt, and the seat belt fastened tightly around him made the smallest intake of breath painful. He smelled something vile, too – he thought it must be the oil and engine fluids oozing out of the front of the car. Slowly the awareness of something wet on his head and the moans of his children in the backseat brought him from a state of floating above it all and down to reality.

He knew that something bad had happened and that he'd eventually have to deal with it. For a time he just sat in the car, trying to make himself open his eyes and face the horrors around him, but he must have slipped in and out of consciousness. Each time he woke up, he smelled the sickening smell again, heard the hissing of the car's engine and remembered that his children were somewhere in the backseat.

He knew that everyone was going to blame him for this later on. They'd say, "What kind of man would teach his wife to drive a car with his two small children in the backseat? What was he doing, taking his wife out on that narrow, two-lane highway where there was no escape but to be driven off the road? Why didn't he react quicker and save them all?"

But it wasn't his fault. Betsy had killed them all. She was stubborn and stupid and had never listened to him even once the whole time they were married. She deserved what she got. He'd tell them. He'd let anyone who thought otherwise know: Betsy had killed them all.

At some point, Ambrose did open his eyes and saw a man standing over him shaking his arm, the man surprised that anyone was still alive.

It was then that Ambrose saw Betsy slumped over the steering wheel next to him and Jeanine, buckled into her seatbelt behind her, bloody and quiet. Jeanine had been moaning in the backseat a while ago, and when she stopped, Ambrose suspected the worst. But where was Mark? Had he ever put his seat belt on? If one of his children was still alive, please let it be Mark, he prayed.

"Hey, what are you doing back here?" a stern, unforgiving voice broke into his thoughts and Ambrose was back in the chair in the library stacks. "You're not supposed to be here. This area is for library staff only."

He looked up and saw a librarian shaking a finger at him. "Get out of here now before I call security."

He wanted to thank her for showing up when she did. His hiding place was gone, but he didn't care. She got him out of that memory, but this time he had learned something he didn't know before. Mark was blaming himself for the accident, and it was clear that was what was messing him up.

Suddenly, Ambrose could see why everything had gone so wrong between him and Mark. Only someone who was there that day could set Mark straight. But how was he going to do that? Abigail was on the alert, and Mark would run away from him again unless someone else came with him to see Mark. Someone who Mark might like to meet and talk to. Someone young and beautiful who took a shine to him. Ten wasn't too early for a boy to notice girls. Mark would think it was cool to meet someone like Lisette. He'd see how good it felt to have someone like her pay attention to him.

So he made a plan. He'd get Lisette to go see Mark with him, and then he'd talk to Mark about the accident. He could kick himself now for running out on Lisette in the cafeteria earlier. If he had told her the rest of the story, he was sure she would see how important it was for Mark to know the truth about what had happened.

He had to find Lisette. If she wasn't down in the cafeteria, he'd go back to her hotel. He'd have to convince her to help him out, but he was good at getting her to do things. And this thing was the most important thing in his life.

Of course she'd help him out.

She'd have no reason not to.

CHAPTER TWELVE

Whose Fault?

Lisette was livid.

She had rushed out of the cafeteria and up the stairs after Ambrose, but by then it was too late. He had disappeared, and she stood there in the middle of the lobby of the library feeling like an idiot.

What had she missed? One minute he was telling her about the accident, and the next minute he was gone. Even while he was telling her, he was acting like an idiot, calling his wife a cow. So he didn't have a happy marriage – he didn't have to run off like that. What was she supposed to do now? Go chasing all over the place looking for him? Screw him! She didn't need this shit.

She huffed out of the public library and down the long, white steps in the front of the building where she and Ambrose had stood a while ago. As she got to the curb, a voice called out from behind her.

"He took off on you already, did he?"

Lisette spun around to see Abigail standing there.

"He's like that," the woman went on. "Never takes responsibility for anything. But you look like a smart girl. Don't get fooled by him."

She glared at the woman. "Haven't you caused enough trouble for one day?"

Abigail's voice fell. "So he *has* gotten to you. He told you some story and now you think it's my fault. He's good at blaming everyone but himself for his problems."

"Yes, he told me everything," Lisette lied. "How he lost his wife and daughter in a car accident, and how you won't let him see Mark."

Abigail grunted with disgust. "It's incredible to me how you women get taken in by guys like Jeffrey and you don't even know it."

"I haven't been taken in by anyone!" Lisette protested.

"I saw how he picked you up and hauled you into the library like a sack of potatoes. Like he could control where you go and who you talk to."

Lisette laughed. "Nobody controls me. They don't even try."

She put her hand up to hail a cab, hoping that Abigail would go away, but the woman didn't move.

"Look," Lisette said firmly. "Leave me alone, or I'll call the police."

"I'm not here for you, my dear. It's him I want to get my hands on. You don't know by any chance where he's living now, do you?"

Lisette eyed the woman. Did she really think she'd tell her that, even if she knew? "Lady, leave me out of this, okay? I'm not snitching on Ambrose to anyone."

Abigail looked confused for a moment. "So that's what he's calling himself these days? Ambrose. Isn't that odd?"

"What do you mean?"

Abigail's voice got quiet. "Ambrose was his grandfather's name, and he was a real mean son of a bitch. Beat his wife, too, or didn't he tell you that either?"

Lisette's head was in a whirl, and she looked at Abigail in bewilderment. "But Ambrose didn't hit Betsy. It was an accident. He told me so. He was teaching Betsy how to drive, and his kids were making a racket in the backseat."

"So now it was Mark's fault?" Abigail exploded. "Is that what he said?"

"No. I don't know exactly how the accident happened, but…"

"Technically," Abigail broke in, "they were forced off the road by another car. But knowing Jeffrey and his need to control everything, he had a hand in it."

"What do you mean?"

"I know my daughter wouldn't let that car go off the road, not with her kids in it."

Lisette didn't know what to say. Did Ambrose make up that part of the story, or was Abigail trying to get him in trouble?

"What do you know about it, anyway?" Lisette finally sputtered. "You weren't there. Neither was I. You can't know."

"All I know is that if I had been there, my daughter and grand-baby would be alive today and Mark wouldn't be a mess. You can't imagine how this has affected him." Abigail's voice trailed off for a moment, and then she went on angrily, "I've done everything I could to keep that man away from Mark." She shook her fists up into the air. "So long as I am alive, he'll never lay a hand on his son again."

"He hit Mark? Is that why Mark was taken away from him?"

Abigail's face broke into a broad grin. "You aren't as stupid as I thought. Yes, after such a horrendous crash, father and son should be together. But that's not how Ambrose played it."

"But I don't understand." Lisette was desperate now to know the truth.

Abigail reached back down into her bag and pulled out a piece of paper. "Here," she said, shoving the page at Lisette. "It was in all the papers. Read it for yourself."

Lisette looked down at the sheet and felt herself starting to panic. She couldn't read this. She couldn't tell her that without feeling like an idiot.

"Take it with you, my dear," Abigail said, as if she sensed her uneasiness. "It might save your life. You never know."

Just then, a cab pulled up to the curb, and Lisette gave Abigail a pained look. "I don't know who to believe. I thought he was telling me the truth."

"You can believe what you want, but *I'm* telling you the truth."

Then Abigail turned and walked away. Lisette looked after her for a moment and then climbed into the cab. As it sped back to her hotel, she sat in the backseat feeling miserable and confused.

What was she supposed to do with this damn piece of paper? It would take her hours to look up all the words she didn't know, and she couldn't ask Ambrose to help. Still she had to know what he hadn't told her.

Who could she get to read it to her?

Erick popped into her head. He'd help her understand what it said, but she didn't have a phone number for him. She didn't even know where he lived.

"Driver," she said, tapping her finger on the glass between them. "I want to go to the Bare Bottom Dance Club instead. Do you know where that is?"

The cab driver nodded and made a quick U-turn. Lisette wondered if Erick would be there this early on a Tuesday morning. Wouldn't he have classes during the week? What were the chances she'd be able to find him? When they arrived at the club, she paid the driver and got out of the cab.

"Erick's not here right now. You'll have to talk to the manager about getting his phone number," the guy behind the bar told her. "But I wouldn't do that if I were you," he added.

"Why not?" she snapped. Who was he to tell her what to do?

"Aren't you the girl who danced here last week and quit on him?"

"Yeah. I got mobbed on the stage, so I had every right to quit."

"I believe you. But the owner lost a lot of business before he could replace you, so I wouldn't ask him any favors." Then he went on, trying to be more helpful, "Come back on the weekend. Erick will be here."

Damn! she thought as she turned and marched out of the club. If she weren't so anxious to read what was on that stupid piece of paper, she would have taken on that asshole club owner right now. But she knew he wasn't going to give her what she wanted. She'd have to get someone else to read it for her.

Lisette walked down the street, hating that she couldn't figure out what one lousy newspaper article said without needing someone's help. She could go up to someone on the street and ask them to help her. But what if they couldn't read either? They'd be embarrassed, too. She knew how that felt.

If only Lacey was around, Lisette sighed. Lacey could see through Lisette's eyes, and she could read this paper for her. But Lisette had told her to go away this morning, and she wasn't sure when or if she'd be back.

Not sure what to do, Lisette walked for a while. Soon she noticed she was in the neighborhood of the college that Lacey had attended, surrounded by students carrying books and backpacks. One of them could read the article to her without being embarrassed, she thought. Then it came to her. Sophie! Sophie could help her. Lacey had bugged her this morning about going to see Sophie, and now would be a perfect time to find her.

But how could she do that? She didn't even know Sophie's last name. So she walked up to several students and asked them if they knew anyone named Sophie. One of them gave her an angry look and turned away. Others said they didn't know any Sophie, and one guy went on about a Sophie he knew in high school. Ready to give up, Lisette asked a girl crossing the street, and to her surprise, the girl said, "Yeah. I know Sophie."

"Do you know where I can find her?"

"Sure," the girl said easily. "She's got an appointment with Professor Morris right after lunch."

Lisette was stunned. "How do you know that?"

"I was just in class with her. She said she needed to talk to him about setting up the symposium next week. His office is in that building." The girl pointed to the other side of the street and then looked Lisette up and down. "What do you want with her?"

"I need to ask her something," Lisette said uneasily, afraid the girl would have some problem with that.

"You should know that Sophie's having a tough time. Her roommate was killed last week. Sophie is taking it hard. We all are." The girl's voice dropped off for a second, then continued. "You aren't going to bum her out any more than she already is, are you?"

"Oh, no," Lisette said quickly. "I won't. I promise."

The girl frowned and then continued. "They want us to forget it happened, you know. But those of us who knew Lacey liked her a lot. That's why we want to have the symposium. So no one forgets her."

"You knew Lacey? And Ari too? What did people think of him?"

The girl frowned again. "He's a different story. I didn't know him very well. No one did. He was moody and a little creepy. We were all surprised that Lacey even went out with him and glad when she broke it off. She deserved better." Her voice cracked for a moment. "I've got to get to class. Hope you find Sophie."

"Okay," Lisette called after her. "Thanks! You've been a big help."

But Lisette didn't want her to go. She had so many more questions. Like what was a "symposium" and why exactly was that going to help everyone not forget Lacey. It sounded important, Lisette thought, and she had to find out why.

Sophie was the key to it all and she had to find her now.

Ambrose was getting frantic.

As he raced through the library looking for Lisette, starting in the cafeteria, he mulled over how he would have to apologize to Lisette when he found her and give her an explanation for his behavior. But damned if he knew why he had taken off like that! Suddenly, it had felt like the room was closing in, and he knew that if he stayed one second longer telling Lisette how he lost his family in such a terrible way, he'd go crazy.

That was good, he thought and he grinned. She'd like that explanation. But first, he'd have to find her. Having no luck in the library, he pushed through the front doors and raced down the steps, when he suddenly saw Abigail.

"Ah ha!" she shrieked, jumping out and grabbing his arm. "I want to talk with you, Jeffrey," she demanded. "And don't run away this time."

"Get your hands off me, you old bag!" Ambrose flung her hand off his arm and rushed by her in a rage. "You've caused me enough trouble for one day!"

"If you are looking for her, she's gone."

He turned and looked at her, suddenly interested in what she had to say. "Which way did she go?"

But Abigail didn't respond. He stepped closer and added, "Tell me, old woman, or so help me God, I'll hurt you!"

"You can't hurt me anymore," she sputtered. "You've already killed my daughter and my grandbaby! What more is there?"

"I didn't kill anyone. It was Betsy's fault."

"Isn't that just like you? Blaming someone else. I told her all about you."

Ambrose's eyes lit up. "Where did she go?"

"She didn't believe me," Abigail went on. "Not yet."

Suddenly Ambrose realized what Abigail was saying and grabbed her by the arm. "What did you tell her? If you mess up what I've got going with her, I'll…" His voice dropped off, and he gripped her arm even tighter.

"What are you doing with a girl like that anyway?" Abigail said, wrestling her arm away from him. "You're old enough to be her father. You're disgusting!"

"What I do with her is none of your damned business!"

"I know you. You've got a get-rich-quick scheme going with her. Like that would get you Mark back."

He pulled her up close to him and glared down at her as if he could do her some serious harm. Why did she hate him so much? he fumed.

"Mark is all I have left," she went on, her voice shaking. "As long as I'm breathing, you're not coming near him! Do you hear me? Don't even try!"

"You think you've got it all figured out, but you don't even have a clue," Ambrose snarled at her. "If you think I'm going to let you keep destroying my life, you're wrong!"

"It's already done. You can't do anything about it."

He glared at her. "What are you talking about? What did you tell Lisette?"

"I didn't have to tell her anything. She'll read all about it, and she'll know."

Ambrose felt the blood rise into his head. "What did you give her?"

"Something that appeared in the paper during the trial," she said with a laugh. "I keep copies of it in my purse. You never know when they'll come in handy."

"You old fool." Ambrose laughed. "She can't even read. She'll toss that paper the minute she gets away from you."

"No," Abigail said defiantly. "I saw her looking at it as she got into the taxi."

"Taxi? Which way did she go?"

"Like I'm going to tell you!"

"Tell me! Or I'll make you sorrier than you've ever been."

He pulled her up against his body and held her close, but instead of being intimidated by him, she screamed in his face, "I'm already sorry you were born, that you came into my daughter's life, that Jeanine and Mark had you as a father. Tell me, how much sorrier am I than that?" Then her body sagged under his grip and her voice got quieter. "Go ahead. Tell me something I don't know."

"Damn you!" he snarled and pushed her away with such force that she fell into a heap on the ground. "If you've screwed up things between me and Lisette, I'll find you and you'll be sorry."

She yelled something back at him, but by then he had crossed the street in front of the library and was out of her sight.

Okay, so he'd have to find Lisette all by himself. No problem. First, he'd go to her hotel and see if she was there, and if not, he'd go to the club and wait for her. He had to get to her and find out what Abigail had given her to read about him. Maybe she was looking for him right now, wanting him to read it to her, not believing anything of what Abigail had said.

That was it, he decided. Abigail had put her off as much as she put him off, and soon Lisette would return and help him get his son back.

It was as easy as that! No one would believe a crazy old woman like Abigail.

Least of all Lisette.

That was it, he decided. Abigail had put her off as much as she put him off, and soon Lisette would return and help him get his son back.

It was as easy as that! No one would believe a crazy old woman like Abigail.

Least of all Lisette.

Twenty minutes later, Lisette sat on a bench in a dark corner near the door to Professor Morris' office, waiting for Sophie and about to go crazy.

Not only did she need someone to read this article to her about Ambrose, but she also needed a cigarette badly. With "No Smoking" signs everywhere in the building, she didn't dare light up, and yet she couldn't go outside either because she didn't want to miss Sophie. So she sat there, tapping her foot and staring at the clock on the wall across from her. It was after one o'clock and still no Sophie.

Lisette got worried. What if she didn't show up? Who would she get to read the story to her? Someone needed to tell her more about this symposium thing, too. Suddenly, she heard footsteps coming down the hall toward her, and when she looked up she saw the girl she sat with at Lacey's funeral moving down the hall and stopping in front of Professor Morris's office.

"Hey, Sophie," Lisette yelled out to her as she was about to knock on the door.

The girl jumped and let out a yelp. She spun around and looked at Lisette. "You scared me half to death!" she said, gasping for breath. "I didn't see you."

"Do you remember me, Sophie?" Lisette said anxiously, getting off the bench and moving out of the shadows into the light.

As she did, Sophie gasped and then blurted out, "Lacey? Is that you?"

"No, I'm Lisette. You don't know my name, but I sat in the same pew with you at Lacey's funeral. Do you remember?"

Sophie drew back from her and looked at Lisette with wide eyes. Then she stammered, "I'm sorry. For a moment there I thought…" Her voice trailed off. "I thought…" she stammered again.

"I'm Lisette," she said quickly. "I'm a friend of Lacey's."

"You look just like her. I thought you were a…" Sophie's voice trailed off again.

"A ghost?" Lisette broke in. She didn't think she looked like Lacey, although they both had long blonde hair and were the same age. But Sophie did.

"It's just that…that…" Sophie struggled for words. "For a second, I thought, Lacey is alive! The nightmare is over. We can all go on with our lives."

Lisette came closer and saw the tears coming down Sophie's face. She reached out and touched Sophie's hand, saying softly, "Lacey's safe. No one can hurt her anymore."

"I miss her so much," Sophie cried out. "When I think of what he did to her…" Sophie wiped the tears from her face with the back of her hand. "It happened so fast. One minute she was alive, the next minute dead. That bastard didn't even stay around to tell us why. How could anyone do that to another human being?"

Then Sophie took a hard look at Lisette, "I do remember you. You sat next to my Gram at the funeral. Then you got up and ran off." Sophie paused and then went on, "Funny, Lacey never mentioned you. How did you know her?"

Lisette hesitated and then said, "I know her father. Too bad about what happened to her mom." At least that was the truth, Lisette told herself. She had met Lacey's dad at the funeral, and Lacey had told her about her mother.

"How did you find me?" Sophie asked. "What do you want?"

"Lacey told me you're studying to be a social worker. I came across this in the newspaper. Could you read it and tell me what you think?"

Lisette handed Sophie the paper that Abigail had given her.

Sophie looked at it for a moment and then back at Lisette. "This newspaper article is five years old. What do you care about something that happened so long ago?"

"It's a long story," Lisette said uneasily, not wanting to tell her more than she had to. "I need to know why this guy can't see his son any more."

Sophie looked down at the paper and silently read it to herself. Lisette broke in. "Could you read it out loud? I've read it, but I..." Lisette stammered as she lied. "...I broke my glasses this morning, and I can't remember what it says."

Sophie gave her an odd look. Then she said, "I'd like to help you out, but I've got an appointment with Professor Morris and I'm late."

Sophie turned and put her hand on the door.

"No, please. Don't go. You've got to help me. I'll do anything. Have you eaten lunch yet? I'm buying. I saw a place right across the street. If not for me, do it for Lacey. Please!"

Sophie looked at her and sighed. "I hate to blow off Professor Morris. We have a lot to talk about. The symposium is coming up soon and we haven't even decided on all the speakers. But it doesn't even sound like he's in there." Sophie knocked at the door, listened for a moment and then tried the doorknob. It was locked.

"I must have the wrong time," she said simply. Then she turned to Lisette and said, "I guess now I do have time for a quick bite." Sophie grabbed Lisette's arm and steered her toward the elevator. "That restaurant across the street lets you smoke even in the nonsmoking section. I'm dying for a cigarette."

"Me too," Lisette said, and then she giggled. "Funny, Lacey never told me you were a smoker."

"Funny, Lacey never told me about you, period! That makes us even."

The elevator door opened and they entered.

"Damn!" Sophie said as the doors closed. "I wish we could smoke in the elevator. Lacey and I tried once in our dorm, but we got caught. They've put those damn smoke detectors up everywhere and one puff sets off the bells and whistles like you're a criminal. It's just a cigarette! What's the big deal?"

Lisette smiled knowingly. Spoken like a true smoker, she thought.

She liked Sophie.

She liked her very much.

CHAPTER THIRTEEN

It's the Tease

By the time Ambrose had caught a taxi to take him across town to Lisette's hotel, he had his story straight and he was sure it would work.

He'd tell Lisette that if she helped him with Mark, she'd be helping out a kid who was damaged the way she was. He had a tough exterior, just like her, but underneath he was wounded and vulnerable.

As he jumped out of the taxi, raced up the steps into the hotel lobby and headed toward the front desk, Ambrose had another story ready. This one was for the desk clerk and it was about his "niece" who was staying at the hotel, but he had forgotten her room number. He was sure that one would work, too.

Soon he was inside the elevator, punching the button to the fourth floor where Lisette was staying. As the elevator ascended, Ambrose stood there, lost in a fantasy of what it would be like to have Mark back. They'd be a family again. What a victory that would be for him! He'd show Abigail. He'd show them all. He'd be on top again.

When the door of the elevator opened to Lisette's floor, Ambrose stepped out and walked up the hall to find her room. When he got to the door, he knocked confidently, sure that Lisette would immediately come, open it wide, and invite him in. Why did he run off like that, she'd want to know. Was it something she said? He'd explain everything, and the disasters of the morning would be forgotten. But Lisette didn't come to the door, so Ambrose waited for a moment and then knocked again. This time his knock was louder and more insistent, but still there was no answer. He didn't understand it. She had to be there. Where else could she have gone?

After a third try, rapping his knuckles hard against the door this time, he lost it. "Goddamn it, Lisette!" he screamed, kicking the door with his foot. "I know you're in there. Open the damn door!"

He jammed his right foot, then his left, against the door, one after the other until sweat poured down his face, which was bright red now. The door shook but never opened.

Suddenly, a woman's voice with a thick Spanish accent yelled at him from down the hall. "Stop that! Get away from there!"

A maid rushed toward him with a cart of towels, sheets, and bottles of cleanser. "What are you doing?" she demanded as she got closer.

Ambrose's mind whirred as he concocted a story, knowing that with his rumpled clothes and two days' growth of beard, he didn't look as though he belonged there. "I'm waiting for…" he stammered "…for my wife. This is our room."

He pointed at the door and then thrust his hands in and out of the pockets of his pants. "I've lost my key."

The maid wagged her finger in his face. "No banging on the door," she said. "What is your wife's name?"

"Lisette LaTour. She'll be registered under that."

The woman's eyes looked up at the room number on the door and then down at a sheet of paper on top of her cart. Her eyes stopped about halfway down, and she smiled. Ambrose sighed with relief. Lisette's name must be on that list. The maid grabbed a ring of keys hanging from her belt and said, "I shouldn't do this, but..."

She pushed a key into the lock, turned it, and opened the door. "Get another key at the front desk later, okay?"

"Muchas gracias, Senora," Ambrose beamed at her. "My wife thanks you, too."

What luck! he thought as he stepped into the room and closed the door behind him. So he had to lie a little – at least he was in the room. It was better this way. All he had to do now was wait for Lisette to show up.

He walked over to the bed, took his jacket off, and sat down facing the door so he'd be the first thing she'd see when she walked in. Then he waited. A few minutes went by, then ten, fifteen, twenty more, and still no Lisette. Should he be worried? All kinds of horrible thoughts came to him until he made himself stop, take a deep breath, and lay down on the bed. He could rest here a while. No one would bother him. He needed a rest. It had been a crazy day.

He could just close his eyes and rest here for a while.

Sophie and Lisette sat in Murray's Midtown Diner, puffing away on their cigarettes and looking over the menu.

This was fun, Lisette thought, not like being with Ambrose. Suddenly she didn't care if she ever saw Ambrose again. She looked up and smiled at Sophie.

"I can't believe how much you look like Lacey," Sophie said suddenly, breaking the silence between them.

Lisette blushed. "I guess I do. I don't really know."

"And I can't believe how you showed up at Lacey's funeral and then at Professor Morris' office today. It's like Lacey is reaching out to me from the grave." Sophie let out a laugh, as if she were making a joke, but it only made Lisette squirm in her seat.

If Sophie only knew, Lisette thought. Lacey was reaching out, all right, dragging them both deeper and deeper into this mess. Maybe she shouldn't have gone looking for Sophie. Lisette wasn't sure she could keep up with all the lies she had had to tell her.

Just then, the waitress came over and took their order. When she left, the two women sat smoking in silence for a moment, each lost in her own thoughts until the thought that popped into Lisette's head made her ask Sophie a question.

"You said before that you were planning to have a symposium. What's that, and what does it have to do with Lacey?"

Sophie put her cigarette out in the ashtray in front of them and leaned forward in her seat.

"A symposium is like a meeting," she explained. "It's a discussion of a topic by a few speakers and then the audience gets to ask questions or make comments or suggestions. It's to help educate people about an issue and get them concerned so that they'll want to take some kind of action." Sophie's voice rose, full of excitement, as she continued, "I want people to get mad about what happened to Lacey, and I want them to do something about it."

"But Lacey's dead. What's there to do?" Lisette asked, confused.

"There is a lot we can do," Sophie insisted. "I've been researching it on the Internet. Schools and colleges all over the county are already working on the issue of dating violence. Young women – and men, too – need to know the warning signs of abuse in a relationship and how to get help before it's too late. We all missed what was happening between Ari and Lacey. He never hit her or touched her physically, but he did emotionally and psychologically abuse her. Most of all, he was extremely possessive and jealous of her and wouldn't let her go when she wanted to end the relationship. He was always accusing her of seeing other guys when she wasn't doing anything like that, and he tried to isolate her from her family and friends. Until she met Jack, she never even thought seriously about another guy, and by then her relationship with Ari was pretty much over."

"You're talking about that night at The Keg, when Jack was dancing with Lacey and Ari dragged her off the dance floor and made her go home with him."

Sophie looked stunned. "You know about that?"

"Yeah, kind of," Lisette mumbled, afraid that she had said too much.

"I didn't realize how well you knew Lacey," Sophie began, but Lisette interrupted her, changing the subject and offering enthusiastically, "I want to help with this symposium. It sounds really important."

"Yeah, it is. We need to get the entire campus to demand some action or the college will just sweep the whole thing under the rug. We need more discussion on this campus about how to identify abuse in a relationship, and we need to have a central place where students can go if they need help. We have to make sure that what happened to Lacey won't happen to anyone else. If it can happen to her, it can happen to anyone!"

By now, Sophie was practically shouting, and she seemed embarrassed.

"Sorry," she said with a quick smile. "I can get a little carried away about this, but you get the idea. We need to have this symposium on the topic of dating violence on campus in order to get things moving. We have a lot of work to do. Some members of the faculty are behind us. That's why I was going to talk to Professor Morris today. He said he could help us get some of the city leaders involved. A real community effort! Everyone needs to help, he says."

Lisette looked wide-eyed at Sophie. She really was worked up about this symposium thing. Lisette hadn't seen anyone have so much passion about anything in a long time. Then suddenly

Sophie got very quiet. She sat back in her seat and, as she did, she pulled out the paper Lisette had given her out of her pocket.

"Sorry, I don't want to forget about what you asked me to read to you. You said this newspaper article was about a friend of yours, right?"

Lisette smiled to herself and watched Sophie unfold the paper in her hands. She liked that Sophie hadn't forgotten about why they had come to lunch and how important it was to Lisette to find out the real story about Ambrose. It was about as important as the symposium was to Sophie.

"Okay," Sophie began. "Here's what the editorial says."

Lisette wanted to stop her right there because she didn't know what an editorial was, but she didn't. She let Sophie to continue.

"'Attorney Jeffrey Jerome Alexander has a fool for a client,'" Sophie read aloud, "because today he was the one representing himself in the criminal case against him this week in the County Court. He's being given some leeway by the Honorable Jenny Jablonski, since he is a prominent member of the bar, but anyone who's been in that courtroom over the last few days knows that Attorney Alexander has finally gone too far.'"

Jeffrey Alexander, Lisette thought. That must be Ambrose's full name.

Sophie read on, "'What started out as a case of suspected abuse by Attorney Alexander of his six-year-old son, Mark, has ballooned into a full-blown 'he-said, she-said' debate. Except that now it's a battle between Attorney Alexander and his dead wife, Betsy, who was killed several months before in a car accident, and, by proxy, Betsy's mother, Attorney Alexander's mother-in-law, Abigail Derocher, who has been in the courtroom fighting for her grandson.'"

"What's a 'proxy'?" Lisette asked Sophie quickly. She didn't want to miss out on anything.

"A 'proxy' is someone who stands in for someone else. So here, this Abigail person is standing in for her daughter, Betsy, who's dead."

"Okay. I got it," Lisette replied. "Go on."

Sophie continued. "'What Attorney Alexander thinks he is doing is presenting evidence that he did not abuse his son. He claims instead that he was properly disciplining Mark in response to his son's behavior after the car accident that almost killed him – and did kill his mother and his younger sister, Jeanine. Not that one thing has anything to do with the other, as the prosecutor in the case has pointed out repeatedly, but Attorney Alexander has insisted on bringing it up at every turn as the excuse for his conduct toward his son. The prosecutor has strenuously objected whenever that issue has been raised and the judge has ruled such evidence irrelevant, but Mrs. Abigail Derocher, the prosecutor's own witness, opened a Pandora's Box upon cross-examination. She blurted out how Attorney Alexander was abusive to her daughter Betsy during their marriage and how, according to Mrs. Derocher, he had insisted on taking Betsy out on a learner's permit before she was ready to drive on a narrow, two-lane country highway in car with a manual transmission. He caused the accident that day. Her daughter would never have driven off the road with her children in her car.'"

Isn't that what Abigail had said to her earlier today, that Ambrose was responsible for the accident? But Lisette thought Ambrose made it sound like the accident had happened because his kids were acting up in the backseat of the car. What was the truth? What did Sophie think about that? Lisette didn't want to stop and ask her. She needed her to read on.

"'That opened the door for Attorney Alexander to refute the statement, and he has gone after it like a pit bull. The idea that anyone would blame him for having any part in this nightmare is apparently so abhorrent to Attorney Alexander that he has turned the trial into a crusade to exonerate all men wrongly accused of abusing and exerting undue control over their wives. But all he has managed to show is how men operate when they deny they have been abusive, and how women and children suffer as a result.'"

Sophie stopped for a second and looked up. "We've been studying about the impact of spousal abuse on the children in sociology class. This guy sounds like a real power and control freak!"

Lisette rolled her eyes and said sarcastically, "Tell me about it."

Sophie continued reading. "'Judge Jablonski has done her best to rein in this proceeding and focus the parties on the young boy who is now in the custody of his grandmother. But who knows how this trial will turn out? Whatever the outcome, let's hope Attorney Alexander will remember that what's at stake here is the future of a young boy who lost his mother and younger sister in a terrible accident. Now is not the time to blame others, but to heal and reconcile so that the best interests of this child – and not his pompous father or his accusatory grandmother – are served.'"

Sophie stopped reading and looked at Lisette. "What happened to this Mark? He must be, what, about ten years old now."

Lisette sighed, "He's still with his grandmother, but Ambrose wants him back."

"Who's Ambrose?" Sophie asked, confused.

"I mean Jeffrey," Lisette said quickly. "He calls himself Ambrose now."

"You know this guy?" Sophie was incredulous.

"Yeah, he wants to be my business manager."

"What do you need a manager for?"

"My act," Lisette said simply, but there was a hedge in her voice. She wasn't sure how much she wanted Sophie to know about what she did for a living. "But I didn't know this about him until today."

"I don't know what your act is about, but this guy could be dangerous. If he could hurt his wife and kid, he could hurt you, too."

"Goddamn it!" Lisette suddenly exploded. "I wish everyone would stop saying that. Ambrose isn't a killer. Not like Ari. And Lacey knows that too!"

Sophie gaped at Lisette, stunned, as if she wasn't sure she had heard Lisette correctly. "Are you saying Lacey knew Ari was going to kill her?"

"No, that's not what I meant. If she did, she never would've gone to his room that night. Not after what happened at The Keg."

"What do you know about that night?" Sophie asked, her eyes glued to Lisette. "You two were that close? How did you meet Lacey anyway?"

Lisette didn't know what to say. She hated to lie to Sophie, but she didn't think Sophie was ready to hear the whole truth.

"I only met Lacey recently," Lisette said softly.

"How recently?" Sophie quizzed her.

"That's hard to explain," Lisette said, her voice shaky now. "I mean…." she stammered, then blurted out, "What do you think happens to people after they die?"

"After they die, they're dead. They leave this physical plane and their spirit goes somewhere else. Like heaven or hell, whatever you believe."

"But what if they get stuck?" Lisette offered. "What if you don't have a body anymore, but you aren't some place else either? What if Lacey is, you know, stuck and needs our help?"

Sophie gulped. "You mean like she can't move on? I've heard about that."

"What if Lacey's stuck and it has something to do with Ari? What happened after he put his hand through the window at The Keg? How did things get so bad between them?"

"I can tell you what happened. Ari was acting like a complete jerk at The Keg, and when we got to the emergency room that night, things only got worse. But it wasn't Lacey's fault. Jack and I saw it all."

Jack was with her? That surprised Lisette. She thought Jack had left Lacey on the dance floor that night and that was it. Now Jack had something more to do with this, but what? Sophie was fighting back her tears now, but Lisette knew she had to push on. "You've got to tell me what happened."

Sophie gave her a desperate look. "It's so hard to remember." Her voice was choked with tears, but she went on. "Now I can see it all so clearly, but then none of us saw what could have helped poor Lacey."

Suddenly the waitress' voice broke in.

"Who's got the double cheeseburger, no onion, with fries?"

"It's mine," Lisette said, thankful for the interruption. They both needed to stop and get something in their stomachs. As Sophie wiped away her tears, the waitress put the cheeseburger deluxe in front of Lisette and the one with all the works in front of Sophie.

"The food looks great," she said to Sophie as the waitress walked away, and then added with a smile, "Pass the ketchup, would you?"

As Sophie finished the last bite of her cheeseburger at the Midtown Diner, she sighed. "Do you really want me to tell you what else happened the night Ari put his hand through the window at The Keg?"

"Yes," Lisette said eagerly, swallowing the last bite of her burger. Then she added, more thoughtfully, "If it's not too hard."

"No, it's just that…" Sophie's voice dropped off and her face went pale. "Every time I think about what that bastard did, I get so mad. How could he… he…" Again her voice trailed off. Then

Sophie began to cry and Lisette felt terrible. She liked Sophie. She liked her very much. Maybe she shouldn't push her for the whole story right away.

"Look," Lisette said, trying to make it easier. "Tell me this. You read the article I gave you about Ambrose. Do you think what happened to Lacey could happen to me?"

"It depends," Sophie said, her voice thick and mysterious.

Lisette screwed up her face. "On what?"

"On the kind of guy this Ambrose is. You see, Ari was a manipulator. He counted on Lacey being kind to him and trying to let him down easy after she broke up with him. That's how he got her to come to his room that night, and when she wouldn't go along with what he wanted, he killed her."

"Do you think that every guy who doesn't get what he wants from a girl could kill her?" Lisette laughed. "If that's true, I'm in big trouble. I play the 'tease' with every guy in the audience. So far nothing bad has happened." Lisette paused. "Except that lately I've been attacked on the stage – and off – but that only started when…"

Suddenly Lisette stopped. Oh my God! she thought. It had all started when Lacey came into her that night at the Bare Bottom. The guys attacked Lisette on the stage, the man with the knife cornered her at her dressing room door, and then she had to leave that job. When she went to the Pussycat, strange things happened to her there, too. Was all this connected to Lacey being inside her? Lisette couldn't believe it! She wanted to tell Sophie everything now and hear what she thought, but when Lisette looked over at Sophie, she saw she was playing with the last of the fries on her plate, dipping them into a pool of catsup and then staring off into space. Sophie wasn't with her right now. She seemed lost in thought and still struggling with how and why Ari killed Lacey.

That became clearer when suddenly Sophie looked up at Lisette and said, "Let's get back to what happened that night at the hospital. It is a good example of what a manipulator Ari was."

"If you think that will help," Lisette said quietly, her thoughts still in confusion.

Sophie nodded and began. "When Jack and I got to the hospital that night…"

"Jack was with you?" Lisette broke in. She couldn't help herself.

"Yeah. He felt bad about what had happened on the dance floor, so he came looking for Lacey, but by then she had left with Ari, stranding me and the other girls at The Keg. Jack found a ride for the girls and drove me to find Lacey. After we heard about all the blood from the cut on Ari's hand, we figured she had taken him to the hospital.

"Sure enough, we found her in the emergency room at St. Joe's. While Jack parked the car, I went inside. She was there in the waiting room, and when I came up to her, she looked at me as if she was expecting me, like the whole thing was no big deal."

"But it was," Lisette said. She got it. Why didn't Lacey?

"Sure, it was," Sophie went on. "She had driven off with that lunatic, Ari, without her purse, driver's license, the keys to our dorm, money, or anything. I was so relieved to see her that I pulled her out of her chair and hugged her hard.

"'Thank God, you are all right,' I said to her. 'Where's Ari?' She flipped her hair over her shoulder and scowled. 'He's in the suture room,' she said, 'getting his hand stitched up.' 'Is he okay?' I asked. 'What the hell happened?' She laughed. 'You know Ari. All drama, no substance!'"

"What did she mean by that?" Lisette broke in.

"Oh, Ari was always so dramatic. *He* loved her *so* much, *he* couldn't *live* without her, and *he* wanted her with him *all* the time. It was always about him. But this time, it got to her. She told me she was fed up and wanted nothing more to do with him." Sophie shook her head with disgust. "Not that I hadn't told her a thousand times that Ari was creepy and that the way he treated her was weird. This time, I let her know that he was trouble, big trouble, but she begged me not to lecture her. She said she felt bad enough, leaving me and the other girls stranded at The Keg. Then suddenly she asked, 'How did you get here?'"

Now a smile came over Sophie's face. "That was the cool part. I looked over my shoulder, just as Jack was walking in from the parking lot, and Lacey's face lit up when she saw him. 'He insisted on helping me find you,' I whispered to her as she waved him over. When he got there, Lacey gave him a big hug and they held each other for a long moment. I could see what a great couple they were."

"So, he really liked Lacey?" Lisette asked, trying to imagine the two of them together. Was Jack the one for her? she wondered. Had he just shown up at the wrong time and place?

"He was completely taken with her," Sophie said, smiling again. "He told her, 'This is all my fault. I shouldn't have asked you to dance.' 'No,' Lacey insisted, 'I asked you and dancing with you was the best part of the night. It was Ari who was the jerk.'"

"Wow!" Lisette said. "So she really liked Jack, too, didn't she? Did they hook up that night?"

"I wish. Then Lacey would be here telling you the story, not me. No, Ari was still in control."

"But I thought you said that she and Ari were through that night, right?" Lisette asked. "That she didn't want anything to do with him anymore?"

"Yes, but that didn't mean that he couldn't still get to her."

"But how? What did he do?"

Sophie frowned and went on. "Suddenly, we heard a voice call for Lacey from across the room, and we looked up and saw Tom,

Ari's friend from school. He came right up to Lacey and screamed in her face, 'Where's Ari?' Then he looked at Jack. 'Is he your new boyfriend already? You can't keep your hands off other guys, can you? You're nothing but a whore!'"

"Jesus!" Lisette exclaimed. "What was it with this guy Tom?"

"I don't have to tell you that he and Ari were thick as thieves, but Jack was on Tom in a flash. He grabbed him by his shirt and yanked his face up close to his. 'Don't talk to her like that,' Jack yelled at him and then pushed him back against the chairs and onto the floor. Tom looked up at Jack and yelled back at him, 'You're screwing her already, aren't you? That's why you're all hot to protect her.' Jack lunged at Tom, punching him in the face and stomach. Lacey and I tried to stop them, but we couldn't. Suddenly a nurse came running in and went right for the two of them and pulled them apart. 'Haven't we had enough male testosterone for one night?' she said. Then she looked at Tom. 'Are you the friend Ari called?' Tom nodded as he wiped blood off his lip. 'Then come with me,' she barked.

"As Tom was being led away, Lacey jumped in, 'How come he gets to go when I've been waiting here for an hour?'

"'That's not my problem,' the nurse replied. 'Your friend asked to make a phone call, and this is who he called to take him home. I suggest you go home, too.' That infuriated Lacey, and she sputtered, 'Fine,' and then added, 'Tell Ari…' She stopped for a moment and blurted out, 'On second thought, don't tell him shit. He doesn't deserve to know how the hell I feel.' By then, Jack and I had grabbed her by both arms and steered her out of there. When I got into the backseat of Jack's car with her, she was sobbing.

"'How could I have been so stupid to fall for such a creep?' she said. 'What am I going to do? How am I going to get away from him?' I didn't know what she meant by that at the time, but some part of her must have known that breaking up with Ari wasn't going to be easy. And it wasn't. For about a week after that, Ari kept calling and emailing her, tormenting her. Half the time he would be apologizing to her, and the rest of the time he was blaming her for everything. I know, because when she wouldn't talk to him, he'd call or email me. She refused to see him until the night he killed her. I wasn't in our room when she left. I wish I had been – I would've stopped her. But she thought she could deal with him, so she just left me a note. All it is said was, 'Gone to see Ari. Back in ten minutes.' I never saw her again."

With that, Sophie's voice shook, and she stopped talking.

Lisette looked at her blankly. "But I don't understand. If Lacey knew Ari would never let her go, didn't she get it that she was in danger?"

Sophie slowly shook her head. "You have to understand Lacey. She thought she could solve the problem all by herself. That if she went there and told him one last time to leave her alone, it would work." Sophie was silent again and then gave Lisette a long, hard look. "You know how he killed her, don't you?" Sophie swallowed hard. "He shot her twice. Once in the back and then again…" She took a deep breath before she went on. "He shot her in the face." Her voice cracked. "He destroyed her beautiful face!"

Oh, God! Lisette pulled back in horror. No, she didn't know that. Oh, Lacey! Lacey! No wonder she was afraid for Lisette. Not just because of Ambrose but because of what she did up on that stage every night.

Lisette felt a shudder go through her body. She played the tease with those guys every night, and she never felt any danger. The job was just something her mother had done and she had fallen into, too. But was there a man out there who could do to her what Ari did to Lacey? Was Ambrose that man?

If it could happen to Lacey, it could happen to anyone.

Oh, Lacey! Tell me it isn't true!

Where was Lacey? Lisette hadn't felt or heard her voice inside her for a long time.

Now, just when she needed her, Lacey was gone.

CHAPTER FOURTEEN

From the Beginning

Lacey wasn't going to give up on her father.

For a while now she had been sitting in the diner with Lisette, listening to Sophie telling her about that night in the emergency room with Ari. But Lacey knew how the story ended, and while she was glad to see that Sophie and Lisette had finally gotten together, Lacey had other pressing things to do.

She had to get the real story of her mother's death out of her father or she'd never get out of Lisette's body. That knowledge, she believed, was key to her understanding and forgiving both her parents so that she, like her mother, could move on. Determined to break into her father's thoughts, she suddenly found herself with him sitting on the grass in front of her mother's grave. He was crying and emotionally vulnerable, and of course that was always Lacey's way into what went on inside her father's head.

With tears streaming down his face, he was telling himself, and Lacey suspected his dead wife at her grave too, how good it was that no one alive knew how Marge had died. He had vowed to Marge on this very spot, right after her funeral, that Lacey and Jimmie would never know.

Yeah, Lacey thought. He sure kept that promise although it had caused her a lot of pain when she was alive. But now that she was dead, she listened as her father remembered it all from the beginning.

On the day of his wife's death, Howie came home early from work because he was worried about his son, Jimmie.

His son's full name was James Howard, after his grandfather and father, but Jimmie was the name that stuck with him. Howie remembered how proud he was of having a son, and although he told himself he loved his daughter, Jimmie was indeed very special to him.

It had only been six weeks since they had brought him home from the hospital and Howie wanted to stay home all day, every day, and be with Jimmie. But in those days, paternity leave was unheard of, and it was considered out of the question for a man to be so preoccupied with a baby. Babies were for the mother to take care of, but Howie wasn't sure that Marge was up to that task.

Howie remembered how Marge had had some problems with depression after Lacey was born, but not like this. It was as if Marge knew how attached Howie was to this baby and she resented him – no, he'd have to use a stronger word – she *hated* him for it. Suddenly, everyone's attention moved from her, the pregnant mother, to Jimmie, the exciting new baby. Even Lacey, then five years old, was entranced with her new baby brother.

The first few weeks of Jimmie's life didn't go well. Marge needed a lot of help with the baby and in taking care of herself. Her labor was hard, harder than with her firstborn, and she was more exhausted. At first, she let one of the grandmothers come and help her, but eventually she insisted she was fine and reluctantly everyone went away.

Thinking back on it now, Howie was the one who wanted another baby, not Marge. But he thought once the baby came, she'd come around. She was a woman. Women were naturally supposed to be mothers.

That morning, Marge woke up early with Jimmie and seemed rather vague when Howie asked her before he went to work what she was going to do that day. With Lacey in school and someone coming to do the weekly clean, he didn't see this as a particularly hard day for his wife. She could take care of the baby and she'd be fine. He called her a few times from work that morning to check in but got Myra, the cleaning lady, instead. Myra assured him that all was well and told him that both Jimmie and Marge were taking naps. Howie was relieved.

Still, he made the effort to finish what he needed to do at the office and came home early that afternoon. He called his mother to pick up Lacey at school and keep her until dinner time so he could spend some time with his son and with Marge. They really hadn't had time together since before Jimmie's birth and that might help their strained relationship.

He left the office, confident that his idea of coming home early was a good one and he looked forward to surprising Marge and being with the baby. But when he reached the house and pulled into the driveway, he saw someone at the back of the house, standing by the garage window and looking inside. He got out of the car and walked in that direction when he saw the figure move slightly and he realized it was Marge. She was alone, standing there barefoot in her robe and nightgown and she had a blank look on her face.

He wanted to yell out to her, but he was afraid if he startled her she'd scamper off like a frightened rabbit. He needed to find out where Jimmie was. If he wasn't with her, where was he? So, he moved slowly and quietly toward her until he stepped behind her and encircled her with his arms. Then he spoke softly into her ear.

"Marge, honey! What are you doing out here? Where's Jimmie?"

She turned her head to look at him and then back at the garage.

At first, he thought she was trying to avoid him, and that pissed him off, but then he realized that she was, in fact, answering his question with a gesture. For when Howie looked in the direction of the garage, he could see Jimmie in the car lying quietly in the backseat. His arms were raised up outside of the blanket wrapped tightly around his body, but he wasn't moving. It was as if he had been suddenly overtaken by sleep, his arms in mid-motion reaching out for something.

What was going on? Had Marge put Jimmie to sleep in the back of the car? That didn't make sense. According to the doctor, she wasn't even supposed to be outside for another week, let alone driving with Jimmie somewhere.

Suddenly Howie felt a vibration inside the garage and realized that because it was a big old building, it had muted the sound of the car running inside until now. Then he realized that Jimmie was inside a car spewing out gas fumes while all the doors and windows of the garage closed. No wonder he wasn't moving.

"Oh my God! Marge!" Howie screamed as he flew to the side door of the garage and grabbed at the handle. "What the hell is going on here?"

The door was locked, and he turned in panic to Marge.

"Where's the key? Give me the key to the garage. Now!"

She looked at him and then back at Jimmie. "I'm sending him back, Howie," she said in a dull, flat voice. "He's not supposed to be here."

Howie ignored her and threw his whole body against the door but it wouldn't budge. Quickly he moved around to the front door of the garage and pulled on the door handle there. As he tugged, he prayed it would be open, but it too was locked. By now, Marge had walked over and was standing next to him with an empty, blank look on her face.

He grabbed her around the shoulders and shook her.

"Where's the key, Marge? What have you done with it? You know we never lock these doors. I have to find the key."

She gave him no response.

Howie was frantic now. Who knew how long Jimmie had been in there? There wasn't time to call anyone. Jimmie could already be dead. He had to do it. He had to save Jimmie.

"Please, God, I'll do anything," he muttered. "Just let Jimmie be alive. Take me. Take Marge, but not Jimmie. Please, God. Not my son!"

He looked around quickly and saw a small wheelbarrow leaning up against the side of the garage. He grabbed it, lifted it up over his head, and aimed it at the window in the side door of the garage.

"Stand back," he screamed at Marge, who was hovering behind him now and pulling desperately at his arm.

"He's with God!" she wailed. "Let him go back where he belongs. He'll be a happy baby up in heaven. You'll see. He's going to God!"

"Let go of me, you lunatic," Howie exploded, wrenching her hand off him with a sudden, sharp movement that sent her sprawling on the ground. "If Jimmie is dead, this is all your fault."

Then he heard the simple sound of something metallic hitting the pavement and he looked back to see her scrambling to retrieve a shiny, gold key only a few feet away from her.

"Why, you little…" he screamed, as he dropped the wheelbarrow and rushed toward the key. "You had it in your hand all the time. Give it to me now!"

She screeched in pain as he stepped on her outstretched hand and grabbed for the key himself. With his hand shaking, he took the key, turned back to the garage door, and shoved it into the lock. The door open quickly and he rushed in, but the fumes from the car almost overwhelmed him. His eyes stung and grabbed at his throat, coughing and choking as he pushed himself into the garage toward the car.

Thank God, the back door to the car was unlocked so he swung it open and reached in to grab Jimmie. The child was limp and lifeless in his arms, but he had hope. He repeated his prayer, almost without thinking, Please, God, let Jimmie live. Take me or Marge, but let him live!

He moved quickly to the side door of the garage, but Marge stood in front of it, her arms spread out, trying to keep him from getting out with Jimmie.

"What? Are you totally out of your mind?" he screamed as he rushed at her. "Get out of my way before I run you down!"

But she stood there, so he shoved her aside with such force that he heard her hit the ground with a thud behind him. He didn't look back. All he could think about was getting Jimmie out of there before it was too late.

As he held the baby tightly in his arms, he could hear Jimmie's breath coming in short gasps, his face a bright pink color. Still, he was breathing and that gave him hope, the only hope he had that his son might be all right.

Please, God! he prayed again as he ran down the driveway and jumped into his car with Jimmie. He drove like a maniac down the driveway and out into the street toward the hospital. Please let him live! Please! he pleaded. If there was a God, he'd owe him one for this.

If only his son would survive!

Howie didn't even think about Marge until later.

Of course, he had cursed her all the way to the hospital. What if he hadn't come home early? What kind of a lunatic was she, saying all that crazy stuff about sending Jimmie back to God?

Damn her! Was she doing it to spite him for making her have this baby, this dear, sweet child?

He told the doctors and nurses in the emergency room only what they needed to know. That he had been working on his car in the garage and he didn't realize how close his son was to the fumes. The doctor gave him a look, but it didn't go any further when Jimmie checked out all right. By the time he left the hospital with his son, he had already called his mother and told her that there had been an accident. He'd be there soon to tell her and Lacey about it.

"Are you all right?" his mother asked excitedly.

"Yes," Howie said, "and Jimmie is fine, too."

"And what about Marge? How is she?"

Suddenly, it struck him. He didn't know how Marge was. He wasn't even sure where she was. For all he knew she might be wandering the streets in her nightgown. As he drove home, he realized that all along he expected Marge to have wandered back outside the garage and in the house by now. But as he drove up the driveway and saw the garage, suddenly it hit him. All the garage doors and windows were shut. Had the side door shut behind him as he rushed out with Jimmie? Would Marge have locked herself back in there? Was she crazy enough to try to kill herself if she couldn't kill Jimmie first?

A sinking feeling went through Howie, and he remembered what he had prayed so fervently hours before: "Please let Jimmie live. Take me or Marge. Let him live."

Howie jumped out of the car and rushed toward the garage, leaving Jimmie on the front seat. Frantically, he began bargaining with God. He hadn't meant what he said before. He did want everyone to live. But when he ran to the window of the side door to the garage and peered in, he couldn't see Marge. The car was no longer running – it must be out of gas – but where was Marge?

"Are you in there, Marge?" he cried out, banging on the window and rattling its panes. "Marge! Marge!"

He grabbed the wheelbarrow again and lifted it over his head. This time, he crashed into the window and felt splinters of glass fly at him. He grabbed for the door handle on the inside and opened the door. Trying not to breathe too heavily the poisoned air in the garage, quickly he moved to where he had last seen Marge. But she wasn't there. Instead, he spun around and saw her in the corner curled up with her robe drawn up to her waist and her legs bare. Her face was a bright pink, and as he went over and touched it, her skin was cold.

"Oh, God!" he cried out, bending down next to her, putting his ear to her chest to feel a heartbeat. But there was none. She was dead. He was sure of it. But why? How? What had happened in the garage after he left with Jimmie? Why was he left to try to understand what she had just done? Why did she get to be crazy and he had to worm his way out of it? What could he say? That his wife was trying to kill their baby so he knocked her out and left her in a garage full of deadly fumes? But *had* he knocked her out? She had to have crawled over to this spot, hadn't she? If so, why didn't she get up and turn off the car, or break the window and save herself?

This much he knew. He hadn't intentionally left her to die, but he saved his son. She was the crazy one, the criminal, not him. What could he tell the police – that his wife was a crazy, cold-blooded murderer? No, he couldn't. He could tell them his wife was lost and confused and got locked in the garage. He didn't have to tell them about Jimmie or that he had taken him to the emergency room. They'd have no reason to check hospital records unless he told them – and no one else knew, not even his mother. He'd tell them what he had told her. That there had been an accident, a freak accident in the garage, and that Marge was dead. That was all.

It was a plausible story. He could explain everything and no one would suspect otherwise. That way, Marge wouldn't have committed suicide and she could be buried in the church cemetery and her children wouldn't be stigmatized for life. Lacey and Jimmie would never know what really happened. But what *had* happened? Was she suicidal? Did she mean to hurt Jimmie? He didn't know. He only cared that it was over now. He'd go get Jimmie out of the car, take him into the house, and call the police. He'd tell the story about finding Marge in the garage.

He could do that. He could pull that off. He had to. There was no other way to save his family.

No way.

CHAPTER FIFTEEN

Chasing Spirits

Lisette sat across from Sophie in the diner, watching as she puffed on a cigarette and studied the check for their lunch that the waitress had left on the table between them.

But Lisette couldn't focus on anything as mundane as money, not with the image stuck in her mind of Ari putting the gun to Lacey's head and blowing her face off. How could he do a thing like that? she wondered. What was wrong with him? Surely, he was burning in hell right now. But what if he wasn't? What if he was somewhere wandering around like Lacey was? If he came for Lacey, would he come for her, too? Was that possible? How did all this work? With each thought, Lisette got more and more spooked until Sophie suddenly spoke up and took her mind off these terrifying thoughts.

"I'm sorry I told you about how Lacey was shot. It's hard to hear something like that about someone you know." Then she paused and added, "How do you know Lacey anyway? You never said."

"I… I…" Lisette began, her voice shaking for fear of where this was going. "I was working nearby the night that she was killed."

There, Lisette thought. That wasn't a lie, but it wasn't the whole truth either.

Still Sophie didn't let it go. "And where was that?"

Lisette gulped and took a deep breath. "I was working at the Bare Bottom Dance Club."

Sophie stared at her. "You mean that strip joint near the college? You worked there? Like as a waitress?"

"Not exactly." Lisette hesitated then said quickly, "I was one of the dancers."

Sophie laughed. "You mean a stripper? How could Lacey know a stripper and not tell me about it? What a hoot!"

Lisette took a deep breath. There was no way not to tell Sophie now.

"It wasn't like that. I've only known Lacey since she's been dead."

"What?" Sophie was so startled that she dropped her lit cigarette and had to grab it quickly from the seat of the booth. She stubbed it out in an ashtray and looked at Lisette. "What do you mean you've only known her since she was dead?"

Suddenly, the words spilled out of Lisette's mouth. "Look, I know this sounds crazy, but Lacey's inside me. She's in my head talking to me all the time. I can even see her sometimes. It's weird, but it's true!"

Lisette cringed and waited for Sophie's reaction.

"Are you telling me that Lacey's spirit is inside your body?"

"Is that what it is?"

"Geeze, I don't know anything about spirits. But my grandmother says that spirits can sometimes get stuck between the two worlds and inhabit another person's body. I don't understand how or why. You'd have to talk to her about that." Then Sophie continued excitedly, "But tell me, how does it work with you and Lacey? Is she talking to you right now? What's she saying? Is she asking about me?"

"No," Lisette groaned. "I haven't heard her voice all day. That's the problem."

"Then how do you know she's there?"

"I don't, but she went away before and then came back. I guess I'll hear from her again."

Sophie hung her head. "Jesus! This is so unbelievable. Here I'm thinking Lacey is gone forever, and now I find out that she's stuck in the body of a stripper. How weird is that? Wait 'til I tell Gram! She'll go nuts when she finds out Lacey's still around."

Lisette frowned. "But she's dead, right? We all went to her funeral. Her body was in the casket. So how come I can hear her like a voice in my head?" Lisette stopped a moment, remembering something Sophie had said. "Your grandmother knows about this kind of stuff? Can she help get Lacey out of me?"

"Maybe. She works with dead people's spirits all the time, but I'm not exactly sure what she does. If you want, I can take you to see her."

Lisette's eyes lit up. "Would you? Does she live nearby? Can we go there now?"

"Yeah. She has an apartment not far from here. She's a shaman – that's a kind of a healer. Let me call and see if she's home."

Sophie reached into her purse and pulled out her cell phone. Lisette watched her punch a few buttons and then put it up to her ear.

"Hey, Gram!" Sophie said almost immediately. "You are not going to believe this!"

Lisette listened while Sophie talked, feeling almost hopeful that she had finally found someone who could help her. Maybe this is why Lacey told me to go find Sophie, she thought. Maybe Lacey is still with me after all.

When Sophie flipped her phone shut, Lisette asked eagerly, "What did she say?"

"She says we can come over right away," Sophie said, tossing her cell phone in her purse and pulling some money out of her wallet. "Let's go. I've got lunch covered."

"No, no!" Lisette insisted. "I want to pay. It's the least I can do after all you've done for me."

"Hey, don't get your hopes up," Sophie said with a shake of her head. "I'm not so sure that Radiance has anything in her bag of tricks that can help you."

"Who's Radiance?" Lisette asked, confused. "I thought your Gram's name was Ruth when I met her at Lacey's funeral."

"Oh, I forgot." Sophie sighed, as though embarrassed by the whole thing. "That's the name my Gram uses when she does her shaman work."

"Radiance? What kind of a name is that?"

"You know, it's like a stage name. You must have one of those, too."

"Sure! Mine is Attila the Hunny!"

Sophie gave her a look. "You do a strip act about Attila the Hun?"

Lisette nodded and threw some money on the table for the waitress.

"Oh my!" Sophie said with a laugh. "Radiance is going to love you!"

Ambrose sat in a booth in the hotel coffee shop, sipping a cup of hot, black coffee to clear his head and trying to figure out what to do next.

He had woken up a few minutes ago, after sleeping all afternoon in Lisette's hotel room. He woke up with a start when he heard someone out in the hall and thought it was her, but it wasn't. It was just the maid coming in to clean the room, and that's when he decided he'd better leave.

Now that he had some coffee and felt more alert, he made a list of places where Lisette might be. Obviously, he could find her dancing tonight at the Pussycat Club, but he wasn't sure he'd be able to get near the place with Wiley and Webster on the lookout for him. He could wait outside the club for Lisette, but he didn't want to accost her on the street. She might panic and run away from him forever. No, he needed to appear as normal and calm as he could, he decided, even though he was seething inside with anger at Lisette.

How could she have disappeared? Was she hiding from him? Had Abigail talked to her again and poisoned her against him? He could try to explain to Lisette what had happened between him and Mark, but he didn't want to appear desperate and crazy in front of her. It was bad enough that he lost it when he saw Abigail this afternoon. God! How he hated that bitch! She had made his life miserable ever since Betsy and Jeanine were killed and that wasn't even his fault. He couldn't let Abigail ruin his chances with Lisette. In the short time he had known this girl, she had changed everything for him.

Abigail wasn't going to ruin it. He was determined.

There was no going back now!

Whatever Lisette expected to see when she got to Radiance's apartment with Sophie, it wasn't what she saw when Radiance opened the door and invited them in.

The lady who had sat next to her in the church at Lacey's funeral, the one who kept pushing her black hat down over her bushy red hair was gone, and another person, a wild, crazy person named Radiance, had taken her place.

"Come in, girls! Come in!" Radiance said with a big, sweeping gesture of her hands. Lisette could see that Radiance was still as short and big around as she had remembered her, but today she could see that most of what was big about her was her breasts. They came off her shoulders like two large, squishy masses of gelatin and wiggled around as she grabbed Sophie first and drew her into a big hug. When she turned to Lisette, she didn't know where to look as those two big ones came at her. She thought she had seen every kind of woman's breasts as a stripper, but she had never seen anything like Radiance's huge boobs.

When Radiance finally let go, Lisette was able to take all of her in. Today, she was wearing a long, flowing purple skirt and a colorful top. Her bright red curly hair hung loose down her back in perfect ringlets and didn't look so brassy in this light. On her head, Radiance wore a sequined headband that made Lisette think of her as someone's fairy godmother. Maybe she could wave her magic wand, Lisette mused, and make Lacey disappear from inside her.

"You remember Lisette, don't you, Gram?" Sophie said with an easy smile.

"Of course I do," Radiance replied, as she closed the door behind them. "We were worried about you running out of the church like that at Lacey's funeral. I'm glad to see you are okay."

Lisette wasn't sure how okay she was, but instead of arguing about it, she let Radiance put an arm around each of them and bring them into the apartment. Lisette was curious to see what was there. She was afraid that the place would be dark and full of weird, evil-looking things since, according to Sophie, Radiance hung around with dead people. From the outside, the building looked spooky enough. It had high black iron gates in the front and a dark, muddy river in the back. But once inside, Radiance's apartment was fabulous. As they entered the small, cozy front room, there was stuff everywhere – books and plants, artwork, brightly painted animal figures, and lots of candles. It all fit Radiance so perfectly.

"So, you like it?" Radiance asked, as if she could read Lisette's mind.

"Yes," Lisette gushed. "I love what you've done with it!"

"Then come into my workroom, and we'll get acquainted."

Not sure what to expect, Lisette cautiously followed Sophie down the hall. Stepping inside, she found the workroom to be a magical place. This room had big windows on the far side, and from there Lisette could see some of the buildings on the campus and the lush, green hills that surrounded the city in the distance. On another wall, there were tall shelves of books and mobiles made of paper, string, and other shiny objects hanging from the ceiling. But what really caught Lisette's eye was the large number of drums placed on the opposite wall. Each drum had a different brightly colored picture painted on it, and below them there was a stack of blankets and soft cushions on the floor.

"I've never seen so many drums!" Lisette said. "What are they all for?"

Radiance smiled. "They help me do my work. Drumming is a big part of it."

Before Lisette could ask Radiance more about the drums, Sophie lunged for a low, small table in the middle of the room. "Oh Gram! You made my favorite! Double-chocolate-chip cookies!"

She grabbed a cookie from a plate and stuffed it into her mouth, then fell happily onto the floor where she poured herself a cup of tea from a pot also on the table.

"Sophie!" her grandmother scolded her. "Where are your manners? Pour tea for all of us while I make our guest feel more at ease."

Sophie nodded and poured, while Radiance pointed Lisette toward the couch near the table.

"Why don't you sit there, my dear?" she said cheerily and then added with a wave of her hand, "Just throw those pillows on the floor. Sit back and relax."

Lisette looked at Radiance and managed a smile. She liked that Radiance wanted her to feel comfortable, and the tea and cookies made her feel at home. But she couldn't relax, wondering about the drums and how they were a big part of Radiance's work. Was she going to beat Lacey out of her? Was that what this was all about?

Before Lisette could ask, Radiance settled into the armchair near her and said softly, "Tell me something about yourself."

Startled, Lisette didn't know what to say so she took the cup of tea Sophie offered her and sat back, letting the hot liquid in the cup warm her hands.

Suddenly, Sophie practically leapt up off the floor.

"I can tell you something about Lisette," she blurted out. "She's a stripper. She dances under the name of 'Attila the Hunny.' Isn't that cool? She was working at the club joint near the college the night that Lacey was killed."

Lisette watched Radiance's face, fearing a bad reaction.

Instead, Radiance smiled and asked gently, "Do you like dancing?"

"I guess so. I've never really thought about doing anything else. My mother was a dancer and I sort of fell into it."

"So that explains it," Radiance replied.

"That explains what?"

"Why there is so much male energy around you."

Lisette twisted around in her seat. "There is? Where? I don't feel anything."

"You wouldn't, but it makes sense now why Lacey has taken up in your body."

Lisette's eyes widened. "It does? But I didn't even know Lacey. I'm sorry she was killed, but why me? What does she have to do with me?"

"That's what we're going to find out. We're going to start by having you take a journey today. The drums are going to help you do that."

Lisette was confused. "Am I going on a trip? I thought this was your workroom. Why are we going to go somewhere else?"

"No, it's a journey inside your mind so you won't physically be leaving the room. I'll explain it in a minute. Let's start by getting you comfortable."

Radiance got up from the armchair and walked behind it to the other side of the room. While she did, Lisette reached down and poked Sophie.

"Hey!" she whispered. "I like your grandmother, but what's this journey shit she's talking about?"

Before Sophie could answer, Radiance came back with an armful of stuff and handed a blanket to Sophie and a soft cushion to Lisette.

"Here," she said to Lisette. "Sit down next to Sophie on the floor and take off your shoes. She's going to lay that blanket out for you and I'll give you a quick lesson about shamanic journeying and what's going to happen next."

There's that word "relax" again! Lisette thought. No way was she going to be able to do that! But she slipped down off the couch onto the floor anyway while Radiance picked up a drum and began to beat it softly with a drumstick.

"Do you hear that?" Radiance asked. "It's like the human heartbeat, slow and steady. Shamanic drumming allows you to enter into the realms where human and animal spirits dwell so you can gain wisdom and heal."

Then she stopped drumming and laughed. "Oh, I know that sounds a little crazy but trust me, it works. The drumming takes you under, like into a trance, and then a part of you is going to journey into the spirit realm. It's like a meditation, and you'll feel calm and in control. Are you okay with that?"

"I guess so," Lisette said with a weak smile. "I don't know what else to do. You're the only person who has a clue about how to help me."

"All right, then. When you are ready, you're going to lay down on the blanket on the floor and I'm going to drum like this...." Again, she hit the drum firmly with a slow but steady beat. "Then you'll close your eyes and relax. Take a few deep breaths. Picture some place high up, like a mountain, somewhere familiar to you. Go there, and then launch yourself up to a place above the clouds until you pass over some clear line, and you'll be there in a special space."

Lisette looked at Radiance and smiled, "You mean like in heaven."

"Kind of, except I don't believe in heaven or hell."

"You don't?" Lisette said, surprised. "You don't think my mother went to heaven when she died?"

"She went somewhere, but I call it the Upper World. You see, in shamanism, we believe there are three worlds – the Upper World, the Middle World, and the Lower World. We travel to those worlds on healing journeys and let our spirit guides help give us direction for our lives."

"Don't you believe in God?"

"We aren't a religion; we interact with spirits. For me, there is no 'God' as such involved."

Lisette shook her head warily. "Okay. Just tell me where I'm going to go when I close my eyes."

"To the Upper World, and I want you to look for a teacher."

"You mean like in school? I didn't do well in school."

"No, more like someone who can help you solve a problem."

"You mean like how to get Lacey out of my body?"

"Yes, or anything else that comes up. Let the drums take you to the Upper World. Don't think about anything. Just get yourself there and see what happens. When you meet a teacher, ask for her name, and see if she has a gift for you. Do you understand?"

"Sure," said Lisette. "It sounds goofy, but if it helps, I'll do it."

"Good. Now when it's time for you to return to Sophie and me in this room, I'm going to beat the drums a little faster like this." Radiance did a drumroll and then hit the drum four times very slowly. "That's the call to come back, and you must promise me that when you hear the drums go like that, you will come back. Do you agree?"

"Yes," Lisette said, and then she asked eagerly, "Can we get started now?"

"Wait a minute," Sophie chimed in. "What if she sees Ari in the Upper World? He might attack her, too. Can he do that? What if he tries to hurt her? You can't send her there. You can't!"

Suddenly Lisette could feel Sophie coming unglued, and the mention of Ari's name caused a physical reaction in her own body. There was a pain in her stomach, and her eyes burned as they brimmed with tears. Her words came in short bursts. She could hardly breathe. She cried out, "Lacey's back inside me. I can feel her again. She won't leave me alone. She's telling me there is danger! There is danger. Help me! Help me!"

Sophie grabbed Lisette and put her arms around her.

"No, no," Sophie said firmly, although she didn't sound calm. "It's going to be okay. Gram will help you. Right, Gram?" Sophie looked at her grandmother, pleading, "You've got to help her. Lacey needs your help, too. She's stuck someplace, and I need to talk to her. Why did she go to Ari's room that night by herself? I should've gone with her. I should've…." Sophie's voice trailed off briefly, and then it was hoarse and hollow when she went on. "If only she had let me go with her. If only I could've stopped him. If only…."

By now, Sophie was crying, and Lisette was clutching her stomach and groaning. Radiance got up from her chair and got down on the floor with the two girls. She pulled both of them into her arms and held them tightly against her soft, warm breasts.

"It's all right. It's all right," Radiance cooed in their ears until Sophie stopped crying and Lisette could feel herself breathing again.

Then Radiance said to Lisette in a slow, calm voice, "Lacey's caught between two worlds. She's stuck in the Middle World, what we call the real world, but she no longer has a physical body so she has come into yours. I can help her to leave, but you must trust me and follow my instructions exactly. Do you understand?"

Lisette nodded and sniffed back her tears. "But where's Ari?" she asked.

"I don't know," Radiance replied. "He may be with her in the Middle World or he may be somewhere else. It's hard to say."

Then Radiance turned to Sophie. "I've told you this before, and I'll say it again. Lacey's death is no one's fault except Ari's. This was his doing, not yours. If you had gone with her that night, he would have killed you, too. And what would I do without my little Sophie?" Radiance took Sophie's face in her hand and covered it with kisses. "My Sophie! My dear, dear Sophie!" she repeated.

Tears filled Radiance's eyes, and Lisette didn't even try to stop her own. They were all in so much pain over what had happened to Lacey and yet, Radiance was right. It could have been worse. If Sophie had tried to stop Ari, Radiance would have lost a granddaughter, too.

It was all so sad. Nobody could bring Lacey back, but here they were, taking care of each other and, in that moment, Lisette felt a wonderful sense of belonging. For the first time since her mom died, she was with people who really cared about her and wanted to help her. How amazing was that!

Soon she would lie down on the blanket and with the help of Radiance's steady drumming, she'd journey into the unknown. She wasn't sure how it worked, but she was going to give it a try.

She had to. Lacey needed her help, and maybe all this would help her too. She had to believe that.

From her vantage point inside Lisette, Lacey watched Sophie and Radiance comforting Lisette, and it made her feel terrible.

How come Lisette got to have someone commiserate with her and she didn't? Who was here for her when she had returned from her father's thoughts? Learning the true story about what had happened to her mother in the family's garage was real hard for her. Her mother had died so unnecessarily. It sounded to Lacey like her mother had had severe postpartum depression after Jimmie's birth, but no one had diagnosed it properly. Surely her father must realize that now. If only her mother had gotten the help she needed, what a difference it would have made for all of them. It was so sad. Her father did what he thought was best for his family in the circumstances, and she couldn't blame him for that.

But finding out the truth about her mother and forgiving her father now still hadn't set her free from this crazy limbo state she was in. Instead she returned to Lisette miserable, and the shaman thing she was doing with Radiance made Lacey even crazier. She heard Radiance explaining it all to Lisette, but the part that worried Lacey most was what Radiance had said about Ari.

Lacey could see now how much she had missed about him. He was a master manipulator, making her feel sorry for him and taking advantage of her kindness. He was really two different people – one charming, loving, and attentive; the other angry, possessive, and controlling. He wanted her as his "forever" girl, but what did he really mean by that? Could he really pursue her after death? Could he be here too, stuck in the Middle World? If Ari had never really cared about her, what did he want with her now?

But I did care about you, my angel, a voice said, barely audible but unmistakable. *You are beautiful, so beautiful.*

"Who's that?" Lacey demanded, but she knew the voice was Ari's.

Oh God, Lisette! she cried out, trying to get her attention. *He's back! Just like you said! You've got to help me. Please! Sophie! Radiance! Please help me!*

But Lisette only grabbed her stomach as Sophie and Radiance comforted her. With their attention turned away, the voice continued, even louder this time.

Lacey! It's me. I still love you. I always will. Come to me. I'm yours forever. I need you to forgive me for what I did. Please, Lacey! Please!

His words shocked her, and she felt fear and outrage. How dare he say that he still loved her? How could she forgive him for what he did? How dare he even ask? Lacey fumed. How dare he!

Then, the voice came again, even louder this time, pleading with her to come back to him. As the voice grew stronger, she felt weaker and more defenseless. Maybe Ari was using her emotional state to come into her world the same way that her father's emotions had transported her into his world. Could she do the same? Could she draw herself into Ari's emotional place and move into his space, so they could settle this? She knew that even as Ari told her how much he loved, he was angry and obsessed with her. It was his fury that she could latch onto. It was worth a try. So she filled herself with angry thoughts of Ari. What did he want from her? she fumed. Why was he doing this to her? Hadn't he already killed her? What more did he want from her?

Lacey! Ari's voice called again, even stronger now, and she smiled, pleased that she was right. As he grew stronger, so did she, and she could feel her essence moving from Lisette to another place. Then she heard his voice again. *I don't know why you're so afraid of me, Lacey. I won't hurt you.*

Suddenly she saw him, looking calm and in control, standing there in the workroom where Radiance's drum collection hung on the wall.

Are you kidding? she said, moving toward him. *You killed me. Wasn't that enough? Leave me alone. Do you hear me?* As she moved closer to him, she felt something shift in her. She was coming into her own as a disembodied entity, and she liked the power it gave her. She could see strange beings shimmering and floating around him. All at once it came to her that these were the spirits of people Ari had abused in his short, miserable life. They were all women – which didn't surprise her – women he had loved and hated, screwed and treated like shit. The spirits created such a loud rabble that she almost couldn't hear him when he spoke again.

We can be together for all eternity, if you will only listen to me.

I don't have to listen to you, she said in a strong, clear voice. The energy of these spirits surrounding him now came toward her, and she could feel her own focus sharpened and deepened. These spirits may not have been killed by him, but they were ready for a fight – and this time, unlike the last, she'd win.

She approached him quickly now, reaching up and grabbing a set of drumsticks from the wall. Like him, she had gained some physicality again, but she felt superhuman, stronger than she had ever been in her human life. With that power, she pummeled him with one of the sticks, and he cowered away from her as she forced him back into the corner, trapped and at her mercy.

He cried out as each blow caused a sudden flash and a puff of smoke to come out of him. She was beating the energy out of him, and it felt good. At first, he struggled, but when he realized that she had the upper hand, he stopped fighting and sat there immobilized.

It won't work! he screamed at her, meanness his only defense now. *You can't kill me – don't you know that?*

But I can *hurt you,* she screamed back. *And I will!*

Sticks and stones may break my bones, but names will never hurt me, he recited in a sarcastic, singsong tone.

Jesus! she exploded. *Don't you ever give up? Don't you see what you are?*

I'm a man. I have my conquests. You were one of them.

You certainly feel like you are entitled, don't you? Lacey snarled and pushed herself down against him. *I want you to leave me alone. Do you hear me? I mean it. LEAVE ME ALONE!*

Suddenly his voice changed as he pleaded with her. *But I need you, Lacey. I need your help.*

What makes you think I'd help you? she laughed.

Because I have this. He dangled a heart-shaped locket on a gold chain in front of her.

Horrified, Lacey saw it was her mother's necklace, the one her father had given to her when her mother died. She tried to grab it, but Ari snatched it away.

Not so fast, he said. *You lighten up first, and then we'll talk.*

Reluctantly Lacey stepped back. By removing her energy, she could feel him gain back some of his. Still she hovered close to him.

Where did you find that? she demanded.

Finders keepers, losers weepers, he said in that same infuriating, singsong voice.

Jesus, she swore under her breath. *You are a complete bastard, aren't you?*

He had her going now, and she didn't know how or where this would end.

What do you want? What do you think I can do for you here?

I need your help to get out.

How can I do that?

You can fix me. It's what all you bitches want to do with men anyway. Then I'll leave you alone.

You think it's that easy? I snap my fingers and you're fixed?

No, but I don't have the same advantages you do.

What does that mean?

You've got friends looking out for you, he whimpered. *I've got no one.*

Could that be because you killed me and then killed yourself? she said sarcastically. *That you lied and betrayed me? Betrayed all your friends? Who would want to help a pathetic little bastard like you?*

But you have to help me, he whined. Then he got that lilt in his voice and added, *You're my angel. You will always be my angel!*

You're damn right, I'm your angel, she exploded. *I'm your avenging angel, and I will get my revenge on you! I will!*

Furious now, she stepped toward him and throttled him again and again with the drumstick. She laughed as energy shot off from him like fireworks and buzzed around her. Then suddenly everything faded, and she felt herself rise above where she was, leaving Ari huddled in the corner. She felt Lisette's energy surround her again, and weakened by beating up Ari like that, she didn't fight it. She had to go back to Lisette, but she knew that she and Ari would meet again soon. She hadn't gotten what she wanted from him yet, but she would get it.

She wanted her revenge. He'd pay for what he had done to her and her family. The little bastard!

CHAPTER SIXTEEN

From a High Place

With the insistent beat of Radiance's drumming, Lisette felt herself being lifted now above the chaotic rabble of her own life and pulled into a different time and space.

Radiance had told her to go to a high place that was familiar to her, and to her amazement, Lisette found herself in the mountains of Peru. That she went to the ancient city of Machu Picchu didn't surprise her, though. Even though she had never visited there, that magical place was fresh in her mind, having told Ambrose only a few days ago that when she was a little girl, she and her mother had poured over picture books about this place. Lisette knew it well.

But Lisette didn't linger long there; it was only a launching point, as Radiance had told her it would be. She felt herself go up higher above the cloud line now, going into a space that she had never seen before until she found herself in a deep, dark forest, green and fresh all around her. The only noise in this peaceful, quiet place was the gentle sound of water gurgling in a bubbling brook that flowed down through the piles of rocks at her feet.

At first, as she took all this in, she didn't notice a woman sitting on a rock a few feet away, dressed in a long, flowing green gown, the hues of which blended into the woods around her. When she did, Lisette exclaimed, "Oh my! Who are you?"

"I'm here to greet you," the woman said in a soft, friendly voice.

"But how did you know I was coming?"

"It is as it should be," the woman said, but her words confused Lisette. What did that mean? It sounded so final and that made Lisette panic.

"I'm not dead, am I?" she asked frantically, "A place this quiet is my idea of hell. This isn't that, is it? Did Radiance screw up and send me to hell?"

"No," the woman said gently. "You are where you've always dreamed of being. You are in the Upper World."

Ah! The Upper World, Lisette thought. That was where Radiance sent her to find a teacher. Excitedly, Lisette asked, "Are you my teacher?"

"Would you like me to be?"

"Could you stop with the riddles? Radiance said I'd come here and find a teacher." Then her voice got softer. "I could use some help."

The woman smiled at her. "Then come with me."

The woman stood and a flock of birds gathered around her, lifting her up into the air. Lisette watched in amazement. Was she supposed to follow her? But how? But before she knew it, another flock of birds swarmed around her and lifted her up too. Suddenly she was in the sky, flying over a canyon with such speed that the wind whipped her hair up behind her. It trailed after her like a tail.

This is wonderful! Lisette thought. This is how it feels to fly. Then slowly the birds steered her down to the floor of the canyon where the woman in green was waiting for her. The birds gently put her down and flew off in a clatter.

Lisette smoothed her hair and clothes and looked anxiously at the woman. "Where are we now? What is this place?"

"You'll recognize it in a minute," the woman replied.

But all Lisette could see was something far off in the distance that she couldn't make out. As they walked toward it though, it became clearer and she didn't believe what she saw. Was this some kind of joke?

She turned to the woman and blurted, "That's the trailer I lived in with my mom. What the hell is it doing here?"

Then Lisette rushed towards it, terrified that it would be just as she had left it – on the day of her sixteen birthday and Ralph would be there inside.

"I don't understand," she turned and asked the woman. "Is this a dream? It feels like a nightmare!"

"It's a waking dream," the woman said smiling. "And a chance to review your life's lessons."

"Oh, no!" Lisette snapped back. "The only thing I learned in that trailer was that I didn't want to be there."

The woman smiled again, "Then that's an excellent lesson to learn." The woman leaned closer. "Take a look inside. There's something for you to see."

Lisette glared at her. Didn't she get it? She couldn't bear to see Ralph's face again, and she wouldn't. She was clear about that. But what if her mother was inside? She hadn't come to the Upper World looking for her mother, but if she was there, she had to go see her. That thought made her move toward the window of the trailer and standing on her tiptoes, like she was a little girl again, what she saw inside was amazing. Everything was painted a bright pink, and huge red and white peppermint sticks, her favorite candy, were hanging from the ceiling. The trailer was full of all the toys, dolls, and playthings she had ever wanted. In the middle of it all sat a girl in a bright red dress, much like the dress her mother couldn't afford to buy her. The girl looked so happy! She had everything Lisette ever wanted.

Suddenly, the girl looked up at her, smiled and waved her inside. Lisette felt a shiver run through her. Who was this girl and what did she want from her?

"The girl is you," the woman told her.

"She is not!" Lisette shot back. "Trust me! My childhood was nothing like that!"

"Even if it wasn't, you could still enjoy it now. Why don't you go inside?"

Lisette scowled, but she was curious. So she opened the door and stepped inside. The sweet smell of sugar hit her first. The candy canes hanging from the ceiling were real, and there were bowls full of her favorite candy everywhere. Then she saw the girl in the red dress, sitting on a chair in the middle of the trailer, eating candy from a bag. She grinned at Lisette and asked, "Do you want some?" She held out the bag. "The red gumdrops are the best!"

Lisette's eyes grew big. She loved red gumdrops – they were her favorites. Eagerly, she put out her hand and the girl poured some candy into it. Lisette popped a piece in her mouth, and as she chewed it a wild, wonderful flavor filled her mouth.

"These are amazing!" she exclaimed, tossing the rest in her mouth and putting her hand out for more. "I love candy! My mother used to get mad at me when I was a kid! She'd say…"

"Be careful, baby," a voice called out from behind her. "You'll get a tummy ache if you eat too much!"

Lisette recognized the voice and whirled around to see her mother.

"It's you! You *are* here!" But her mother looked so different! She was so young, so happy, so full of life. The last time Lisette had seen her was in the casket, her body cold and lifeless, but now she could touch her again. What would that feel like? Could she do it? As if knowing her fear, her mother took Lisette's hand and hugged her close. Lisette put her head on her mother's shoulder. Closing her eyes, Lisette let herself feel what it was like to be so close to her mother again. It was wonderful!

"Oh, Mommy, Mommy!" she sighed. "I've missed you so much!"

"Yes, my baby!" Her mother rocked Lisette in her arms. "I've missed you, too. It's been a very long time!"

Then her mother released her and held her at arm's length as she beamed. "Look at you! You are all grown up!"

"You look great too, Mom," Lisette gushed.

"I look pretty damn good, don't I?" Her mother smiled. "This place agrees with me."

"But what is this place?" Lisette was hoping for a straight answer, not riddles. "Where am I, and who is that girl?"

"That's simple. The girl is you."

"But I wasn't that happy, and our trailer wasn't the Candy Land Express!"

Her mother sighed. "It wasn't that bad, my darling, was it? I loved you." She touched Lisette's check softly. "I've always loved you."

"I know." Lisette's voice cracked as emotions welled up inside her. She couldn't blame her mother for everything that went wrong later in her life, but losing her mother when she was only ten years old had been hard. The cancer had spread fast, and her mother didn't have time to put everything right before she died.

"I came back as soon as I could," her mother went on. "I had to heal first and get stronger."

Lisette didn't know what to say. She was happy that her mother had healed, but in the meantime, she had been stuck living with Ralph.

Then, as if her mother had read her mind, she added, "After I died, you went through hell, didn't you?"

"Oh, no, it wasn't so bad," Lisette lied, holding back her tears.

"But you see Ralph was the only one I could leave you with." Her mother gently pushed a loose strand of hair from Lisette's face. "Ralph was the only one who would love you because he was the only one who loved me."

Ralph loved someone! Lisette was shocked at the thought.

"I know you don't believe that, but in the end, he was the one who kept you out of jail for trying to kill him, right?"

"But Ralph didn't do that because he loved me," Lisette insisted. "He did it because…" Lisette's voice suddenly dropped off, and she was lost in thought.

Why did he keep her out of jail? She had always thought it was so that someday he could show up and expect to get something from her in exchange. But he hadn't done that, had he? She hadn't seen him after that day in court when she lied…. No, she couldn't think about that. It made her feel awful. She was still ashamed of herself about that and didn't want her mother to know.

Then suddenly it came to Lisette.

"*You* made him do it," Lisette said excitedly. "It was you, wasn't it? How did you do that? Why did you…"

"Don't try to figure it out," her mother interrupted. "All you need to know is that I have never left you and never will. I've been trying to tell you this for a long time, but you haven't been listening. Since Lacey is with you… "

"You know about Lacey?" Lisette interrupted.

"Of course!" Her mother smiled. "I told you – I'm always with you. It's not for you to figure out. It's for you to live your life right here, in the present. To live in the most conscious way that you can."

Lisette was confused. What was her mother talking about?

"Look, it's simple," her mother went on. "There is a reason you came into this world. There is something you can do that no one else can. You need to figure out what you can do right here, right now to get yourself on the path to finding out your purpose in this lifetime."

Lisette shrugged her shoulders. "I guess I could learn to read better. That would be a start."

"Okay!" Her mother's face broke into a big smile. "I remember how you loved reading all those books about Machu Picchu with me."

Lisette's face brightened. "I miss that. I don't read very much anymore."

"Why not?"

Lisette didn't know what to say. She had come up with reasons before, like she stopped reading because she was mad at her mother for dying and leaving her alone, but now those felt so ignorant and childish that she couldn't tell her mother.

"Oh, don't worry," her mother went on. "You're just out of practice. You learn it again. You always loved to learn."

Lisette stared at her in amazement. "But I don't understand. How could you…" Lisette was interrupted by the sound of the drums beating softly but insistently.

"It's time to go." The woman in green was standing now at the trailer door to warn her, "The drums are calling you back. Remember what you were told. You must go back when the drums call."

"But I don't want to go back," Lisette wailed. "I want to stay with my mother. I have so many things I still need to find out…"

"It's okay," her mother said gently. "Listen for me in the wind. I'll be there."

"I don't get it. What wind? Where? How can you be with me if I have to leave now?" Lisette could feel herself unraveling. She couldn't think of a time since her mother died that she hadn't felt lonely and scared. She needed her mother. How could she leave her now? How could she tear herself away? There must be a way – there must be something she could do!

"No, baby," her mother interrupted her thoughts. "You must go now and trust that you will see me again. If there is one thing I can tell you now, it is to never give up and always believe in yourself. Can you do that for me?"

"But I…"

"You made a promise to Radiance to come back when the drums called, didn't you?"

"Yes, but I didn't think I'd find you here. I didn't believe it was possible."

"Then that's the lesson you've learned. Everything is possible, and you must keep your promise."

"Will I see you again?" Lisette asked, but before she could get an answer, the final call of the drums sounded – four long, hard beats.

"I love you, Mommy," she cried out. "I have to go!"

When Lisette let her mind come back into the room with Sophie and Radiance, she didn't know where she was at first. Slowly she moved on the blanket and then opened her eyes. They were both standing over her.

"How was it?" Sophie blurted out, like she couldn't wait another second to ask. "Where did you go on your journey?"

"Oh God!" Lisette exclaimed, and then moaned as she raised her head up off the blanket. "I feel like my head is ready to explode."

She felt Radiance's hand on her shoulder, pushing her gently back onto the blanket. "Take it slow. No need to get up right away. Take your time."

Lisette moaned again and said in a dazed voice, "I saw my mother. I could feel her. It felt like she was real. Was she?"

"Sometimes when you journey, it can feel like that," Radiance explained. "You have emotional reactions just as in ordinary reality."

"It felt so wonderful," Lisette said wistfully. Then she shook her head and demanded, "Can I go back? I need to see her again. She's the one who got Ralph to keep me out of jail."

"Ralph?" Sophie broke in. "Who is Ralph? And what's this about jail?"

"Ralph was my father," Lisette said bitterly. "And I don't want to see him ever again." She slowly raised her head off the blanket, this time feeling steadier, and then turned to Radiance. "I have so many questions to ask my mother. Please, can I go back now?"

Radiance shook her head. "You need to take a breather. This was enough for one day. Come back tomorrow, and we'll have you journey again."

"Will I see my mother then?" Lisette asked excitedly.

"It's possible," Radiance said. "But you need to get some rest now."

"But I can't," Lisette said with a frown. "I have to work tonight."

"Can I go watch you dance?" Sophie asked eagerly. "Can I, please?"

"You can't be in a bar until you are twenty-one," Radiance said sternly.

"But Lisette's only nineteen," Sophie pleaded. *"She* gets to go there." Then she turned to Lisette. "You can get me in, can't you? Please!"

"Your grandmother is right," Lisette said. "You don't want to go there."

"It's settled," Radiance said. "I'll see you both at eleven o'clock tomorrow."

"I'll have to skip calculus class," Sophie replied. "But that's fine by me. Is that a good time for you, Lisette?"

"Sure," Lisette said, even though on the nights she danced she didn't get up until noon. "If Sophie comes by to get me, I'll be ready. I wouldn't miss it!"

"Then it's a date," Radiance said with a smile. She gave each of them a hug, and Lisette and Sophie raced out of the apartment and into the hallway. There, Sophie broke away from Lisette and squealed, "Last one to the elevator is a rotten egg!" She took off ahead of her.

"Oh, no, you don't!" Lisette shouted and ran after her.

The two of them yelled back and forth at each other down the hall until Sophie reached the elevator door first, punched the down button and sang out, "You're the rotten egg!"

"Jesus," Lisette said, gasping for breath as she came up behind Sophie. "I've got to stop smoking. I can't believe I'm so out of shape."

"And I can't believe that I know a stripper," Sophie giggled. "God, I wish I could be there tonight to see you dance."

"You can come. I can get you in. I said that in front of Radiance so she wouldn't worry." Lisette could see Sophie hesitate and then asked, "Do you think Lacey will be there tonight?"

Lisette laughed. "She never misses a show."

"Really?" Sophie said. "Isn't that just like Lacey? She loved being the center of attention. She'd never miss an opportunity to show off."

Just then the bell on the elevator chimed and the door opened. The two girls entered the elevator and stood in silence for a while.

Lisette figured that Sophie was probably thinking about Lacey, but she couldn't stop thinking about her mother and how great it was to touch her today.

It had been a long, long time since someone loved her like her mother did. She wondered if she would ever find anyone in her life like that again.

"Please, Mother," she said silently to herself. "Come back and help me. I'm so lost."

Lacey wasn't there after all that night when Lisette danced, even though Sophie was watching her from a spot backstage.

It wasn't hard for Lisette to sneak Sophie into the club through the back door and into her dressing room, but getting Sophie behind the stage wasn't so easy. It got more complicated when Erick turned up that night as a bouncer at the Pussycat.

"What are you doing here?" Lisette asked running into him in the hall outside her dressing room. "I thought you worked at the Bare Bottom."

Lisette hadn't seen Erick since Lacey's funeral, and she was embarrassed about how she had gone on about Lacey and then fainted on the sidewalk in front of him.

"I'm filling in for a bouncer tonight," he told her with a big smile that made Lisette feel less nervous. "I hoped I'd see you here. How are you doing?"

"I'm all right," she said cheerfully. "But I could use your help."

"With Ambrose?"

"Ambrose?" Lisette was confused. "How do you know Ambrose?"

"I don't," Erick replied. "I've never even met the guy, but I know that Wiley has banned him from this club. He told me he's given Webster orders to keep him from hanging around inside or outside the building. So he won't be bothering you anymore."

"I couldn't care less about Ambrose," Lisette said flatly. "I've got more important things to think about."

"Like what?"

Lisette hesitated for a moment. Could she tell him? Had he forgotten about what happened the other day? Could she trust him? Why not? So she told Erick that Sophie was there in her dressing room and that she needed his help to sneak Sophie backstage to see her act.

"Who is this Sophie?" Erick asked, sounding confused. "How did you meet her? I thought you didn't have any friends here in town."

Lisette sighed. "Are you going to help me or give me a hard time?"

"Are you in some kind of trouble? Is this about that girl, Lacey, you were telling me about the other day?"

Oh, God, Lisette thought. Erick was trying to rescue her again.

"Look, if you must know, Sophie and her grandmother are helping to get Lacey out of my body. That problem will be solved soon, thank you very much!"

"But you told me she was gone the other day when I suggested you see a counselor. How is her grandmother going to help you?"

"She's a shaman, and she drums for me, and I go on these journeys. Yesterday, I saw my mother and…"

"Whoa!" Erick yelled. "You saw your mother? I thought she was dead."

"She is. But I saw her in this kind of dreamlike state that Radiance – that's Sophie's grandmother – helped me get into. She was banging this drum and we were in her workroom at her apartment. She lives in this old apartment building a few blocks from here that looks pretty spooky on the outside. It has these two big towers in front and you can see the river from out the window of her workroom. That's where we do the journeying." Then she stopped and heaved a big sigh. "I know this all sounds crazy to you, but I think Radiance can really help me."

"She can't! People like that are all quacks. You need someone good to talk to. I can find you someone who…"

Lisette glared at him. "I don't need your help with that. I do need you to sneak Sophie backstage. Could you handle a simple task, Mr. College Guy?"

"I'm worried about you," Erick went on as though he hadn't heard anything she had said. "I need to understand what is going on here so I can help you."

"What is going on is that I need your support. I don't need you to fix anything. I need a friend, and I thought you were my friend."

"I am, but you're not making any sense," he barked at her. Then he said more gently, "Look, let me take you out to lunch tomorrow. and we'll talk about this. I have class in the morning, but I could meet you at noon. How's that?"

Lisette eyed him carefully. "If I say yes to lunch tomorrow, will you help with Sophie tonight?"

"Yes, I can help you with that, and yes, I'd like us to have lunch."

Lisette hated what she was going to do next, but she had no choice.

"Okay," she said firmly. "I'll meet you tomorrow at twelve-thirty in the lobby of my hotel."

Erick gave her a smile. "See, that wasn't so hard, was it?"

"No," she said sweetly. "Not at all."

What Erick didn't know is that come tomorrow he'd be standing there in the lobby all by himself, waiting for her. How long, she wondered, would it take him to figure out that she wasn't showing up? Would he wait? A nice guy like Erick trusted people because usually they didn't lie to him, so she guessed he'd wait for a half hour or so, maybe more. Then he'd be really pissed.

By then, she'd be at Radiance's apartment with Sophie and well into her next journey. She felt bad about hurting Erick, but she couldn't help it.

People like Erick had to learn not to trust everyone they meet. That's why there were people like her.

She could teach Erick that lesson easily.

No problem!

CHAPTER SEVENTEEN

Opening Up

When Lisette got back to her hotel around two o'clock in the morning, she found the floor inside the door littered with papers filled with frantic scribbling and messages from Ambrose.

He had left five voicemails for her, too, on the hotel phone. What was so damn important that he had to talk to her? Was it more important than getting Lacey out of her body? She didn't think so, but she knew Ambrose wouldn't understand it. He didn't think that hearing voices in her head was anything to worry about. He heard them all the time, he had told her, but she wasn't going to end up like him. So she ignored his messages and made a plan to get up early the next morning and leave the hotel by ten o'clock. That way she'd be gone long before Erick arrived to meet her for lunch at twelve-thirty and hopefully avoid seeing Ambrose in the hotel at that early hour. Both Ambrose and Erick were annoying her now, and she didn't need their demands cluttering up her life.

Lisette got to Radiance's apartment building well before eleven o'clock and waited for Sophie in the lobby. When she arrived, Sophie buzzed Radiance's apartment, and they heard her bright, cheery voice over the intercom inviting them up to her apartment on the sixth floor. Riding in the elevator with Sophie, Lisette told her how much she wanted to talk to her mom again today. Sophie, in turn, went on about being at Lisette's club and seeing her act the night before.

"Erick is really nice," Sophie said, practically swooning over him. "He likes you. I can tell by the way he looks at you."

"Of course he looks at me. I have all my clothes off."

"No, I don't mean because of that!" she giggled. "Is he your boyfriend?"

"No, I'd never date anyone from the club."

"I think he's hot!" Sophie continued. "What a body! He's got to be better than that Ambrose character you were telling me about."

Lisette shrugged. "Erick's okay, but I don't have time for a boyfriend. Besides, he's busy taking classes. He's planning to be a psychologist."

By then, they were at the door to the apartment and all conversation about their time at the club had to cease in Radiance's presence. Radiance was delighted to see them both again, and that left no doubt in Lisette's mind that she had made the right call to dump Ambrose and Erick today. Journeying with Radiance was far more exciting and important to her.

First, Radiance wanted to know more about Lisette's journey yesterday, so they talked about that as they sat next to each other on the couch in Radiance's workroom. Sophie took up her perch on the floor in front of the table where Radiance had muffins and hot tea laid out for them.

"Did you find a teacher?" Radiance asked her.

"Oh, yes!" Lisette replied. "She was this very beautiful lady, and she was dressed in this wonderful, flowing green gown."

"Did you get her name?" Radiance asked.

Lisette frowned. "I forgot. You did say to ask her."

"That's okay," Radiance replied. "I know you want to go on another journey today, but I sense that your energy has shifted a lot since yesterday."

Lisette didn't know what to say. What was Radiance talking about?

"You said something yesterday about Ralph and how your mother helped you understand that he kept you out of jail. What was that all about?"

Lisette sighed. "It's a long story, and I'm not in the mood to tell it right now. What my mother said about Ralph has nothing to do with Lacey."

"I think it does," Radiance insisted. "There is a reason why Lacey entered your body. I can't explain it exactly, but I've got a feeling it has something to do with Ralph. We need to clear this up now, or this whole thing may not work."

"What do you mean, 'it won't work'?" Lisette exclaimed. "You promised me it would. You said it. I heard you say it yesterday."

"Calm down," Radiance said gently. "What I said yesterday is that you must trust me and do what I say. And what I'm saying today is that we need to hear the story about you and Ralph. Until you do, you can't journey any further. This is part of the healing that Lacey's presence in your body is prompting you to do. You can do it now or do it later, but I suggest we do it now."

Lisette couldn't believe what she was hearing. There was no way she was going to talk about Ralph. Not today – not ever.

"Come on," Sophie said quietly. "It can't be that bad. We're here for you. You can tell us."

Lisette gave Sophie a scowl and sputtered, "You don't know what I've been through. You don't know anything."

"That's enough, Lisette," Radiance suddenly jumped in. "Even I can feel your resistance. You've got to let it go of it. Surrender."

"Are you nuts?" Lisette spun around to Radiance. "I'll never let anyone take advantage of me ever again. Never!"

"That's not what I mean. You've got to let go of your anger toward Ralph."

"No way! He was a bastard and, thank God, I don't have to look at his mean, ugly face anymore." Lisette was desperate now. She could feel the old bad feelings about Ralph coming up, and she wanted to run away. But Radiance gripped her arm and held it tight. She looked deep into Lisette's eyes, like the truth was somewhere back behind them and she was going to hear it.

But Lisette had never told the truth about Ralph, not even to the police. She stared back into Radiance's eyes, in a kind of tug of war. It was what she wanted versus what Radiance wanted, until Lisette could feel hot tears coming to her eyes. Radiance pulled her into her arms and hugged her to her soft body.

"It's all right," Radiance said softly.

"It's not, it's not!" Lisette sobbed. "Oh God! Please don't make me remember! Please!"

Radiance held Lisette until the crying stopped and then added, in a whisper, "You can tell us about Ralph. I'm here. Sophie is here. She's your friend. She needs a friend, and so do you. You can trust us."

Lisette wanted to believe her, but it had been a long time since she trusted anyone, and even longer since anyone had really cared about her. Not since her mom died and she had gone to live with Ralph.

Ralph! She hated him, but she stayed until she could leave, the day she turned sixteen. How could she ever forget that day?

"Go ahead," Radiance said in a whisper. "Tell us the story. Start anywhere."

"Do I have to?" Lisette moaned.

Radiance nodded her head and held her tighter. It had happened so long ago, and Lisette wasn't proud of it. She had been running away from this part of her life for such a long time.

Maybe it was time to tell it.

On the morning of her sixteenth birthday, Lisette jumped out of bed, pulled on her clothes, and grabbed for the long, thin gold chain that she always wore around her neck. She carefully adjusted the small gold key that hung on the chain so that it rested on her chest and then raced into the bathroom. She washed her face, brushed her teeth, and rushed back into her room. She grabbed her diary with its bright pink cover from its hiding place just as she heard Ralph rustling about in the tiny kitchen of their mobile home.

By this time each morning, she would be out there with him, but today she wanted to go through her birthday ritual, something she had done every year since her mother had died nine years ago.

To begin with, Lisette would take the key on the chain around her neck and unlock her diary. Opening the inside cover, she'd take out the loose pages in the front and unfold them up to see her mother's small, tight handwriting. These were the pages from the first diary her mother had given to her on her seventh birthday. By now, Lisette had gone through several diaries, but she had kept these special pages over the years. She had wanted her mother's words – no, her mother herself, she thought – with her whenever she wrote in her diary.

Although Lisette had memorized the words on the pages long ago, she liked to look at them and imagine that the same hand that had written those words was still there to hold hers.

"Give me your hand, honey," she'd remember her mother saying. "When you cross the street, you need to hold Mommy's hand and look both ways."

Then Lisette would close her eyes and rub her hands over the words that her mother had written. She'd think about how her mother might have looked when she wrote them. She supposed her mother would have smiled when she finished, or she might have had tears in her eyes because the words to her daughter meant so much. Finally, Lisette would open her eyes and read her mother's words aloud, slowly and deliberately, in her most grown-up voice.

To my wonderful daughter: I bought you a diary so that all you want and wish for will fill this book and never be forgotten. Believe that all your dreams can come true and they will. No matter what happens, remember that I am always with you. I have loved you from the day you were born and will love you until the day you die, and then for all eternity. Be a good girl, be bold, and live your dreams! Love, your mother, Marie.

By the time she finished reading these words, she would have also looked at the sketches her mother had drawn for her that she also kept tucked in her diary. Finally, she would pull out the sketches she had made of her mother and other scenes from her childhood. These were important pictures for her, one of the few things she had left of her mother that Ralph had not made fun of or destroyed.

Now, with tears in her eyes, she'd go to the last empty page of the diary and record her dreams for the coming year. This year, she decided, that was not necessary, because the dream she had had since the day her mother died was going to come true today and she didn't have time to think of another one right away. So she snapped the diary shut, locked it, and jumped to her feet. She ran down the hall with the diary in her hand, hoping that Ralph wouldn't have left for work yet.

"Good morning!" she chirped as she entered the kitchen area, relieved to see him seated at the table with a cup of coffee in his hand. "Is there any more?"

Her father grunted and gestured toward the stove without looking up from the racing form he was reading. Putting the diary under her arm, Lisette found a mug among the dirty dishes in the sink, rinsed it out under the faucet, and poured a cup of coffee from the pot simmering on the burner. She pulled a carton of milk from the refrigerator, opened it, and sniffed the liquid to make sure it wasn't sour before putting some in her coffee. She sat down at the table opposite him and tucked her diary under her leg on the chair.

She reached for the sugar bowl and spoon in the middle of the table and stared at him while she added three spoonfuls of sugar into her coffee. She took a sip and then gripped the mug with both hands, using it to warm them on this cool, spring morning. She leaned against the table and flipped her long blonde hair away from her face and over her shoulder before she said with a strained sweetness in her voice, "Today is the day."

"What day?" he muttered, without looking up at her.

"My birthday. My sixteenth birthday."

"Really?"

"You know what that means?"

"It means you're a day older." He finally looked at her and said matter-of-factly, "Happy Birthday." He returned to his reading.

She screwed up her face and was about to speak when he added, "Any coffee left?"

She sighed, dragged herself off the chair, and grabbed the pot on the stove. She slouched over to Ralph's side of the table and poured the remaining hot liquid into his cup. After putting the empty pot into the sink, she grabbed her diary from the chair and sat back down. She took the key from the chain around her neck, put it into the gold lock, opened her diary, and flipped through the pages until she stopped in one particular place. She cleared her throat and read aloud.

"'April 20th – my fifteenth birthday. Ralph and I make a deal. In a year, I can quit tending bar at his place and go off on my own.

I tell him how, when I'm sixteen, I can legally emancipate myself from him. That's what I want, and he agrees to it.'" She looked up at Ralph. "So?" Her voice was calm but insistent.

"So what?" He glared up at her over the top of his reading glasses. "Am I supposed to be impressed that you wrote that drivel down in your stupid diary a year ago?" He wagged his finger at her. "You know, if I'd wanted to, I could've broken into that thing a long time ago. Read all your little secrets." He sneered at her. "Like that part about how you did it for the first time in the back of that asshole's pickup truck when you were only thirteen. I should've sent you back to the foster home for that."

"They wouldn't take me back," Lisette shot back. "Not after I flashed that knife at my so-called foster father." She took a gulp of coffee. "I could have just run away – then you'd be sorry. You'd have to look at my picture on the milk carton. Is that what you want?"

"Did I want you to give away your virginity with that asshole kid? No! But at least you didn't run off with him and make a complete mess of your life."

"But Randy loved *me* and wanted *me,*" Lisette wailed. Then she glared at him. "Until you pulled a shotgun on him and ran him out of town."

His eyes held her eyes and growled, "At least you found out sooner rather than later that he didn't have any guts."

She ignored him and went on, choking back tears. "You promised me that I could leave on my sixteenth birthday. That was our deal. I would be on my own!"

"You've been on your own for years, darling. Haven't you figured that out yet? I never wanted to be a father. Having you was your mother's idea. So what's the difference if you go or you stay? You're still on your own. At least here you have a roof over your head."

"But you promised," she sputtered, tears now cascading down her cheeks. "Why can't you ever keep your promises?"

"Like your mother kept hers to me? You just have to take the deals you're dealt, darling. That's life."

"I want to leave!" she screamed at him, pounding her fist on the table so hard that the coffee cup sitting in front of him jolted up and spilled over, pouring the hot liquid down his paper and onto his lap.

"Jesus!" He jumped up. "What are you trying to do, scald me to death?" He wiped the liquid off his jeans with his hand and slapped at his thigh.

"I wish you *were* dead!" Her face was bright red and her lips quivered as she spoke. "Then I could say I was an orphan – that my dad had gone to be with my mother, who he loved more than me, his own flesh and blood."

She bolted up off the chair and ran out the side door of the trailer. The door flapped open and closed several times in the wake of her departure. He raced over to the door and grabbed it. He screamed after her as she made her way down the path.

"I didn't love her any more than I love you!"

"What do you mean we can't go out tonight, Jake? It's my birthday!"

Lisette stood behind the bar after school at her father's club, talking on the phone to Jake. She had planned for weeks how she wanted to celebrate her birthday this evening, but after this morning with Ralph, all the plans she had made were going very badly.

Of course, she knew she could never count on Ralph for anything, but now she could see that he lied to her when he told her she could be on her own when she reached sixteen. He never really intended to let her go in the first place. Without his approval, she had little chance to get a judge in this county to emancipate her. Her guidance counselor at school had already warned her about that. While a parent's approval wasn't required to get emancipated, without it, the judge would look extra hard at what she had to offer.

Without Ralph's approval, her only choice was to run away, but she hated the idea. Her mother would be furious with her for even thinking such a thing, and besides, someone would only find her and send her back to live with Ralph or, even worse, send her back into foster care again.

Ralph! How she hated him, she thought, as she hung on the phone, trying to think of a way to convince Jake to go out with her tonight. Ralph was the one standing in the way of her getting on with her life, and she hated him with a passion. Not only had he chased away Randy, the only man she would ever love, he had all but pushed her into the arms of Jake. Of course, Jake was a passing fling, but at least Ralph didn't threaten to blow his head off for dating her.

So she pleaded with Jake on the other end of the phone to go out with her. With no family except for Ralph, Jake was her only hope of having any kind of real birthday celebration. If only her mother was still alive, she thought for a moment, what a sweet sixteen party she would have thrown for her! Not that anyone would have come; she had no friends at school and even if she did, they wouldn't come anywhere near her house if Ralph was around. Stories about Ralph and this bar were all over town. How girls danced topless and drinks were watered down. No one in town liked Ralph. Why should she be any different?

"Why can't you go out with me for dinner somewhere nice?" she whined to Jake. "I want to blow out the candles on a birthday cake."

"Your dad won't let me."

"Since when do you need my dad's permission to go out with me?"

Jake was silent for a moment, and then he said, "I guess it's okay to tell you now. You are sixteen, after all – a grown woman." He cleared his throat and said quickly, "It's the money. I haven't paid him for the last few weeks. Your father said no more until I pay in full."

"For what? Ralph doesn't run any bar bills in his joint. Never has – you know that."

"Not for the booze, sugar. For going out with a beautiful girl like you."

"What the hell do you mean?" Lisette's voice went up in volume. She couldn't believe what she was hearing.

"You know what I mean. Why else would you go out with an old guy like me?"

"So you're twice my age – so what?"

"No, sugar. I'm more than twice your age, and I…" Jack stopped for a moment. "Maybe I shouldn't be telling you this. Maybe…"

"No, tell me! What are you talking about?"

"After he ran off that young buck with his shotgun, he told all of us that if we wanted to come near you – if we *dared* to come near to you – he'd know about it and we'd have to pay him."

"That son of bitch!" Lisette muttered, seething as she said the words. "How could he do this to me?"

Suddenly, Lisette's mind was in a whirl. This was what Ralph had stooped to, that snake in the grass. He was no better than a pimp, treating her like she was a whore. For a moment, she couldn't speak or hear anything Jake was saying to her. She wanted to slam down the phone, and go find Ralph and – do what? What did one do when a slimeball like Ralph did something so disgusting to his own daughter? If she hated him before, it was nothing compared to how she felt about him now.

"I thought you knew," Jack stammered. Lisette hardly heard him as he went on. "I guess, er… I only thought about how beautiful you are. And how much I wanted to think that you cared about me even if I had to pay."

"But I do care, Jake," she broke in now. "It's Ralph, that slime-ball, who's the problem. I could kill him for what he's done. The bastard!"

"Now, sugar. Don't go blaming him. He was just looking out for you. It's the only way he could be sure you'd be safe, a good-looking woman like you."

"Bullshit!" Lisette shot back, as she gripped her hands into fists around the bar towel in her hand and squeezed it hard. "He knew exactly what he was doing. He's making money off me, and it's no wonder he doesn't want me leaving now that I'm sixteen. I'm his cash cow! The bastard! Goddamn him!"

Suddenly, it all became quite clear to her. There was another way for her to get what she wanted, an option she hadn't dared to think about until now. But Ralph deserved whatever he got, and if that was the only way that he would ever let her go, then so be it.

She hoped that, wherever her mother was, she didn't know the thoughts flashing through her mind. How she'd do it, she didn't know yet, but with the way she felt right now, she knew she could pull it off. No question about that!

She muttered into the phone. "I've got to go now, Jake. I've got things to do. I'm going to get that son of a bitch. Not with cups of hot coffee, like this morning. No, I plan to light him up like a Christmas tree."

CHAPTER EIGHTEEN

A Fresh Start

When it was all over, she could see that it was meant to be.

Ralph may not have seen it that way, but what did she care? He knew she had done it, and that was all that mattered.

Still, she wanted to think that he saw it coming, because then her revenge would be even sweeter. But she was careful to act as if nothing was wrong from the moment she got off the phone that afternoon with Jake to the time when Ralph came waltzing into the bar about six o'clock, acting like he was king of his world.

Inside, Lisette was still fuming with anger, but in a few short hours, she had slowly and carefully put together a plan to do what would have been unthinkable to her this morning. It was bad enough that he wasn't going to let her get emancipated, but to sell her to the highest bidder was over the top. From then on, she knew there was no turning back.

If she had any doubts, they vanished when Ralph came in smelling of alcohol. He was the only man she knew who was stupid enough to drink liquor at someone else's bar. But she knew he had an afternoon poker game every week at Scotty Holbrook's bar down the street and, true to form, he came back plastered as usual.

That gave Lisette an idea.

"Hey, Ralph. How about I go out and buy myself a cake for to-night? The guys can join in my birthday celebration, and while they're toasting me, you can make a few extra bucks on their drinks."

Lisette had learned years ago from Ralph how to water down drinks without the customer even noticing. He taught her that it was hard for any drunk to know how much alcohol or water had been added to anything.

Ralph gave her an odd look, not sure he had heard her correctly. "That's a good idea," he said finally. "I'm just surprised that you'd think about something that could help your dad out."

"I figure the better business is for you, the better it is for me," Lisette said with a lopsided grin, trying to sound like she meant it.

"I thought that maybe after this morning you'd be angry at me. I should have remembered it was your birthday. I'm sorry about that."

Lisette said nothing but thought what a pathetic liar he was. Of course he had remembered her birthday. He couldn't wait to screw her out of something she really wanted. But that wasn't important to her anymore. She'd be free in a little while, just as long as it would take her to get Ralph even more drunk toasting his daughter's sixteen birthday with his buddies.

"Here," he said, reaching into his pocket and taking out a wad of bills from his wallet. "Take the truck and go buy yourself the biggest, best birthday cake you can find. You like chocolate, right? And some ice cream too. We'll serve up a birthday treat and make all the customers happy."

And what about me? Lisette thought with glee, as she took the money and shoved it into her pants pocket. Little did he know what was going to make her happy tonight.

"And," he added, thrusting some more bills at her, "if you are going by the gas station, could you fill up the truck with gas and the can in the back room, too? I wanted to cut the grass in back today, but I didn't have any gasoline for the mower. I'll do it tomorrow."

Lisette nodded, took the bills, and added them to her stash. Then she reached down for her purse and walked into the back room where she grabbed the keys to the truck and looked around for the gas can. She had watched Ralph fill it up before, and she had been running errands in Ralph's truck ever since she got her learner's permit. Sure, some adult should be driving with her, but the cops in town tended to overlook things like that for Ralph, who let them come to the bar during off-hours and get drinks for half price.

But the gas can didn't mean anything special to her until she found it in the back room and got a whiff of the fumes that were on her hand as she put it into the truck. Her mother had always told her how dangerous it was to play with matches and, even worse, strike a match around gasoline. Gasoline could burst into flames so easily and spread so quickly that everything in its path would be gone in a minute.

Not a bad way to do the deed and hide one's tracks, she thought, and suddenly the plan came to her just as Ralph gave her a wave from the window of his office in the back of the bar. He must think that all was well between them because he had apologized for forgetting her birthday.

The bastard! He knew that today was the day he was going to break her heart before breakfast. How dare he act like that never happened? And how dare he think that she'd never find out about his deal with Jake? She wasn't a stupid little girl anymore who was sad because her mother had gone away and left her with a father who never loved or cared for her.

No, she was sixteen today, and she had a plan. If she couldn't get what she wanted from Ralph, she would take what she could get. It was a bold and crazy idea, but she had thought it all through in her mind. She had even picked out a new name for herself as she began her new life.

Yes, she would start fresh, without Ralph and on her own.

It was her sixteenth birthday, after all, and that was her dream. Hadn't her mother told her to be bold and follow her dreams? It wasn't like her to disobey her mother, now was it?

A few hours later, Lisette lit the match and watched the flames explode under the wooden chair that stood on the gasoline-soaked floor in front of the door to her father's office. While she had tipped the chair under the door handle so as to block the door, her plan was to remove it right before she left the bar and her life there forever. But not before she said one more thing to Ralph, her so-called father.

Although she couldn't see him through the door, he was probably sitting behind his desk, counting his money in the tin box he kept in a locked safe. He was pretty boozed up. She planned it that way. She made him join the celebration of her birthday that night in the bar, doubling up rather than watering down the liquor in his drinks. When the last customer left at two in the morning, she began cleaning up behind the bar as he stumbled into his office with the cash for the night from the register and closed the door. As though he couldn't trust her, he had to count his beloved money all by himself. That was fine with her.

She turned down the lights in the bar and walked into the back room for the can of gasoline she had stashed in the closet when she returned with her birthday cake.

Soon, she'd have the wish she made tonight when she blew out the candles.

She knocked lightly on the door to his office.

"Oh, Ralph. I'm leaving now. You're on your own. Let's see how you like it, darling."

She heard him shuffle up to his side of the door and grab the doorknob. "I smell smoke," he shouted. "I can't get the damn door open. Help me! Please, help me."

As the flames rose on her side of the door, she could imagine how hot and smoky it was in there. She had to stand back as the wooden walls caught fire fast. Soon the smoke was pouring out from under the door, making her cough and gasp for breath. It was time for her to leave. That was in her plan too. She got a pool stick and used it to pull the chair out from under the doorknob. She let it fall on its side in front of the door and stood there for a moment longer, the gas can still in her hand.

It didn't take Ralph long to push the door open and stumble into the darkness and smoke that filled the room. He fell over the chair and landed face down in the flames on the floor. As he screamed, she poured more gasoline around him, careful not to let the flames follow the stream back to her. Then she threw the can next to his hand, turned and walked steadily out of the bar into the cool, spring night.

CHAPTER NINETEEN

Playing the System

"Oh my God!" Sophie exclaimed, her eyes wide and her words coming out in a rush of questions. "You killed your father? How could you do that? Did you get away with it?"

Radiance responded in a quieter but firm voice. "There is more to this story, isn't there, Lisette?"

"How do you know that?" she snapped back at her, but before she let Radiance answer that question, Lisette snarled at Sophie, "Just so you know, I was accused of killing Ralph. The police found me the night of the fire in Ralph's truck just outside town. I don't know why they stopped me, but when they did. I was driving with my learner's permit. That, and an old library card I had in my purse, was all I had that linked me to Ralph by his last name."

"What was Ralph's name?" Radiance asked.

"Rozniak."

"And that was your name?"

"Yeah. I was known as Lisa Rozniak then. For some stupid reason, my mom gave me his name although she never took it herself."

"Your parents were never married?"

"No."

"But you told me your name was Lisette LaTour," Sophie interjected.

"It is now. Even before the fire at the bar I had planned to change it. I wanted a new life. I wanted to be emancipated. But Ralph wouldn't let me. So that's why he had to die."

"But he didn't die, did he?" Radiance asked calmly. "I have been pulling tarot cards for you ever since you started talking." Radiance showed Lisette the deck in her hand. "The card for 'death' hasn't appeared yet so there is more."

Lisette squirmed uncomfortably in her seat. "If you think you know so much about my damn life, why don't you just tell me? Why do I have to spill my guts out to you?"

"If you want me to help you, this is the way I work. I use a number of tools, including these cards, but if you don't want my help, that's okay with me too."

"No, please," Lisette begged. "I need you. There's no one else. Please!" Then she added, "It's just that my mother had her cards read right before she died, and the cards scared me. It was like they were the reason she died."

Radiance gave her a smile. "You know that's not true, but I can ditch the cards. You need to keep talking."

Lisette smiled back.

"Okay, it's a deal. Now, where did I leave off?"

On the morning of the second day of the hearing in front of Juvenile Court Judge Morgan Flaherty, Lisette chewed on her fingernails as she sat waiting at the table in the courtroom for the judge to come onto the bench. She was down to her cuticles and still going at it when Deirdre Kelly, her legal aid attorney, came into the room and slid into the seat next to her.

Deirdre slapped Lisette's hand and hissed under her breath, "Stop that. It makes you look nervous. Nervous people are always guilty."

Lisette frowned and pulled her hands down tightly into her lap, rubbing her fingertips into the soft brown corduroy skirt she was wearing with a yellow blouse and brown cardigan sweater. She liked the outfit even though she had no idea where Deirdre had gotten it. Wearing it, she felt like she was living someone else's life.

"What's taking him so long?" Lisette whispered impatiently to Deirdre. "Why can't we get this over with?"

"I told you that this is going to go on for a while. Since you are sixteen and still a juvenile, it's a more informal hearing, and the judge will want to hear things that might be excluded in adult court. And he's going to let me question you first rather than the attorney for the state."

"But you told me it will never go to a trial."

"Probably not a criminal trial in adult court, but the purpose of this hearing is to find out if you are a juvenile in need of confinement. Fortunately in this jurisdiction, even if you are charged with a crime as an adult on the evidence, you are still a juvenile until you're eighteen."

"But they don't have any evidence." Lisette looked back and glared at the two cops who picked her up after the fire at the bar. They were sitting in the courtroom a few feet away from her.

"Keep your voice down," Deirdre said sharply, and then continued in a hushed tone. "They do have evidence, but so far they haven't been able to point any of it at you."

The court clerk called out, "All rise. This hearing is now in session."

Lisette watched the judge, an old man with a slight limp, step up to the bench, sit down, and look at the group gathered at the tables in front of him.

"Are we ready to proceed?" he bellowed, but Lisette blocked out the sound of his voice and also that of other lawyer for the state that Deirdre told her about. Instead she thought about the life she'd have after these idiots bought her story about how she had nothing to do with what happened to Ralph. She had decided she'd lie about her age and get a job under her new name – maybe working in a bar and get her own apartment. That's more than Ralph ever did for her.

Suddenly, she felt Deirdre's elbow poke her in her side. Deirdre looked up at the bench. "Pay attention. The judge is speaking."

"Today, the court will hear testimony from Lisa Rozniak," the judge said. "Attorney Kelly, are you prepared to proceed?"

"Yes, your honor."

Deirdre motioned to Lisette to go up to the witness chair and be sworn in. After the judge asked her if she would have any problem telling the truth at this hearing and Lisette replied that she didn't, he said to her attorney, "Proceed."

As Deirdre had prepared Lisette, they began with Lisette's childhood and the death of her mother when she was ten.

"Were you sad when your mom died?" she asked Lisette.

"Yes."

"How else did you feel?"

"Like she left me all alone. But she didn't want to. She died of cancer."

"Did your mother work?"

"Yeah, in a bar. She was a dancer. That's how she met my father."

"Before your mother died, were she and your dad getting along?"

"That's hard to say. He wasn't around much. He only came around certain nights, mostly to see her and – you know – do it."

"You mean have sex?"

"Yes."

"Were you there? Strike that. Where did they have sex?"

"In our trailer."

"In your mother's bedroom."

"Yeah, in the back. I usually slept in the little room next to hers, but nights when Ralph came, Mom made me sleep out on the couch in the living room."

"Ralph – that's what you called your dad, didn't you?"

"Yeah. Although I usually didn't call him much of anything."

"You didn't like your dad, did you, Lisa?"

"No."

"Did he ever beat you?"

"No."

"Hit you?"

"No."

"Did he ever sexually abuse you?"

"No, not really."

"What does 'not really' mean?" Lisette looked up at Deirdre with panic in her eyes. Lisette knew that this answer was not one they had rehearsed, and she hoped Deirdre wouldn't push her about it. It had just come out of her mouth that way.

"He never touched me like that, if that's what you mean."

"That's what I mean. He never tried to touch your breasts or private areas or have sex with you, right?"

"Yes, that's right. He never did that."

Lisette was relieved when Deirdre let it go. Then she continued, "What happened after your mother died?"

"I got sent to a foster home."

"Your father didn't want you to come live with him?"

"Hah!"

"I take it that's a 'no.'"

"He didn't want to have anything to do with me."

"What happened to you in the foster home?"

"I was okay for a while. I liked the lady who took care of me. But her husband – now he sexually abused me."

"Did you tell anyone about it?"

"Oh, yeah. But no one believed me. Not his wife or my social worker. They told me I was just projecting my feeling of abandonment onto him and that I wanted him to pay attention to me. So I went after him with a knife."

The judge shifted in his chair and leaned down to look at Lisette.

Deirdre continued. "When you did that, did his wife see you?"

"Oh, yeah, she saw me, and the other kids saw me. Hey, I didn't deny that I went after him with a knife – a big kitchen one. I wanted him to stop diddling me and if I had to cut off his balls – excuse me – I mean…" She quickly looked up at the judge.

"It's okay, Lisa," Deirdre reassured her. "Just tell me what you were thinking."

"I thought that either I'd scare him away from me forever or at least I'd get tossed out of that home by trying to stab him in front of everyone."

"And did it work?"

"Yup, but no foster home wanted me after that. The social worker didn't know what to do with me, and I didn't have any relatives. So she tracked down my dad to see if he wanted me."

"And then what happened?"

"Well, he wasn't sure at first until he learned that they would pay him like a foster parent, since my parents weren't married or something like that. Anyway, once he heard about the money, he wanted me all right."

"So that's how you came to live with your father. He was living in your mother's trailer by then, right?"

"Yup. He told me she promised it to him when she died. But I think he just moved in one day and began paying rent to the owner of the lot where the trailer was sitting."

"How was it that you started working in the bar after school?"

"Ralph told me I had to. To pay my room and board, he said.

But it wasn't a big deal. I learned to make drinks and wait tables. It wasn't hard. Just long hours, particularly on school nights, but then I never did very well in school anyway. I never liked reading or writing very much after my mom died. Can't do it very well." Lisette tugged at the gold key on the chain around her neck. "I try to, but I can't really."

"Did anyone ever come in and tell Ralph that you were too young to tend bar?"

"You mean those folks from the city? Ralph paid all those guys off. You know the liquor inspectors. They never came in except to have a few drinks themselves."

Deirdre moved on. "What happened the night of Friday, April 20?"

"It was my birthday, and we were celebrating at the bar. Ralph liked to celebrate so he could drink. He had me go out and get a cake, and I blew out the candles and all."

"So you left the bar that night and bought a cake for yourself. Did you drive your father's truck?

"Yes."

"But you don't have a license, do you?"

"I had a learner's permit. I took driver's ed in school and got my permit."

"But you were supposed to drive with an adult."

"Yeah."

"But you weren't with an adult."

"Nah. Ralph taught me to drive a long time ago, so I drove by myself."

"Did you buy some gasoline for the truck when you went out?"

"Yes, Ralph told me to. He gave me the money."

"Did he also tell you to fill a can of gasoline?"

"Yes."

"Did you do that?"

"Yes. I always did as I was told."

Deirdre ignored that response and continued. "What happened after you came back with the can of gas?"

"Ralph told me to put it in the closet in the back. I cleaned up and left the bar when I was done."

"Did he tell you what he wanted the can of gas for?"

"No."

"Was it unusual that he asked you to get a can of gas? I mean, he hadn't asked you to do that before, did he?"

"No."

"And how did he act when he asked you to get the can of gas?"

"A little strange. He told me to make sure it was full to the top and then sneak it into the bar so that no one else saw it."

"So he was secretive about it. What else was strange about him that night?"

"When I was leaving, he followed me out to the truck and told me that he was sorry but I'd have to go away for a few days. He gave me some money to get some clothes and food for myself because he told me that he didn't want me to go home first. He wanted me to drive out to the motel on Route 23 and stay there until he came to get me."

"Did that surprise you? That he wanted you to go off by yourself?"

"Yeah. But he was drunk and saying some other crazy stuff too."

"Like what?"

"He was slurring his words and talking really fast. He kept saying how he had to do what he was going to do and he didn't need me around to see it."

"What did you think he meant by that?"

"I didn't know what to make of it. But he scared me, so I took off."

"But you didn't go to the motel. When the police officers picked you up in the truck, you were miles in the other direction, weren't you?"

"That's because I decided not to go to that motel. I was mad at him for making me leave like that in the middle of the night without any of my things. But I was afraid to go home, so I just got in the truck and started driving. I didn't know where I was when those two officers stopped me."

"Why did you ask one of them if you were under arrest?"

"Because I watch all those cop shows on television. I know what it means when they tell you to get in the squad car. It means you're under arrest. And he didn't even read me my rights."

"Lisa, did you try to kill your father?"

"No." The word came out quickly and very elongated.

"Did you make a call from a phone booth that night saying that there was a fire at the bar and that you suspected arson?"

"No."

"Who would have made such a call? Strike that. Lisa, did you love your father?"

"Yeah… well, sort of. I didn't like him much, and he wasn't a warm, fuzzy kinda guy. But he never did me any real harm."

"Did he ever make you really mad?"

"No. Well, maybe when he ran off one of my boyfriends with a shotgun. But he showed me that the guy had no guts anyway."

"Did he ever make you so mad that you wanted to kill him?"

"No," she said, as a sweet smile came over her face. "After all, he was my father – and besides, he's not dead."

Then she turned slowly toward the judge and did the very thing Deirdre told her not to do. She changed what they had practiced endlessly for the last few days.

She spoke now directly to the judge with that sweet smile still plastered on her face. "And I'd sure like to see Ralph when he's able to talk to me. He's all I've got left in the world, and like my mother always said, 'Blood is blood, no matter what.' He's my dad."

After lunch, Lisette's attorney called her next witness.

"Please state your name for the record," she began after the witness was sworn in.

"Detective John J. Charbonneau, County Police Department," he replied.

"You are the detective in charge of investigating the fire in the club owned by Lisa Rozniak's father, Ralph, is that correct?"

"Yes, that is correct."

"I would bring your attention to last Friday night. Did you get a call from the hospital in regard to this investigation?"

"Yes. I was called by one of the nurses in the burn unit that one of the witnesses to the fire wanted to make a statement."

"And that witness was Ralph Rozniak, was it not?" Deirdre asked.

"Yes."

"Can you tell us what happened when you got to the hospital?"

"Yes. Well, Mr. Rozniak was barely conscious, but he was asking for his daughter, Lisa. He was driving the nurses crazy about it until one of them called me to see what could be done. I had already tried to question him about what happened that night, but he wouldn't say a word. Now he was insisting upon seeing Lisa."

"So you talked to him that night?"

"Yes. I entered Mr. Rozniak's room and identified myself. I asked him if there was something that he wanted to tell me. And he kept repeating 'See Lisa' in this almost delirious state. I told him that I couldn't bring Lisa to see him because she was in detention, awaiting a decision by the judge as to whether she had tried to kill him."

"And what did he say to that?"

"He grew quite agitated and kept saying, 'Not Lisa, not Lisa.'"

I asked him what he meant, and he replied in a whisper, 'She didn't. Me! Me!'"

"And what did you take that to mean, Detective?"

"I asked him, 'Are you saying that you did this to yourself?' and I pointed to the bandages covering the burns on his face, hands, and chest. He looked at me for a minute, and I repeated, 'Are you saying that Lisa didn't do this to you?' His response was quick and his voice was getting more agitated. 'Yes! Help her, please!' Then his voice faded and he passed from consciousness. The nurse came to his side and told me I had to leave; she said that he had had enough."

"And that was it? That was all he said to you?"

"Yes, and I think he was trying to say she didn't do it."

The detective stopped talking, and Lisette sat there, holding her breath. Was it possible? Had Ralph really said that? Had he tried to save her from going to jail? Then, just as Lisette thought Deirdre was finished asking questions, the detective added, "Of course, you could take what he said either way. Either he's a hero or a good liar. But he is her father. Wouldn't you want your father to do that for you?"

By then, Deirdre was shouting over the detective's voice, saying something to the judge about disregarding the detective's last statement as speculative and how based on what Ralph said, any charges against Lisette should not be pursued.

Four days later it was all over, and Lisette was glad.

Judge Flaherty made his decision, and Deirdre explained it to her this way. Although the circumstances of the fire at the bar cast some suspicion on Lisette, the judge took into consideration the statements made by Ralph to the police that she was not involved in the incident. But since she was a minor, and since Ralph was severely injured and unable to take care of her, leaving her now without any living relative, the judge did find that she was in need of confinement. 'Confinement' didn't mean in jail or a treatment center, but while waiting for a foster care bed to open up, Lisette would be staying in an emergency shelter for kids in the next county. No one would know her there, Deirdre assured her, or have heard about her father and what happened to him that night in the bar.

"But I don't want to go to a foster home again!" Lisette told Deirdre. "I want to be emancipated. I know all about how to do it. I heard about it from someone at school. She did it, and that's what I want."

"But *you* have a judge on your tail, as well as the media," Deirdre explained. "You can't walk out of this mess with no one watching you. The judge wants you under a watchful eye in case the police or the arson squad finds some evidence that clearly points to you starting that fire. He's worried that the public won't want you to get off so easily and he won't be a judge much longer."

"I don't care if he gets reelected; I want to get on with my life!" Lisette eyed Deirdre and then added, "Unless you don't believe that I didn't try to kill my father?"

"You know I believe that you didn't," her attorney shot back. "Look. Be patient. It will all work out."

So Lisette was patient, and everything was quiet – until Jake got arrested. His arrest had nothing to do with Lisette, but when Deirdre came to see her one afternoon, the news was not good.

"I went to see Jake in jail this morning. He told me what he told the police. It doesn't look good for you."

"He's lying," Lisette hissed. "Jake doesn't know anything about what went on between my father and me."

Deirdre looked Lisette squarely in the eyes. "Jake knows enough to save his butt on a drug peddling charge by telling the police everything he knows about you. It's the deal he's made with the cops, and I'm telling you it looks bad for you."

Deirdre paused for a moment, and then continued in a stern voice that Lisette hadn't heard before. "Not only did he tell the cops things you didn't tell them, but what he said contradicts what you told the cops *and* me."

"I didn't lie to you! Jake and I were lovers. There's no crime in that."

"Yeah, let's forget about statutory rape for a moment," Deirdre snickered. "Jake tells a convincing story about how on the afternoon of the fire you found out for the first time that your father was prostituting you to Jake and the other men in the bar. He said that when you found out, you told Jake that you were going to kill your father by – and I quote – 'by lighting him up like a Christmas tree.' Are you telling me that Jake is wrong about all of that? That this doesn't give you both the motive and the opportunity to kill your father several hours later?"

Lisette looked at Deirdre. "What makes you think that Jake isn't telling you all that to make it sound like he is such a stud? I'm beautiful. I could have any of those guys in the bar. My dad didn't need to be a pimp for me."

"He wasn't running a dating service for you, and you know it. He was making money off of your young flesh, and when you found out, you got mad at him – and you wanted to kill him, didn't you?" Deirdre yelled at Lisette. "You had a plan figured out in advance, and when you found out about Jake, you just put it into motion. Didn't you?"

Lisette responded without emotion, "I plead the fifth!"

"You little bitch! You can't plead the fifth with your own attorney. You can't incriminate yourself with me. But all of this lying is certainly making my job harder. What is going on in that mind of yours? How did you think that you were going to get away with this? You are just lucky that Ralph didn't die, because a first-degree murder charge is a very, very serious one."

"I have faith in you as my attorney." Lisette's voice was calm. "Ralph didn't die, and I didn't try to kill him."

"You know, I actually think you believe that. It must have been horrible going through life with a man like Ralph as your father. And then to find out he was selling you to those creeps – I'd have tried to kill him too."

Lisette looked at Deirdre, frustrated because it would have been so easy for her to tell her attorney everything, to come clean and let her guard down, but she couldn't. She couldn't trust anyone about this, just like she could never trust Ralph. He may have saved her in the end, but she wasn't about to forgive him just because of that. No, she wasn't taking the bait. Not this time. She had learned her lesson. She was sticking with her story. Her attorney be damned!

"I didn't try to kill Ralph," she repeated. "And no one, not you or anyone else, can prove it!" Lisette held her breath as she held her emotions in. She couldn't let them out. She couldn't and wouldn't.

"I don't want to prove that you tried to kill him," Deirdre shot back. "I just want you to tell me the truth so that someone else won't prove that you did. If I prove it, that only makes it look like you lied to me and that makes me mad, but if they prove it, you'll go to jail for a long time. Or maybe you'll get off lightly. Maybe the judge will take into consideration what a hard life you have had. It's all a crapshoot now, and whatever happens next is really up to you. It's your life."

"You don't know shit about my life," Lisette said with clenched teeth. She wanted to cry so badly, but she wouldn't let herself. She had to be strong. "I need you to clean this mess up and get me what I want," she went on vehemently. "I want out of here, now! Do you understand?"

Then her voice went shrill. "Or do I have to get another god-damn stupid asshole lawyer? What is wrong with you people? Why can't you just leave me alone?"

CHAPTER TWENTY

Pushing a Limit

By the time Lisette had finished telling her story, Sophie and Radiance were on the edge of their seats.

Lisette was exhausted. She had never told the whole story to anyone, and it made her sick to think of all that she had gone through.

"So you were quite angry then," Radiance finally said in a calm voice, breaking the silence between the three of them. "Did you really say all those things to your lawyer?"

"Yes," Lisette said, almost proudly, and then she sighed. "I know she was only trying to do her job, but I was scared of Ralph. Who knows what Ralph might have done next? I never trusted him, and I still don't."

"Is he still alive?" Sophie asked curiously.

"I don't know. I never saw him again, although one of the social workers at the school I attended wanted me to. I refused – what could I say to a man like that? 'Gee, thanks, and oh, by the way, I forgive you.' Never! I'll never forgive the bastard!"

"But he lied for you and saved you from going to jail," Sophie replied. "He could have hated you for trying to kill him, but he didn't." Then she lowered her voice and added, "He must have loved you. Don't you see that?"

"No!" Lisette said vehemently, her face turning bright red with agitation and rage. "Ralph never loved me or my mother. He got what he deserved!"

Sophia fell back on the sofa, like she had been whiplashed by Lisette's anger. Lisette looked at her and sighed, "Oh God! I'm sorry. I didn't mean to yell at you. It's just that any mention of Ralph and what I did to him sets me off. It's not like it's my fault, but I can't help how I feel about him."

"I'm not surprised that the spirit of a young girl like Lacey is inhabiting your body," Radiance broke in. "You've been stuck in a lot of anger toward men who have abused you and treated you badly ever since your mother died. Remember what I said about Lacey being attracted to your energy? It all lines up."

"That's just great," Lisette said sarcastically. "But at this point, I don't really care why Lacey is in my body. I just want to get her out."

"Knowing why she is there can help get her out," Radiance said simply.

"Is that it? You want to analyze me, figure me out, do some psychological mumbo jumbo on me like everyone else."

"No, I am trying to help you, and this information about Ralph is important as we journey today. I can promise you that."

Lisette looked at her for a moment. "What do you mean, 'we'? I thought I was going on the journey alone, like I did yesterday."

"No, this time I'm going with you. This time, we're going to look for Lacey."

"All right!" Sophie said. "This is exciting!"

"I'm not sure if we will find her or she'll find us," Radiance added cautiously. "Are you ready to begin?"

Lisette nodded enthusiastically. She could hardly wait. She stepped out of her shoes and knelt to lie down on the blanket.

"Wait a minute," Radiance said. "I want to go over the ground rules again. It's important that we are clear here."

Lisette didn't really want to hear it all again, but she had agreed to trust Radiance and do what she wanted her to do, so she sat quietly on the floor as Radiance talked.

"In a few minutes, we're both going to lie on the blanket, and Sophie is going to drum for us like I did for you yesterday. But we won't be going to the Upper World like you did yesterday."

"Where will we go this time?" Lisette asked.

"To the Middle World, where we'll look for my power animal, Raven. We'll stay there and see what happens."

"What's a power animal?" Lisette asked.

"They are spirits in animal forms that guide us and guard us when we are on our journeys. Trust me, you'll want someone like Raven to protect us from the spirits in the Middle World."

"What is this Middle World like?"

"It is the most like our everyday or 'ordinary' reality," Radiance explained. "It's like a spiritual counterpart to this world; things will look familiar yet a little different, so don't get freaked out."

"Why do you think we'll find Lacey there?"

"Because when people die, their spirits can get stuck in the Middle World. Sometimes they don't believe they are dead, or they need to resolve something. Lacey knows she's dead, but for some reason, she can't – or won't – go forward. That's why she'd been hanging out with you."

"Can Raven really take us to Lacey? How will he know where she is?"

"Don't worry. Power animals have extraordinary abilities. That's why you want them around you," Radiance said with a grin. "And remember, we'll be entering a world that looks very much like this one, so the first thing we'll do is leave this apartment, go downstairs, and out into the street. From there, Raven will take us to where we need to go. Do you understand?"

Lisette nodded and gripped Radiance's hand tightly.

"When it's time for us to return to Sophie and this room," Radiance continued, "you must return immediately. Sophie will roll the drum very fast and then hit it four times very slowly. By the end of those last beats, we will be back in this room. That's the call to come back, and you must promise me that you will come back. Do you agree?"

"Yes," Lisette said, and then asked eagerly, "Can we go now?"

"Sure," Radiance said and sat down on the floor next to Lisette. "We're going to lie next to each other on the blanket with our hands and feet touching."

When Lisette settled down next to Radiance, Sophie called out cheerfully, "I'll be here when you get back. You can tell me all about it. Don't forget to say hi to Lacey for me."

"I will," Lisette said, but she realized that all this was easy for Sophie. All she had to do was drum. *What am I getting myself into?* Lisette wondered, some of her fears from yesterday coming back. But before she could say anything more, the drumming began, and Lisette let herself get into the beat.

Slowly, the room and everything around her faded away. The adventure had begun.

Oh my God! Lisette thought, her heart thumping. They were on their way to find Lacey. She had wanted so badly for all this craziness to stop and her life to be normal again. Thank God! She was finally getting somewhere!

That morning, Ambrose woke up, groggy and feeling like an idiot.

Yesterday he hadn't come anywhere close to finding Lisette. Last night he was at the men's homeless shelter, but it was too noisy there for him to get a good night's sleep. Even the nap he had taken yesterday afternoon in Lisette's hotel room wasn't helping him today. So, less sharp and more anxious this morning with a lack of sleep, he headed toward Lisette's hotel, chastising himself for how bad things were going. Not only had he scared Lisette off at the library yesterday, but last night he didn't dare get near The Pussycat, worried that Webster would be watching for him. He needed to set the record straight with Lisette about the accident and explain what had happened between him and Mark or she'd be lost to him forever. She'd never do the performance art act with him or help him make peace with Mark. She was his one salvation, and he wasn't about to let her go without a fight.

As he neared her hotel, Ambrose thought about all the messages he had left for her yesterday, some on the hotel's voicemail and others that he had slipped under the door to her room. She hadn't answered any of them, so he would have to try something else today. His plan was to call her from the lobby before noon and invite her to come down and have a late breakfast with him in the hotel coffee shop. He suspected that she slept in late if she danced the night before, so his timing just might work. If it didn't, he'd go up to her room and break down the door if he had to get to see her. He was that desperate.

Ambrose got to the hotel about eleven-thirty that morning and went right to the house phone to call up to Lisette's room. There was no answer. Then he approached the desk clerk and asked him to ring the room, but again, there was no response. The clerk invited him to leave a message, but Ambrose was afraid that after leaving so many messages yesterday with no response, leaving more might only irritate her. Finally he took the elevator up to Lisette's room and knocked on the door himself, but no one answered.

Agitated but not defeated, Ambrose took a quick walk over to the Pussycat to see if anyone was there this morning, but the place was locked up tight and no one was around.

About quarter to one, Ambrose stumbled back into the lobby of Lisette's hotel and practically fell over a big lug of a guy who was standing by the door, looking lost.

"Sorry!" the guy said and stepped to one side to let Ambrose go by.

"What the hell are you doing crowding the door like that?" Ambrose growled as he pushed past the guy and headed into the lobby.

Any other time, he might have taken on a guy like that who pissed him off, even if he was a kid with big broad shoulders and huge forearms. But today, Ambrose didn't have the time or patience for such nonsense. His plan was to sit down in the lobby near the front desk so he could see and hear what was going on without attracting too much attention and simply wait for Lisette to turn up. As he did so, he saw the young guy he almost tripped over at the door standing near the elevators now and scrutinizing every person who came off into the lobby. Each time the doors opened, he seemed disappointed and he'd shuffle his feet impatiently, check his watch and wait until the elevator bell rang again.

He was waiting for someone, Ambrose decided, and that someone wasn't showing up. As the minutes ticked by, the guy looked more and more disappointed and distracted. God! Ambrose thought, he knew that feeling, waiting for Lisette to show up. But did he look as lost and forlorn as that kid did?

Finally, the guy walked briskly toward the front desk.

"Excuse me," Ambrose heard him say to the desk clerk. "I'm waiting for someone who is staying at this hotel. Could you ring her room for me?"

The desk clerk nodded and the guy went on, "Her name is Lisette LaTour."

At the sound of Lisette's name, Ambrose perked up. Could this guy be looking for Lisette too? But who was he? What did he want with her?

"And who shall I say is calling?" the desk clerk continued.

"Tell her Erick is waiting for her in the lobby."

Jesus, Ambrose fumed. Is Lisette dating this kid? Is that why she hasn't been around to meet with him? "Damn it!" he muttered.

While the desk clerk rang Lisette's room, Ambrose watched with growing agitation as Erick drummed his thick fingers on the wooden front desk.

"I'm sorry, sir," the desk clerk finally said, hanging up the phone. "There is no answer in Ms. LaTour's room. Would you like to leave her a message?"

"No," Erick said, and then scowled and turned away from the desk. He turned back suddenly and asked, "Do you know, by any chance, if there is an apartment building nearby with two big towers and the river running behind it?"

An apartment building? Ambrose wondered. What did that have to do with Lisette? The desk clerk thought for a moment and then replied, "There is an old apartment building that used to be part of a gated community. It's on Alba Avenue. It might fit that description. You can walk there from here."

What did Erick know about Lisette that he didn't know? Was Lisette in that building? Bingo! Ambrose thought with glee and then listened as the desk clerk gave Erick directions. If he followed him, he might find Lisette. It was that easy.

"Thanks," Erick said as he walked quickly across the lobby and out the front door. Ambrose was right behind him, undetected and at a distance, trying to keep himself calm.

He didn't care what this Erick was to Lisette. He would use Erick to find Lisette and once he did, he'd deal with Erick as he had to.

It was as simple as that.

CHAPTER TWENTY-ONE

Between the Boundaries

As she and Radiance settled down on their blankets, Sophie began drumming and Lisette felt herself go into a panic.

Maybe Erick was right after all. She was making a mistake. This crazy shaman stuff that Radiance was doing was not what she needed. She had to get out of there, now, before this journey began. But as she moved to get up off the blanket, Radiance squeezed her hand tightly and held her there. The warmth of her touch filled Lisette's body, and she loved how that felt.

Lisette sighed and the feeling lingered for a moment longer while the drum's beat pulled her down into a fuzzy place, one that had no real shape to it at first. But then it was like Radiance had said it would be: They were there in the real world, but everything looked slightly different. She felt Radiance grabbing her arm and pulling her out the door of the apartment and into the hall. There in the Middle World, this hallway was longer, darker and more mysterious. She expected that they would wait for the elevator, but that didn't seem necessary. They were both lifted up and out a window in the hall and then down into the street.

"Wow!" she said as she landed next to Radiance on the sidewalk in front of the building. "You didn't tell me you could fly in the Middle World."

"That's nothing," Radiance said with a grin. "In the Middle World, all kinds of things can happen. I've seen spirits fight and even kill each other."

"But they are already dead," Lisette said, sounding confused.

"Yes, but they can still act in physical ways."

Suddenly, a large black bird soared around above them, the sound of its wings so loud it was deafening. The bird dove down toward them, and Lisette gasped. She was relieved when it glided past her onto Radiance's shoulder and sat there quietly.

"Thank you for coming to help, Raven," Radiance said to the bird. "We need to find Lacey. Do you know where she is?"

Raven jumped off Radiance's shoulder and onto the ground in front of them. The bird grew bigger and bigger until it was larger than both of them.

"Oh my God," Lisette cried out, stepping back in horror.

"Don't be afraid." Radiance grabbed her hand and pulled her toward Raven. "Let's get on his back. Grab his feathers and hold on tight."

Lisette tried, but before she could grab on, the bird took off. Lisette fell backward, and Radiance grabbed her and pulled her onto the bird's back.

"I meant it," Radiance shouted over the loud flapping of Raven's wings. "You've got to hold on. This bird waits for no one."

Lisette grabbed a fistful of feathers and clung to them while Raven squawked beneath her as if he had enjoyed giving her a good scare. Soon, she relaxed a bit and looked down on the ground beneath them. She was amazed to see that they were flying over her hotel, and she could see Erick walking down the street with someone who looked like her.

"Hey!" she called out to Radiance. "Who is that down there with Erick?"

Radiance looked and then yelled back, "I forgot to tell you. Sometimes in the Middle World, you can go back in time. Were you walking here recently?"

"Yeah, the night Lacey was killed, Erick walked me back to my hotel. That night was the first time I heard Lacey's voice in my head."

Radiance smiled and yelled back. "That's a good sign. Raven is on Lacey's trail. It shouldn't be long now."

Lisette didn't know how Radiance knew that, but at least they were close. Otherwise she would have asked if Raven could slow down so she could see what was going on between her and Erick down there. They looked so happy, walking hand in hand, like he was her boyfriend. She didn't remember holding hands with him that night, but maybe Sophie was right. Erick was more interested in her than she thought. But by then Raven was circling another building, and she recognized it as the library where she and Ambrose had been yesterday morning. It, too, looked different.

"Oh my God!" Lisette cried out. "The library is shimmering! It's so beautiful!"

Suddenly everything around her shifted. No longer was she perched on Raven; instead, she was in a hole, all cramped up in a small, enclosed space, not able to stretch her legs. It was exactly how she had felt when she and Ambrose sat at the low table in the kiddy room and she had read to him from the books he had picked out about Attila the Hun. She looked up to see Lacey sitting across from her at the same table with a book in her hand. Lacey looked up at Lisette and smiled.

"Hi, Lisa Rozniak. How are you doing?"

"My name is Lisette!" she snapped back.

"Don't be so touchy! I heard the story you told Sophie and Radiance about Lisa."

"How did you know that? Were you with me? Where have you been?"

Lacey laughed out loud. "I've been spending time with my dad. And I had this harrowing experience with Ari. It was awful."

Lacey's voice broke, and she looked like she was going to burst into tears. Feeling bad for her, Lisette reached out to touch her and when she made contact, Lisette had the same warm feeling as she did yesterday when she hugged her mother in the Upper World.

"He's stalking me," Lacey said, her lips trembling. "Just like before. I tried to make him go away. What am I going to do?"

"But he killed you! What more could he want from you?" Lisette turned to Radiance, desperate for an answer. Radiance stepped forward and gently brushed Lacey's long hair away from her face.

"There, there," Radiance said softly, comforting Lacey. "We can help you."

Lisette winced. She wanted to help, but she didn't want to meet up with Ari. She remembered how scared she was when the man came at her with the knife in the hallway at the Bare Bottom. But Lacey had saved her then, and now she had to be there for Lacey.

"We're here to help," Lisette said to her. "Whatever it takes, we'll do it."

"Is he here now? Is that why you are so afraid?" Radiance asked Lacey.

"No, but he was before, and I'm afraid that he'll…."

Lisette turned to Radiance. "What can he do? What kind of monster is Ari?"

"Not one we can deal with," Radiance replied. "We can only help those who reach out to us, and right now, that's Lacey."

"We have to do something for her," Lisette said, desperation in her voice.

"We can escort her to the boundary between the worlds and see if someone on the other side is willing to help her cross over."

"Cross over?" Lacey broke in. "What does that mean?"

"It's the passing from one world into another," Radiance explained. "In that world, you will be welcomed as having completed your transition from the physical world on earth to the nonphysical world. In the Middle World, you've just been prolonging that physical life; you have been living it in a distorted fashion through Lisette."

"Like when you've been hanging out in me," Lisette interjected.

"Yes, but she wasn't really in you," Radiance clarified. "More like in your head, in your mind. In any case, now she needs to break free and move on."

"I want to, but I don't know how," Lacey whimpered. "There's so much going on. I found out that my mother… she… she…."

"What about your mother?" Lisette asked, then listened as Lacey told her about getting into her father's thoughts as he remembered that day in the garage and how he rescued Jimmie but couldn't save her mother's life.

When she finished, Lacey burst into tears.

"All these years," she said between sobs, "I thought my father wasn't telling me how my mother really died because he hated her – or, worse, because he didn't love me. But he did it to protect me and Jimmie. Could you imagine Jimmie finding out that his mother tried to kill him? How horrible is that!"

Lacey collapsed into Radiance's arms and sobbed into her chest.

"But it sounds like your mother wasn't well," Lisette broke in. "Isn't there some kind of depression women get after they have a baby?"

"It's called postpartum depression," Radiance said, stroking Lacey's head and comforting her. "Some women get it so bad they want to kill their babies."

"See?" Lisette said to Lacey, trying to make her feel better. "It wasn't your mother's fault. She didn't know what she was doing. Luckily, your dad showed up and took Jimmie to the hospital."

"Yes, but what about after my father left? Did she kill herself? Or did he knock her out when he pushed her aside getting Jimmie out and she never got up? Oh God! I'll never know what really happened. Even my dad doesn't know."

"That's not true," Radiance said. "You can ask your mother."

Lacey pulled away from Radiance and gave her a wild look.

"How can I do that? I haven't even seen my mother. She must have killed herself. She's in hell, and so far I haven't been there!"

"I suspect your mother is in the Upper World," Radiance said calmly, not reacting to Lacey's idea of hell, which Lisette knew that Radiance, as a shaman, didn't believe in.

"And where is the Upper World?" Lacey asked. "Can you take me there?"

"Yes, but you can't cross over until you've cleared up a few things. How do you feel about your father now?"

Lacey smiled for the first time. "I've forgiven him. My mother's death wasn't his fault, even if he's still not sure how she died and blames himself."

"That's for your father to resolve," Radiance said firmly. "All you can do is know that he was acting in his children's best interest."

"I know," Lacey said softly.

"Good," Radiance replied, sounding encouraged. "That leaves finding out from your mother how she died and then clearing up things with Ari."

"Oh, no, not with Ari!" Lacey moaned at the sound of his name. "I can't…" she began, but Radiance interrupted her.

"Don't worry about him now. We'll focus on your mother first."

Lacey looked relieved, and Lisette was, too. Then she had a thought.

"If we're going to the Upper World, will I see my mom too?" Lisette asked.

"Maybe. We're going to a special part of the Upper World where spirits go to cross over," Radiance explained. "If you cross over there, it will be very hard to come back, because the energy is so intense."

Lisette sighed with disappointment, but then another thought came to her.

"Oh my God," she squealed and turned to Lacey. "Your mom and my mom might know each other in the Upper World. Wouldn't that be cool?"

Lacey smiled at Lisette. "It would be way cool."

"All right," Radiance said. "We'd better get going."

Lisette climbed up on Raven and sat between Radiance and Lacey. Suddenly she felt very happy. She and Lacey were off to find their mothers.

What a trip! Lisette thought, Radiance had called it a journey.

Whatever it was, she hadn't felt this happy in years.

When Raven put Lacey, Lisette, and Radiance down at the boundary between the two worlds, Lisette looked around at the amazing place they had come to. She gazed at the tall green trees that towered over them and the lush plants and shrubs at their feet. There was a cool, light mist in the air that felt good on her face, hot and flushed after the wild ride on Raven's back. The mist swirled around their feet as they walked steadily, with Radiance in the lead, toward a small clearing in the trees just ahead of them. It was like being in paradise, Lisette thought.

"I could stay here forever!" she sighed with delight.

"Exactly," Radiance said. "That's what I meant when I said that the energy in this place is intense. The pull is so strong that we'll want to stay, so we must take care."

But Lisette didn't want to be careful. She wanted to stay here where she felt peaceful and happy. Lacey, on the other hand, was fidgety and restless as she followed Radiance out into the clearing. The three of them stopped at a spot near a large rock.

"Is this where I'll see my mother?" Lacey asked Radiance impatiently. "You said I'd see her here, right?"

"She'll come soon," Radiance assured her. "We are at a place where the veil between the two worlds is very thin and it's the easiest for those in the Upper World to communicate with us in the Middle World."

"But what if she doesn't come?" Lacey asked. "What if she doesn't want to?"

"Of course I want to see my baby!" a voice from beyond the rock called out. Lisette could see by the look on Lacey's face that she recognized the voice immediately.

"Mom? Mom?" Then Lacey turned excitedly to Lisette. "It's her. It's my mom. She's here!"

"What is your mother's name?" Radiance asked quickly.

"It's Marge. My dad called her Margie sometimes." Lacey giggled and squealed, "Oh my God! It's my mom."

Lisette looked up to see a figure emerge from the mist right beyond the rock. It was a woman dressed in a long, white, flowing gown with red and white flowers braided into her long, brown hair.

"She looks so beautiful," Lacey cried out. "Mom, Mom! Is it really you?"

Lacey made a move toward the figure, but Radiance put a hand out to stop her.

"Not yet," Radiance said. "We must find out first if she is willing to help you cross over."

Lacey looked at Radiance like she was crazy. "Of course she'll help me cross over. She's my mother."

Lacey stepped forward again, and again Radiance pulled her back.

"I know this doesn't make any sense to you, but we must do this right. You must trust me, Lacey. Please."

Lacey sighed and stepped back. "All right," she muttered, and Radiance moved forward.

"I'm looking for Marge, mother of Lacey. Is that you?"

"Yes," the figure replied, facing Radiance across the narrow expanse that separated the two worlds.

"Lacey is here, wishing to cross over," Radiance went on solemnly.

"And I am here to help her, if she is ready," Marge replied.

"She has a question for you, and she needs to know the answer," Radiance went on. "She needs to know how you died, and if she caused your death. She also needs to forgive you for leaving her and Jimmie all alone."

Lisette watched Lacey's face as Radiance spoke, although she wanted to see if her mother was there in the mist too. But this was Lacey's moment, and she didn't want to upstage her.

Marge sighed deeply and looked beyond Radiance to Lacey.

"Oh, my dear one! You didn't cause my death," she said in a soft, clear voice. "How could you have? You were just a child. I loved you so much. And I loved Jimmie, too. I don't know what happened that day, but something snapped in me. I thought I was protecting Jimmie by putting him in the garage. I thought there were people out to get him, and when I saw your father, I thought he was one of them. I fought him. I tried to keep him from Jimmie, but I couldn't, and when I couldn't, there was nothing left for me. I was the worst mother in the whole world, and I deserved to die."

Tears welled up in Lacey's eyes as her mother went on.

"I thought of you, and I wanted to live. I didn't want to leave you or Jimmie. I wanted to get out of the garage, but I couldn't. The door had locked behind your father, and as I watched him walk away, I yelled at him to come back, but he couldn't hear me. I took it as a sign that it was my time to go, and so I went."

"But you could have turned the car off," Lacey shouted across the clearing. "You could have yelled louder. Someone would have heard you."

Lacey was almost frantic now. Lisette could see that she needed an answer from Marge, and she didn't like the one she was getting so far.

"Why didn't you?" Lacey went on. "Why did you leave us? Why?"

"What I could have done or should have done is not important now," Marge said patiently. "The fumes overtook me and lulled me into a place where all my pain was gone. It felt so good, Lacey, so wonderful. I forgot all about how much you'd miss me. I'm sorry. It was my doing, not yours."

Lacey looked at her mother and wailed, "But Daddy thinks he's to blame."

"Yes, he would," she said sympathetically. "He had so much guilt about our relationship that it was easier for him to blame himself and live in misery and regret. Your father should have moved on after my death years ago, but that's not your problem. Do you see?"

Marge gave Lacey a patient look, as though she had been angry about all this in the past but wasn't anymore. Lisette wondered how she had gotten beyond her rage. That wasn't an easy thing to do.

"He thinks he killed you," Lacey blurted out. "And that's something he's never forgiven himself for."

"But I have forgiven him, and that's why I'm here now in this wonderful place," Marge said. "If I blame myself for anything, it was that I needed help after Jimmie was born and I didn't get it. People in the physical world talk more freely about things like postpartum depression now. If it had been that way back then, things would have been different."

Lacey stood there for a moment, taking it all in. Then she sighed and said quietly, "I can understand that. I forgive you and

Daddy – and Jimmie, too. I thought it was all about me, but it wasn't."

Lisette spoke up impatiently from behind her. "Is that it? Can she cross over now? I mean, she said the magic word, right? It sounds like she forgave them all. Isn't that what she had to say?"

Radiance ignored Lisette and looked at Marge. "Your daughter would like to cross over. Will you help her?"

"Yes, of course," Marge said. "I'm ready to receive her into the Upper World." Then she turned and said directly to Lacey, "I have never stopped loving you, baby. I've been waiting for you to come so we can be together again."

Lacey was smiling now, and Lisette was ecstatic. She couldn't believe it was finally going to happen. Lacey was going to move on, and she was going to have her life back. Thank God! Lacey looked so happy.

Suddenly a voice behind them barked out, "So here you are! I've been looking all over for you, and you're not going anywhere until I say so!"

Lisette turned around and saw a young man. She recognized him immediately. Though the pictures she had seen of him before were fuzzy and grainy, there was no mistaking Ari. He was stalking Lacey all the way to the boundary between the worlds. He was going to ruin everything, and Lisette wasn't going to let him.

She was so angry with him, she forgot her fear, put her face right up to his and screamed, "What is your problem?"

"My problem? What's yours, stripper girl?"

"You!" she shot back. "Can't you just leave her alone?"

Ari jabbed his finger into Lisette's shoulder so hard that it pushed her away from him. "It's none of your business," he growled. "I know who you are and what you do. Go back to that silly tease you do, girl. You're out of your league here."

Lisette was furious. She threw her whole body at him, not sure what was going to happen. She couldn't imagine fighting with someone who was already dead, but Radiance had said that spirits could do battle and kill each other in the Middle World.

To her surprise, Ari's body was like a solid rock, and she bounced off it so hard that she fell backward.

"Hey, that hurt!" she yelled from the ground, rubbing her behind and groaning.

Ari glared down at her. "Don't get in my way, or I can, and I will, hurt you more." He stomped past Lisette and headed toward Lacey.

Lisette wasn't going to let him go that easily. She grabbed his leg and hung on. "No!" she screamed. "I won't let you spoil this."

But Ari kept going, shaking her off his leg like she was a fly. Lisette fell back to the ground and as she looked up, she saw Ari wave something right in front of Lacey's face. It was the same heart-shaped locket Lacey had been wearing that night at the Bare Bottom when her image flashed into Lisette's head and saved her life.

Lisette watched now as Lacey tried to grab the necklace from Ari.

"Give me that! It's mine," she hissed.

But if it was hers, what was Ari doing with it?

What the hell was going on?

Standing in the narrow expanse between the two worlds with her mother just a few steps away from her, Lacey was furious when she turned around and saw Ari.

He had rushed past Lisette who had tried to stop him and then came towards her. She looked over quickly at her mother, but Lacey knew that her mother couldn't help her with this. She had to face Ari alone one last time.

She felt her anger toward him rise from deep inside. She was going to the Upper World to be with her mother, and he was trying to stop her. That wasn't going to happen. But did she have the strength to fight him? When she had tried before, she didn't and it still appalled her that her need for revenge was so strong that she wanted to kill him. But he was already dead by his own hand. He had beaten her to the punch. Was there no justice even in this, the Middle World?

She turned to Radiance, who leaned over and whispered as if she knew what Lacey was thinking, "Ari has the power to keep you in the Middle World forever. Don't be fooled by him or underestimate his power. He'll use any trick to stop you. Be careful."

"But why can't he leave me alone?" Lacey cried out in frustration.

"Because this is where it must end. It has to, or you can't move on."

By now, Ari was there, waving the heart-shaped locket again in her face. She snatched at the gold chain, but he pulled it away, cackling and dancing in front of her.

"I've got your necklace. Come on, Lacey! You can have it – and so much more. We can be together. This is our forever."

She glared at him, knowing that he was trying to make her come after it again, and suddenly it dawned on her. The last time she saw the necklace, it was in her jewelry box in the dorm room that she shared with Sophie. There was no way Sophie would ever let Ari, dead or alive, get anywhere near that box or her necklace. So it was a trick, just an illusion, one more of Ari's lies. He wanted her to believe this locket was hers, but it wasn't. It was a fake.

She wondered why she had believed anything he had ever told her, and what he didn't tell her had killed her. Like about the gun, for instance. He had tricked her that night. He got her into his room with a story about how he wanted her to read his paper. Then he closed the door and sat down near it so when he pulled out the gun, she'd have to walk past him to get away. If she tried to go through the bathroom door into his suitemates' room, he had a plan for that, too. That was the one that worked. So he had it all figured out that night, but this time she was on to him.

"You think you're so smart, don't you?" she said, eyeing him carefully. "That if you push me long and hard enough or make me feel sorry for you, I'll give in. That may have worked before, but it won't now."

She glared at him. "And you knew I wouldn't be able to live with knowing you killed yourself because I dumped you. Did it make you feel like a real man to shoot me while trying to get away from watching you do that?"

Ari grunted but didn't speak. Lacey moved around behind him now, sizing him up. "Sophie was right about you," she went on.

She stopped behind him and poked him several times in the back.

"She told me that guys like you are vultures, but I didn't see the wings on you until now!" She cackled and then her voice got serious again. "Sophie told me that you'd keep picking at our dead relationship until there was nothing left but a carcass. She told me not to trust you, to treat you like a stranger, but I thought, 'Ari would never hurt me. He loves me.' I was wrong, dead wrong!"

Lacey made a full turn around Ari and stopped in front of him, staring him in the eye. The last time she stared into them, she was begging for mercy. He had the gun in his hand, aimed right at her, and she remembered the blood.

Blood – red, red blood – splattered everywhere – his blood, her blood. The images came fast now, and she couldn't stop them. The fear she experienced that night gripped her again. What happened came back to her from the beginning in a flash.

He had the gun to his head, his finger on the trigger, and she wouldn't watch it. This bastard wasn't going to kill himself in front of her. But as she stepped away, toward the bathroom door, the first shot rang out, and she couldn't believe what was happening.

The bullet hit her in the back and she fell to the ground. She felt something gushing out of her and she turned and looked up at him, dazed. She told him she was sorry, so sorry. For what, she didn't know. It was no use. He scowled at her, showing no mercy, and said, "If I can't have you, no one can." The coldness of his voice terrified her. How could the man she had loved so much and who had said that he loved her point a gun at her and then pull the trigger?

The second shot came, and the red, red blood was everywhere. He shot her in her face. Her face, her beautiful face, was gone. Could she ever get it back? Now in a panic, Lacey put her hands up to her head and felt how whole and complete her face was, but she knew the form she had in the Middle World wasn't really her anymore. He had destroyed who and what she was, and yet now he wanted more. What more could she give him? She wanted something back. She wanted to save her face and get her revenge.

"But you came to me that night, my angel, didn't you?" Ari said, his voice sounding so sweet and yet so insincere that it jarred her back into the moment. "You made your choice, and I made mine," he went on, cocky now and so full of himself that she wanted to slap him silly, but she held herself steady. When Ari reached out to touch her, she jumped back.

"Don't you dare try to touch me!' she screamed. "You shot my face off! You didn't want to kill me – you wanted to destroy me."

"It was our fate to die together," he said solemnly.

"We didn't die together," she screamed at him defiantly. "You killed me, and then you killed yourself. You are a murderer and a coward. You caused our families and friends so much pain! You betrayed us all. You took everything away for your own selfish reasons. Everything!"

"Not everything," her mother's voice said calmly from across the clearing. Lacey spun around to look at her. But in that moment of vulnerability, Ari took the opportunity to grab her arm and pull her up against his body, with one hand at her throat and the other across her mouth so she couldn't speak. She could only struggle against him.

"Shut up," he yelled back at her mother. "We don't need to hear from the 'Other Side,' because Lacey isn't crossing over now or anytime soon."

"You're wrong about that," her mother replied. "You've underestimated my daughter this time."

With that, Lacey went wild, grabbing at Ari's hands, trying to pull them away from her throat and mouth. Suddenly she had strength, more strength than she had before, but still it didn't make a difference. He had her in his grip and she couldn't break it. She scratched, jabbed and even tried to bite his hand, but nothing released her.

Then something came to her. It was what her mother had just said. Ari hadn't taken everything away from her. She had something left, something that he could never have. True, when they were physical beings together, Ari had a strength superior to hers, but now it wasn't his physical strength that was keeping her there locked in his arms. Her body had died, but her spirit – her soul, as they called it at St. Mary Magdalene's High School for Girls – was immortal. That would never die, and it had a strength and a power all its own.

Her spirit was strong, stronger than Ari's, and she knew it. It gave her the courage to forgive her father and now her mother. All that was left for her to do was to release Ari. If she overcame her fear of Ari and let go of her anger, she could do anything. That was where her power was, and she put all her focus there.

First, she signaled Raven with her eyes that she needed his help. Quickly the huge bird flew up and over them and then circled around, dive-bombing at Ari, pecking madly at his head and hands.

Before long, Ari screamed, "Goddamn it! Get that bird away from me!"

He still didn't release her, but it did distract him and with a burst of energy, Lacey pulled one more time at Ari's hands, and this time she broke his grip.

His hand fell away from her mouth, and she screeched at Raven, "Enough! He's all mine now."

Suddenly, things were reversed and she was holding him from behind with her two hands tight around his neck, ready and able to snap it like a twig.

"Good girl!" her mother called out to her from across the divide. "I knew you'd find your power."

"I could break your miserable neck, but I won't," Lacey screamed into his ear. "You aren't worth it. I'm leaving you here to wallow for all eternity. See if I care!"

But that was too vengeful, she realized suddenly, and she looked up at her mother for help.

"Think about how you feel about him," her mother yelled out to her. "You can't change who he is, but you can change how you feel about him. Acknowledge who and what he was to you in this life and then move on. Just think. You get to move on, and he doesn't. Isn't that your best revenge? Did you ever hear that saying in the physical world, 'Living well is the best revenge?' That's what this is about. Where I will take you after you cross over is so magnificent I can't even describe it to you."

Lacey considered this for a moment. The best revenge! Yes, that was it! She would get the best of him after all. She would have what he would never be able to have. If only she could reach for the highest, best thought she could have about him. But what was that?

It was difficult, but after a moment of agony, she did come up with something. For one thing, she could appreciate the fact that, without him, she wouldn't be here now with her mother. She wouldn't have gotten to ask her about what happened that day in the garage and finally deal with all the ways her mother's death had changed her relationship with her father and her brother. She was grateful that all was forgiven now and cleared away.

What else?

She thought again for a moment. She didn't know how much of this life with Ari she would remember, but she did know this. Whatever her future might be, including another physical life to come, she would recognize and act on the warning signs of power and control, obsession and possession, without fail. She'd never make that mistake again, and she'd inspire Lisette to educate women back in the physical world not to make the same mistake either.

"I can see you are ready," her mother said gently, and Lacey looked up to see her moving slowly toward her from behind the large rock, reaching her hand out toward Lacey.

Lacey looked at her with surprise. "How did you know?"

Her mother smiled. "I know. In the Upper World, you'll get to know too."

Lacey smiled back and then said to Ari, "I'm going to let go of you now. You have no power over me anymore, and I release you. I have compassion for you, but I can't fix you. You can only fix yourself."

Then she relaxed her grip on him, and he fell to the ground in a heap.

Quickly he grabbed her leg and begged, "Please, Lacey. Let me go with you. I can't bear to be here alone."

"No," Lacey said firmly, shaking him off. "This is not about me. It's about what you need to resolve before you can cross over. I hope that one day you will do so."

Ari scowled and muttered, "It's not fair. You get to go, and I don't. Why do I have to be left behind?"

But Lacey ignored him and turned back to her mother. She held her hand out and moved toward her mother's own outstretched hand. This time, Radiance did not stop her.

"Thank you, Radiance, for all your help," Lacey said, smiling back at her. "Please tell Sophie that I'm sorry I can't be with her and that I love her."

Radiance smiled and nodded. "I will."

Suddenly Lisette rushed past Radiance toward Lacey.

"Wait!" Lisette cried out. "I'm going to miss you. I know I made a big fuss about you being in my body, but you've helped me a lot."

Lacey turned and smiled at Lisette. "And I have one more thing that I can help you with. Stay away from angry, controlling men. Think about it, Lisette. You have been in their clutches for too long. You have to find your own power, as I finally did, and then you'll be fine."

"But how can I do that without you?"

"You can," Lacey assured her. "You have Radiance and Sophie to help you. Tell Sophie that she's the best and she was right about everything. She likes it when she's right!"

Lisette tried to smile, but Lacey could see the tears welling up in her eyes.

"I'm going to miss you too," Lacey went on. "We had some pretty wild times together, didn't we? Don't worry. We'll meet again."

For a moment, Lacey envied Lisette for the physical life she would live out as she could not. She had been so young when Ari killed her, and she had felt she had so much more to see and do. But now, as she approached her mother, she was so happy, happier than she had ever been, and she knew this was right.

"Good-bye, Lisette!" Lacey said, turning back and waving. "When I see your mother in the Upper World, I'll tell her you love her and miss her very much!" Then she added, "Remember, you are the avenging angel, and living well is your best revenge!"

Then Lacey moved into the mist and, with her mother, walked toward a light that shone like a beacon marking the path to the Upper World.

"Good-bye, Lacey. I love you!" she heard Lisette cry off in the distance behind her. As she let the sound of that voice fade, her mother's came to her loud and clear.

"Welcome, my child, to your new home. It is truly paradise!"

CHAPTER TWENTY-TWO

Letting Go or Not

As Lisette watched Lacey disappear into the mist, she couldn't help but cry. Radiance came up next to her, put her arm around her shoulder, and drew her close.

"Don't worry! She'll be very happy," Radiance said softly. "You'll see her again."

"But I miss her already! I didn't think I would, but I do."

"That means she brought something good into your life. Celebrate that."

"Are you always so cheerful? Doesn't anything ever get you down?"

Before Radiance could answer, Lisette heard the drum calling them back, and Radiance turned to look at her.

"We can't stay here," she said quickly. "We must go back. And it's very important that you do not try to contact Lacey for a while. It's still too easy for her to come back to the Middle World to be with you. She needs to get settled in the Upper World first."

Lisette sighed. "I feel so weird, like I'm lighter without her, but not better. Does that make sense?"

"It won't seem right now, but you'll figure it out," Radiance said, and then added more firmly. "We must go back now."

Lisette heard the call of the drum again, and Raven suddenly appeared and swooped down in front of her feet. Radiance grabbed Lisette by the arm and guided her onto the bird's back.

"There's nothing back there for me anymore," Lisette lamented, as Radiance sat down next to her and Raven took off. "I'll just be miserable again."

"Nonsense! You don't know how it's going to feel when you return. This experience could have shifted all the energy in your life."

"I doubt it! Like Attila the Hunny is going to get a whole new life just like that!" She snapped her finger in Radiance's face and gave her a forlorn look.

"Trust me. Things can change. Besides, Sophie is waiting, and she'll want to know everything. She'll be so happy to know Lacey is safely on her way."

"And," Lisette said with a smile her faced brightening, "she'll be pissed she missed the big fight between Lacey and Ari."

As Lisette snuggled down into Raven's coat of feathers, she tried to feel positive and full of hope. Maybe Radiance was right. Her life could change. It could get better. But it never really had, and she couldn't imagine that changing.

Nothing ever changed in her life.

Nothing ever got better.

Nothing!

As Ambrose followed Erick to where Lisette might be, he wondered how Erick was going to get into the building, let alone find the exact apartment once inside. But, as he was soon to learn, Erick was a very resourceful guy.

Standing around the corner hidden from view, Ambrose saw Erick on the top step outside the locked front door push every damn doorbell on the panel until the door buzzer went off and Erick quickly stepped inside, the door slamming behind him. Encouraged by this stunt, Ambrose bounded up the steps himself and tried the same thing. To his surprise it worked, and he too moved quickly inside the building, looking down the hall for Erick. As luck would have it, the elevator in the old building was slow and Erik was still waiting for it. Ambrose strode nonchalantly up to him, pushed the up button, already lit, and stood there quietly. He hoped that Erick wouldn't recognize him from the hotel earlier. But Erick had seemed so focused on finding Lisette back then that Ambrose doubted if he even noticed him in the lobby. At least they had that in common. They were both looking desperately for Lisette.

When the elevator door opened, Ambrose purposefully stepped in first, pushed the first button he laid his finger on and then asked Erick, ever so politely, "What floor for you, sir?"

Erick gave him a quizzical look. Maybe he was surprised at Ambrose's graciousness, which even Ambrose had to admit was laying it on thick. But Erick simply said, "Six," and Ambrose obliged him by pushing that button. As he stepped back in the elevator, Ambrose went on in a friendly voice, "Have you lived in the building long?"

Erick looked at him distractedly. "No, no," he stammered, then he managed to say, "I'm just visiting someone on the sixth floor... I think."

"You're not sure?" Ambrose detected an opening here. "Why is that?"

"I'm looking for someone named Radiance, but I couldn't find anyone with that name on the doorbells downstairs. So I picked a woman with a name that started with R. Ruth, I think it was. If she's not who I'm looking for, I'll go back downstairs and try again."

"And who is it that you are looking for?" Ambrose said again in that polite but friendly voice that was working so well for him.

"Actually, I'm trying to find a friend of mine who is with her.

It's all very complicated," Erick said with a sigh and a twinge of embarrassment.

"No need to be embarrassed," Ambrose came back amiably. "Odd things happen to me every day too."

"This day *is* certainly an odd one," Erick replied. "A real doozy."

Ambrose went on with a smile. "I haven't lived in the building long, but I'd be glad to come upstairs with you and assist with any introduction you may need with this person. Did you say her name was Ruth?"

"Radiance is her name actually. My friend says she's a shaman, so I think she's a little weird. But all I want is to get my friend out of there. She needs professional help."

"I see – that is rather complicated," said Ambrose, turning his head so Erick wouldn't see him as he smiled, bit his lip, and rolled his eyes. He wanted to burst out laughing at Erick's preposterous view of the situation, but he got himself under control as the elevator bell rang and the door opened onto the sixth floor.

Ambrose and Erick got off the elevator together.

"I'm looking for apartment 608," Erick muttered as they walked down the hall.

"This is it," Erick said suddenly and stood in front of a door almost at the end of the hall. He was about to raise his hand to knock on the door when suddenly he jerked it away. "Wait!" he said, listening intently. "There's someone drumming in there. It's a steady drumbeat. I think that's the kind shamans use." Then he lowered his voice. "Yeah. This is it. It's the right apartment."

Ambrose could hear the thumping of a drum in there, too, but he didn't think it was not loud enough to drown out any noise out in the hallway.

But Erick had different idea. "I don't want to knock until the drumming stops. They'll never hear me," he said, and then he slid down the wall and sat on the floor.

"Are you sure?" Ambrose wasn't so patient. He had to know if Lisette was inside. So he persisted. "I can't wait all afternoon to introduce you to this woman."

"You don't have to," Erick replied easily. "I'll be all right. Thanks for your help."

"I could wait for a while," Ambrose hedged. "I've got nothing else to do."

"No, I can take it from here."

"But I..." Ambrose paced in front of the door, his agitation growing. Then he heaved a sigh. Shaman or no, he had to get inside and talk to Lisette.

He had waited too long as it was.

He had to find her *now.*

Lisette felt Radiance get up off the blanket next to her when they returned from their journey to the Upper World, but Lisette couldn't move yet.

She felt lightheaded and fuzzy, and her mouth was dry. She heard Radiance say something to Sophie, but she couldn't catch what it was. Then Sophie said something that sounded like, "Gram, you look as white as a sheet."

Lisette lay there, trying to remember what had happened, but all she could think of was how wonderful Lacey looked walking toward her mother. Would she ever feel such joy? Was that possible?

Then she heard Radiance's voice in her ear. "It's okay, Lisette. You can get up now, but take it slow."

Lisette tried to move her hands, but she felt a numbness in them that frightened her. Her legs felt the same and she panicked. Oh God! Was she all right? She had to get up. She had to be sure she was okay. Her eyes flew open and she sat up in a quick, jerky motion, but immediately fell back down.

"Whoa! Not that fast!" Radiance said as she grabbed Lisette's shoulders, steadying her before gently putting her back down on the blanket. "Lie here for a bit. I'll get you some water. Sophie will take care of you. I'll be right back."

Lisette nodded and closed her eyes, relieved that slowly she was feeling her hands and feet again. She felt Sophie sit down next to her and take her hand.

"I got scared." Lisette opened her eyes and looking up at Sophie. "I couldn't feel anything. Am I going to be okay?"

"Sure," Sophie reassured her. "You'll be fine. Sometimes these journeys can be intense, and you have to reenter slowly."

"You won't believe what happened," Lisette said excitedly. "We saw Lacey, and she's all right. She looked so happy when she crossed over."

Tears came to Lisette's eyes, and Sophie leaned down to stroke her brow.

"You should be proud of yourself. You helped Lacey so much. You're a true friend to her."

Lisette sighed. "I wish I was as brave as she was. Ari showed up at the last minute and tried to stop her, but she got him. You should've seen the look on his face when he realized she was moving on and he wasn't going anywhere!"

Lisette took a deep breath, as a wave of emotion came over her and her eyes filled up with tears.

"She got him good, Sophie," she went on, her face beaming now. "Really good and he deserved it."

"What's happening?" Ambrose asked excitedly, as Erick suddenly jumped up from his place on the floor at the door of Radiance's apartment, ready for action.

"The drumming stopped," Erick replied. "I hear two, maybe three voices, all female."

"Are you sure? You should knock now! Your friend must be in there."

Erick looked at him blankly, like suddenly this was none of his business.

"Look, I can handle this now," Erick said, his voice stiff and controlled. "I appreciate all your help, but I don't need it anymore."

Ambrose ignored Erick's brush-off and went on, "Knock and see who answers the door. Here, let me do it." Ambrose pushed Erick aside.

"No," Erick said, pushing him back more forcefully, his voice hoarse and his taut body tensed up, ready for a fight. "This is none of your business!"

Then Erick went to the door and knocked vigorously on it. He waited for a few seconds and knocked again, this time even harder. Then he turned to Ambrose, his face was flushed with an odd mix of determination and patience.

All right, Ambrose thought letting himself take a breath. He'd give Erick a chance to do this his way, but that didn't mean he was backing off. He couldn't, not now. He wasn't giving up on working with Lisette. If she was inside, Ambrose wasn't leaving the building until he talked to her.

Suddenly, there was a noise on the other side of the door, and slowly it opened, the chain lock still on. An older woman's face showed through the crack.

"Who is it?" the woman said irritably, like she was being inconvenienced by whoever was in the hall. "I'm not expecting anyone. Who is it?"

Erick spoke first. "I'm looking for someone. I thought she might be in there with you. Can I come in and talk to you for a moment? My name is Erick. Are you Radiance?"

"Who are you looking for?" the woman replied. "No one here but me."

Ambrose could feel his blood pressure rise. Obviously she was lying. They had just heard more than one voice in that apartment. He had to get inside!

Ambrose pushed his way past Erick and yelled, "I'm looking for Lisette. I know she's in there. Open up!" But the woman slammed the door shut and Ambrose pounded on it until Erick grabbed his hand and the two of them struggled out in the hallway until Erick threw him on the ground.

"What the hell are you doing?" Erick screamed down at him. "Who are you? How do you know about Lisette?"

"Go away!" the woman yelled from behind the door. "Or I'll call the police."

"See what you've done!" Erick glared at Ambrose and then turned back to the door, yelling to the woman behind it. "No, please don't do that. Open the door. We can talk about this. I know Lisette, and I know about Lacey too. I know that she's there to get your help. I want to help her too."

With that, the woman opened the door a crack again, the chain lock still on it, and began to talk to Erick in the same tone that irritated Ambrose before.

But he didn't have time to listen. Enough of all this dancing around, he fumed. Enough! Ambrose bolted up from the floor, shoved Erick aside and burst his way into the apartment. He crashed through the door, wrenched the chain lock off its hinges, and pushed the door with such force that it hit the woman and sent her sprawling to the floor.

She let out a loud shrill scream as Ambrose looked wildly around the room, yelling, "Where is she? Where's Lisette?"

But she wasn't there. He'd have to search for her. As he turned to go down the hallway, he felt the woman on the floor grab him by the leg. She hung on so tightly that when he moved she went with him.

"Let go, you bitch!" he yelled down at her. He shook his leg, trying to get her off him, but she was a big woman and she hung on.

"Lisette! Lisette!" Ambrose went on, screeching now. "I'm here, Lisette. It's me! It's Ambrose!"

In all the commotion, Ambrose didn't see someone running toward him, screaming like a banshee.

"EEEE AW!"

The yell jolted him even before he felt the pain of the karate kick that landed on his knee, and he went down like a tree.

"My knee, my knee," he yelled, grabbing it and rolling on the floor, writhing in pain. He looked up and saw a girl standing over him. "You broke my knee!" he screamed. "You broke it!"

Then Erick rushed through the door, and Ambrose watched as he surveyed the scene and went over to the woman still down on the floor. "Are you all right?" Erick asked her.

"Go ahead and help that bitch," Ambrose raged at him. "This is all your damn fault!"

But the pain in his knee was nothing to the desperation he felt inside. Lisette wasn't there, and, with his knee mangled, how was he ever going to find her? Screw Erick and his being so damn nice. Ambrose should've done it his way from the start.

The right way!

Stupid!

How could he have been so damn stupid?

CHAPTER TWENTY-THREE

Doing It Right

Lisette couldn't believe what she saw when she got to the front room of the apartment.

Back in Radiance's workroom, she and Sophie had heard the voices at the front door, at first muffled and then much louder. But it wasn't until Radiance screamed and Lisette heard her name being called out that she and Sophie went into action. Sophie jumped up and ran out of the room. Lisette struggled off the blanket and made her way more slowly down the hall, her legs still shaky and her knees wobbly. By then, Lisette had recognized the voice that was screaming out her name.

She couldn't believe it. Ambrose! What the hell was he doing here?

When she finally got to the front room, she saw Radiance on the floor with blood covering her face and Sophie kneeling next to her. Nearby on the floor, Ambrose was screaming and grabbing his knee as if it might fall off.

To add to her shock, Erick came rushing out of the kitchen with a look of total panic on his face and a wet dish towel in his hand. As he handed it to Sophie, he saw Lisette and the look on his face changed to embarrassment.

"I can explain all this," he began, his words coming in between gasps of air. "Really, I can."

Lisette glared at Erick, turned to ask Sophie. "Is your Gram going to be okay?

Sophie looked up as she wiped the blood from Radiance's forehead. "I hope so. We've called 911. Help is on the way. Erick's been great!"

Lisette stared back at Erick, still not convinced he was the hero of the day.

He must have seen the doubt in her eyes, because suddenly he gushed, "It was all a mistake. I'm sorry. It wasn't supposed to happen this way."

"That's it? That's all you have to say for yourself?" Lisette responded.

Erick looked crushed, but she didn't care. Her friend, Radiance, was hurt and she wanted to know why.

Erick went on painfully. "I was mad because you didn't show up for lunch. I had to know why. I remembered what you said about where Radiance lived, so I came here." Erick shook his head and pointed at Ambrose on the floor. "I didn't realize who he was until he barreled through the door like a madman. He was in the elevator with me on the way up and offered to help me find this apartment. This is all my fault! I never should have come looking for you. What was I thinking? If your friend, Radiance, is really hurt, I'll never forgive myself!"

He sighed deeply now, and Lisette had to feel sorry for him.

"Look, I shouldn't have stood you up this afternoon, but I wanted to go on another journey with Radiance today, and I didn't think you understood how important this was to me." She paused, and then twirled around in front of him. "Do you notice anything different about me?" She didn't wait for his answer. "Lacey is gone. I watched her cross over. It was so wonderful! Her soul is at peace now! I couldn't have done it without Radiance."

Lisette beamed at him, and Erick gave her a smile. "I'm glad. This was the right thing for you to do, and I shouldn't have interfered. Sometimes I just get all tangled up in trying to help, and I didn't see that…"

But Lisette had had enough of his explaining. Instead of letting him go on, she did something crazy. She reached up and kissed him on the lips. That surprised him, but he liked it, she could tell. He looked down at her, and then he kissed her back. As they held the kiss for a moment, Lisette felt a surge go through her. It was something magical, more than a sexual thing. Suddenly she was very attracted to this big lug of a guy who was into helping people.

And it sure felt good.

Lisette and Erick sat in the kitchen of Radiance's apartment long after the ambulance left that took Radiance and Ambrose to the hospital.

Sophie had gone in the ambulance, too, and although Lisette wanted to go, Sophie insisted that she stay at the apartment. Radiance was too confused to tell Sophie where she kept the keys to the apartment so she couldn't lock up. Besides, there wasn't room for all of them in the ambulance, anyway. Sophie gave them her cell phone number and promised to call them when she knew how Radiance was.

As they waited for the call, Lisette made tea and told Erick about her journeys to the Upper World over the last two days. He heard about how Lisette saw her mother and felt her loving presence. He also learned how Lacey had talked to her mother, found out how she died, and forgave her for leaving her and her brother, Jimmie, behind. She told him, too, how courageously Lacey banished Ari to his own misery and crossed over so triumphantly to be with her mother. By the end, Lisette's face was streaked with tears, and Erick wiped them away with the back of his hand.

"You are an avenging angel!" Erick said. "No doubt about that." His face beamed as he took her hand in his and held it firmly. "You helped Lacey avenge what Ari did to her and find peace. I'm so proud of you!"

Lisette gave Erick a look of surprise. "How did you know that Lacey told me that I should be my own avenging angel?"

"No, I didn't know that." Eric shrugged. "It just came to me."

"Then it's a sign," Lisette decided. "The one I have been looking for."

It means that this was right, she thought. She was exactly where she was supposed to be. She had everything she needed right inside of her. Just like Lacey said she did.

She squeezed Erick's hand and said in a strong voice, "Thank you, Lacey, and thank you, Mom. Everything's going to be fine now. Just fine, you'll see."

Erick leaned closer and stroked her hair.

"Sounds like you're praying. You aren't going religious on me, are you?" A big grin filled his face. "Because I like you the way you are."

"You do?" Lisette said, looking at him sweetly. "I kind of like you, too."

He stroked her hair again and sighed. "This is getting better and better. Of course, I can't expect a headline stripper like you to hang around this town for much longer, not for a guy that you 'kind of' like. How soon will you be leaving?"

"Actually, sitting here with you like this in this grand apartment makes me think that it's time to stop all this traveling and stay in one place for a while."

"Really?" Erick seemed surprised.

"In a few years, I'd be retiring anyway," she went on. "I don't want to be doing this when I get really old, like twenty-five or twenty-six."

"Is there something else you've wanted to do?"

"Not really." She paused for a moment and then added, "There is one thing I should do."

"What's that?"

"I'd like to go to this thing called a symposium next week at the college where Lacey was killed. Sophie told me about it, and she and Radiance could use my help to get people there. Sophie says the college must do something so what happened to Lacey won't happen again. Unless the entire community demands some action, they'll just sweep the whole thing under the rug. They want to request more programs for the students to learn how to identify abuse in a relationship. And Sophie says there are lots of other things the college could do, things other schools around the country are doing. There's no reason Lacey's school couldn't be an example of how to do it right. Wouldn't that be great? Then her death would mean something, something important. It's what she would have wanted, don't you think?"

Erick nodded in agreement, and then looked into Lisette's eyes. "I think there is something else she would have wanted from you."

"What's that?"

"To finish what she couldn't and graduate from college yourself."

"Who, me? Go to college? I dropped out of high school!"

"So what? You could get your GED and go to a community college for a few years to get your grades up. It's not an impossible dream. Why not try?"

Lisette stared at him. "You're serious about this, aren't you?"

"Yes, and I think you should be serious about it, too."

Lisette felt panic well up inside her. Didn't Erick understand how hard this was for her? Did he know what she was asking of her?

"What?" He stared at her like he was trying to read the look on her face. "Is that so terrifying?"

"No, but…" she said quickly, then blurted out, "Jesus, Erick! I can't even read. How would I ever get through college?"

"What do you mean, you can't read?"

"Look, don't go crazy about this," she warned him, remembering how when she told Ambrose she couldn't read he got all involved and made a mess of it. "I can read just fine," she went on. "This is not your problem. You don't have to do anything about it."

"I wasn't planning to," Erick said glibly. "There are literacy programs around that can help you. You'll find them and figure it out. I have great faith in you. You give everything you do one hundred percent."

Then he smiled at her, and she saw a twinkle in his eye.

"Do you really think so?" she asked him because she was curious, not just fishing for a compliment.

"Sure. I've never seen anyone be so passionate about what they do. Take your act. You really want it to be artistic and sexy at the same time. Most strippers don't care a hoot about that, but you – Attila the Hunny – you are really something!"

"You're just saying that so I'll go to bed with you," she teased. But as his face grew red, she knew she had hit on something. Maybe it wasn't so long before she and Erick had an understanding of some kind. But could she really settle down in one place, with one guy? Maybe. For Erick, she might give it a try.

"There is one more thing," she said quickly as if the thought had just popped into her head. "I want to go see Lacey's father, but I'll need some help from you."

"What kind of help?"

"You're studying to be a psychologist, right?"

"Yeah, right."

"I need help convincing Howie that he wasn't responsible for Lacey's death, or for her mother's. If he could forgive himself, he and Jimmie could have a much happier life. Lacey would've wanted that. I feel it's something I could do for her."

"Nice!" Erick said with a smile. "I like how you are thinking about this. I like how you see something in this for you – opportunity coming out of loss, positive energy replacing the negative, good stuff like that. You are an amazing person, and you could have an amazing life, even more than you have ever imagined."

She looked at Erick and gave him a half smile. "Yeah, I don't know if I'd go that far, but you know what's funny about this? I don't know how to put it into words, but I have this feeling I've never had before. It feels like I have been sleeping for a long time, lost and alone, but now I'm awaken, like Sleeping Beauty in the fairy tale and I have people who …who …"

Her voice caught, and she couldn't go on. There was a big lump in her throat, and tears came to her eyes. She didn't know how to say it until now. It was like Erick, Sophie and Radiance were becoming a family to her in a way that she never felt before, not even when her mother was alive.

Suddenly she turned and said to Erick in a hushed voice, "Isn't it amazing how sometimes people have to die so others can learn how to live? Why is that?"

Erick just shook his head like he didn't know either, but she could feel the heat of his hand in hers and they sat there together, being very quiet and peaceful. Soon Lisette got that wonderful feeling again. She felt like she belonged to something bigger than herself and that she could do something good with her life.

After a while Erick turned to her and gently said, "Maybe we should call and see how Radiance is doing. Sophie might have gotten hung up in the emergency room and forgotten that we were waiting to find out."

Lisette nodded and reluctantly let go of Erick's hand. He took out his cell phone, flipped it open and pushed a few buttons.

When the phone connected, Lisette listened as he talked to Sophie. By the smile on his face, she could tell that Radiance was going to be okay. A rush of good feelings washed over her again, and she smiled back at Erick.

She gave him her best smile, the one that she knew lit up her face and showed him that she really and truly believed that, perhaps for the first time in her life, things were going to go her way.

She felt happy, really happy.

At last!

Ambrose felt miserable.

Not only did his knee hurt like hell, but ever since the cops and the emergency medical people had arrived at the apartment, everyone was paying more attention to that Radiance woman and what she needed than to him. Like this was all his fault! How was he supposed to know that she'd be there behind the door when he came through the door of her apartment looking for Lisette? She shouldn't have gotten in his way.

Now that he was in the hospital, though, someone was finally giving him what he needed too. He had been screaming for drugs to take away the pain ever since he had been put in the ambulance. He felt the pain not only from that crazy girl kicking his knee, but also from the fact that somewhere out there, Lisette was living her life without him. She was supposed to be with him, not that stupid kid Erick, who would probably convince her to marry him and have his babies. Soon Lisette would end up just like Betsy, a bossy ballbuster who didn't care about anyone but herself. Wasn't that what all women were like deep down inside? Wasn't that why all marriages were doomed to fail? What was the world coming to? Where had all the real men gone? What happened to guys like him who could take control and keep women in their place?

He hated to think that way about Lisette. She was so young and beautiful and talented. He knew he could make her a star if she would only give him a chance. But Abigail had fed her so many lies, how would he ever be able to set the record straight with her? Still, he wanted to crawl out of this hospital bed and try. He was the one who had the power to set her on a course of true creativity, enlightenment, and knowledge. That's what he had always wanted for himself. That's what Attila the Hun had taught him as a boy. Be strong and wield your power with impunity. Don't let anyone stand in your way. If only Lisette could see him that way – strong, virile, and in command! This was his Attila energy, and he loved it!

But the thought of going anywhere, even to see Lisette, was too much. He was humiliated and embarrassed by being brought down by that girl, the one that Lisette had called Sophie. He heard Sophie admit to the cops that she had trained in marital arts. But he'd show her. She was a menace. She shouldn't be allowed to go around hurting people. When the cops came back to question him again, he was going to have her arrested. He'd teach her a lesson. Then he'd sue her in civil court too. There had to be some good case law about the unreasonable use of force. She had caused him great harm when the risk of harm to herself and her grandmother was negligible. He liked that word "negligible." He liked how it rolled off his lips now that the injection the nurse had finally put into his arm was kicking in.

All he had to do was lie back and float like this for a while, and when it wore off, he'd scream bloody murder for another dose. This could go on for some time, he thought, and no one would be the wiser. He was on painkiller drugs now, and it wasn't a bad way to go! It was so much better than booze. It made him forget everything. Lisette and Erick were gone, and so was that awful creature, Radiance. How did someone like her ever come into his life? Of course, he barely remembered what his son, Mark, looked like – and Betsy and Jeanine where just a blur in his memory.

But he didn't care. The drugs were great, so much better than being in pain. It was nice to be on such a buzz.

Why hadn't he thought of this sooner?

October 17, 2009

The Anniversary

Lisette wasn't thrilled about coming back to this place.

She had never felt comfortable here, given her less-than-adequate education and her chosen profession at the time. It was Sophie who had called her, asking her to come back to celebrate, if that was the right word, and Lisette couldn't say no.

It was the tenth anniversary of Lacey's death, and Sophie wanted to gather all those who had helped her be so successful in her work. Lisette was not sure that she was the person to thank, but she did want to see how everyone and everything was. She had heard so much about all of it from Sophie. She had to see it with her own eyes.

Driving up to the school in a taxi wasn't exactly the best way to take it all in, Lisette realized later. She could see that the buildings looked the same, but the students seemed so much younger than she remembered them. But you are so much older, she told herself, and not getting any younger. For someone in her line of work, she had to know that age was everything.

Still, after the taxi stopped in front of the large, open, green space on the campus where the student center and chapel were located and Lisette took a moment to pay the driver, she couldn't help but wonder if anyone on the campus would actually recognize her. She had gone through quite a transformation, and she wasn't sure who would remember her from that part of her life. She wished that her boyfriend could have joined her, but he... well, he was quite busy these days with his own things.

"Go! Have a good time!" he said to her, as he hugged and kissed her that morning, holding onto her for a moment as if he didn't really want her to go. But then he added, "Come back and tell me what's going on with everyone. I want a full report."

That was so like him, Lisette thought. He always let her do what she wanted, but then he'd want to know what it meant to her. She was very lucky and she knew it.

As she stepped out of the taxi and walked past the student center toward the chapel on the hill in front of her, she was filled with amazement. What she saw she could never have imagined ten years ago, and yet there it was right before her eyes.

My God! Lisette marveled. Lacey would be so proud of all of them! They had indeed found the best revenge.

But where was hers?

Would she ever get there, too?

THE END

DISCUSSION QUESTIONS
A Reader's Guide
For Individuals and Groups

Awaken, the first book in *The Best Revenge Series*™, is a novel about two young women, Lacey and Lisette, who are on a healing journey from victim to survivor to "thriver." It is also a story of how Lacey missed some of the warning signs of dating violence and did not have a safety plan in place to keep herself safe.

1. What did Lacey miss about Ari's behavior?

2. Make a list of the ways that Ari abused Lacey from the *Warning Signs of an Unhealthy, Abusive Relationship* listed on the following page.

3. What advice would you have given Lacey about Ari? What could she have done to keep herself safe?

4. Has anything ever happened to you that is similar to what happened between Ari and Lacey in the book? How did you then or would you now react to it?

5. Both Lacey and Lisette lost their mothers at a young age. How do you think that affected their lives?

6. What else did Lisette and Lacey have in common? What made Lisette decide to help Lacey?

7. How would you rate Ambrose, Howie, and Ralph as fathers in the book?

8. Did Ambrose, Howie, and Ralph grow and change as men because of what happened to them? What is their path forward? What would change look like for each of them?

9. If "living well is the best revenge" is the theme of this book series, did Lacey get her "best revenge" from Ari, even after death? What would be Lisette's best revenge?

10. What scene was the most important for Lacey and Lisette in the healing journey? How did you react to it personally?

11. What important role did Radiance and Sophie play in helping Lacey and Lisette heal?

12. What did you learn about the healing process from this book that has been most helpful to you?

13. What would be the best way for Sophie and Lisette to remember Lacey and give her a lasting legacy on that campus?

14. How could a community such as Lacey's college work to prevent dating violence?

15. Who was your favorite character and why? What do you think is next for this person?

WARNING SIGNS OF AN UNHEALTHY, ABUSIVE RELATIONSHIP

He is controlling, possessive and overly demanding of her time and attention. He appears at times to be two different people: one, charming, loving, and kind; the other, abusive, vicious, and mean. He has what is called a "Dr. Jekyll and Mr. Hyde" dual personality. He keeps her on edge, not knowing who he'll be at any moment. He manipulates what she feels for him and makes her feel bad about herself.

He will at times be sorry for what he has said and done and will promise never to do it again, but he will also deny, minimize, or blame others for his behavior. She will feel it is her fault, that *if only* she had done something else, pleased him more, been more compliant, she would not be treated this way by him.

EMOTIONAL
- He insults her, calls her names and belittles her in private and in public with her family and friends.
- He isolates her from family and friends, forbidding her to see them or limiting her access to them.
- He is jealous of her contact with others, particularly with other men. He exaggerates her relationships with other men, accusing her unfairly of having affairs outside of their relationship.
- He wants to know where she is at all times, calling or texting her to find out who she is with. He invades her privacy by checking her cell phone, viewing her email, or monitoring her Web pages.
- He refuses to accept when she ends the relationship and may stalk her long afterward.

PHYSICAL

- He yells, screams, and loses his temper easily, sometimes disproportionately over unimportant things.
- He destroys her things, kicks, or breaks other property, making her fear that he could hurt her, too.
- He intimidates her, making her afraid of him by his looks, actions, and gestures.
- He grabs her, kicks her, slaps her, punches her, strangles her, draws a gun or weapon, and threatens to kill her. He harms her pets or threatens to hurt or harm her family or friends.
- He stalks her with unwanted phone calls, visits to her house or job, and secretly monitors her actions.

ECONOMIC

- He controls her access to money, even her own money or money she has earned herself.
- He refuses to pay bills or let her know about family income, investments, or property.
- He keeps her from getting or keeping a job, and he refuses to support their family or children.
- He makes all the big decisions, using male privilege to get his way and insisting on rigid gender roles.

PSYCHOLOGICAL

- She feels like she is going crazy, that his view of the world is not reasonable, but she will have little chance of convincing him otherwise, and he demands her absolute loyalty to his way of thinking.
- He says he can't live without her or will kill himself if she leaves, so she fears ending the relationship.
- He pushes the relationship too far, too fast, and is obsessed with her and wants her for himself.
- He has unrealistic expectations and demands, and she feels it is her fault he's not happy.

SEXUAL
- He demands to have sex forcibly without her consent with him or with others.
- He withdraws sex from her or makes it conditional on her compliance to his demands.
- He calls her crude names, implying she is promiscuous and unfaithful sexually to him.

Signs of a Healthy Relationship

In a healthy relationship, two people are on an equal footing, and they respect, trust, and support each other. They are honest with each other and take responsibility for their actions. They are good parents, sharing responsibility in raising their kids. They have an economic partnership in which the best interests of both are considered, and they communicate, negotiate, and treat each other fairly.

Reprinted from
Entering the Thriver Zone: A Seven-Step Guide to Thriving After Abuse
by Susan M. Omilian, JD
For more information on Susan and her work, visit *thriverzone.com.*

RESOURCES

As you read this book, you might find a need for the resources below. It is important to view violence and abuse seriously in a relationship and take care. Stay safe!

Crisis Intervention
Contact these national resources for information about immediate crisis intervention services in your local community:

- The National Domestic Violence Hotline 1-800-799-SAFE (7233) **www.thehotline.org**

- National Sexual Assault Hotline at 1-800-656-HOPE (4673) **www.rainn.org**

- National Center for Victims of Crime 1-855-4VICTIM (1-855-484-2846)
  www.victimsofcrime.org/help-for-crime-victims

- Office for Victims of Crime, U.S. Department of Justice
  www.ovc.gov/help/tollfree.html

Dating Violence and Stalking

- Break the Cycle: Empowering Youth to End Dating Violence **www.breakthecycle.org**

- Love Is Respect – National Teen Dating Abuse Help Line 1-866-331-9474 **www.loveisrespect.org**

- End Stalking in America **www.esia.net** provides information and assistance to potential victims and those being harassed, including list of state laws against stalking.

- The Sanctuary for Victims of Stalking **www.stalkingvictims. com** offers sanctuary and resources on stalking to victims, how to identify stalking, and how deal with it through an online support group.

- Women's Law.org **www.womenslaw.org** is a project of the National Network to End Domestic Violence, providing legal information and support to victims of domestic violence, stalking, and sexual assault.

Domestic Violence

- National Network to End Domestic Violence (NNEDV) **www.nnedv.org** offers support to victims of domestic violence who are escaping abusive relationships and empowers survivors to build new lives.

- National Coalition Against Domestic Violence (NCADV) **www.ncadv.org** works closely with battered women's advocates around the country to identify the issues and develop a legislative agenda.

- **www.domesticshelters.org** Free, online, searchable national database of domestic violence shelter programs.

- National Resource Center on Domestic Violence (NRCDV) **www.nrcdv.org** is a source of information for those wanting to educate themselves and help others on the many issues related to domestic violence.

Sexual Assault

- RAINN — Rape, Abuse & Incest National Network **www.rainn.org** operates the National Sexual Assault Hotline and has programs to prevent sexual assault, help Victims, and ensure they receive justice.

- National Sexual Violence Resource Center **www.nsvrc.org** provides leadership in preventing and responding to sexual violence through creating resources and promoting research.

- The Victim Rights Law Center **www.victimrights.org** is dedicated solely to serving the legal needs of sexual assault victims. It provides training, technical assistance, and in some cases, free legal assistance in civil cases to sexual assault victims in certain parts of the country.

Child Abuse

- Childhelp USA National Child Abuse **www.childhelp.org** directly serves abused and neglected children through the National Child Abuse Hotline, 1-800-4-A-CHILD® (1-800-422-4453) and other programs.

Post-Traumatic Stress

See information listed at National Institute of Mental Health website, **www.nimh.nih.gov**

BOOKS BY SUSAN M. OMILIAN, JD

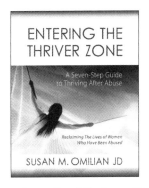

Entering the Thriver Zone
A Seven-Step Guide to Thriving After Abuse

NEXT in the *Thriver Zone Series*™

Staying in the Thriver Zone
A Road Map to Finding Your Power and Purpose

Living in the Thriver Zone
A Celebration of Living Well as the Best Revenge

NEXT books in *THE BEST REVENGE SERIES*™
Emerge and Thrive

For updates please visit www.ThriverZone.com

ABOUT THE AUTHOR

An attorney, author, and motivational speaker, Susan Omilian has worked extensively as an advocate to end violence against women for the past four decades. In the 1970s, she founded a rape crisis center and represented battered women in divorce proceedings in the early 1980s. She also litigated sex discrimination cases including helping to articulate the legal concept that made sexual harassment illegal in the 1990s.

Since her nineteen-year-old niece Maggie was shot and killed by her ex-boyfriend in 1999, Susan has worked extensively with hundreds of women who have experienced abuse helping them take the journey from victim to survivor to "thriver."

A recognized national expert on the process of recovery after violence and abuse, Susan is the author of two book series, *The Thriver Zone* and *The Best Revenge*.

For more about Susan, her books and further resources, visit thriverzone.com.